Nineteenth-Century Southern Gothic Short Fiction

Anthem Studies in Gothic Literature incorporates a broad range of titles that undertake rigorous, multi-disciplinary and original scholarship in the domain of Gothic Studies and respond, where possible, to existing classroom/module needs. The series aims to foster innovative international scholarship that interrogates established ideas in this rapidly growing field, to broaden critical and theoretical discussion among scholars and students, and to enhance the nature and availability of existing scholarly resources.

Nineteenth-Century Southern Gothic Short Fiction

Haunted by the Dark

Edited by
Charles L. Crow and Susan Castillo Street

ANTHEM PRESS

Anthem Press
An imprint of Wimbledon Publishing Company
www.anthempress.com

This edition first published in UK and USA 2021
by ANTHEM PRESS
75–76 Blackfriars Road, London SE1 8HA, UK
or PO Box 9779, London SW19 7ZG, UK
and
244 Madison Ave #116, New York, NY 10016, USA

First published in the UK and USA by Anthem Press in 2020

British Library Cataloguing-in-Publication Data
A catalogue record for this book is available from the British Library.

Library of Congress Control Number: 2021930108

ISBN-13: 978-1-78527-974-4 (Pbk)
ISBN-10: 1-78527-974-2 (Pbk)

This title is also available as an e-book.

CONTENTS

Acknowledgments vii

Introduction 1

I The Tales

Chapter One — Victor Séjour, "The Mulatto" (1837, new English translation by Susan Castillo Street) 7

Chapter Two — Edgar Allan Poe, "The Fall of the House of Usher" (1839) 19

Chapter Three — Edgar Allan Poe, "The System of Doctor Tarr and Professor Fether" (1844) 33

Chapter Four — Henry Clay Lewis, "A Struggle for Life" (1850) 47

Chapter Five — George Washington Cable, "Belles Demoiselles Plantation" (1879) 55

Chapter Six — Lafcadio Hearn, "The Ghostly Kiss" (1880) 69

Chapter Seven — Thomas Nelson Page, "No Haid Pawn" (1887) 71

Chapter Eight — Charles Chesnutt, "Po' Sandy" (1888) 83

Chapter Nine — Grace King, "The Little Convent Girl" (1893) 91

Chapter Ten — E. Levi Brown, "At the Hermitage" (1893) 97

Chapter Eleven — Kate Chopin, "Désirée's Baby" (1893) 109

Chapter Twelve — M. E. M. Davis, "At La Glorieuse" (1897) 115

II Background

Chapter Thirteen — J. Hector St. John de Crèvecoeur, from *Letters from an American Farmer*: Letter IX (1782) 135

Chapter Fourteen — Thomas Jefferson, from *Notes on the State of Virginia*: Query XVIII (1785) 145

Chapter Fifteen — Jean-Jacques Dessalines, "Liberty or Death: Proclamation, 28 April 1804" 147

Chapter Sixteen	Charles Brockden Brown, "On the Consequences of Abolishing the Slave Trade to the West Indian Colonies" (1805)	151
Chapter Seventeen	Leonora Sansay, from *Secret History; or, The Horrors of St. Domingo*: Letter II, Letter XXI (1808)	159
Chapter Eighteen	Thomas Ruffin Gray, from "The Confessions of Nat Turner" (1831)	165
Chapter Nineteen	Lafcadio Hearn, "St. Johns Eve—Voudouism" (1875)	175
Chapter Twenty	George Washington Cable, from "Salome Müller: The White Slave" (from *Strange True Stories of Louisiana*, 1890)	181
Chapter Twenty-One	George Washington Cable, from "The Haunted House in Royal Street" (from *Strange True Stories of Louisiana*, 1890)	197
Chapter Twenty-Two	Charles W. Chesnutt, "Superstitions and Folk-Lore of the South" (1901)	207
Chapter Twenty-Three	W. E. B. Du Bois, selection from "Of the Black Belt" (from *The Souls of Black Folk*, 1903)	213
Index		225

ACKNOWLEDGMENTS

We would like to express our gratitude to the following scholars for their expertise on the Francophone Caribbean, their collegiality and their invaluable assistance: Thomas A. Klinger, William Marshall, Martin Munro and Richard H. Watts.

Thanks are due as well to Matthew Sivils for discovering the few known facts about E. Levi Brown. Thanks to David Bean for proofreading.

We are also grateful to Carol Margaret Davison, series editor of Anthem Studies in Gothic Literature, for her unflagging support of this project.

INTRODUCTION

Charles L. Crow and Susan Castillo Street

The Gothic is a dark window into the fears and taboos of a culture. This collection brings together a dozen chilling tales of the nineteenth-century American South with nonfiction texts that illuminate them and ground them in their historical context. The tales are from writers with enduring, worldwide reputations (e.g., Edgar A. Poe), and others whose work will be unknown to most readers. Indeed, one of the stories has not been reprinted for over a hundred years, and little is known about its author, E. Levi Brown.

Similarly, the historical selections are from a range of authors, some canonical, others not, ranging from Thomas Jefferson and the great historian and sociologist W. E. B. Du Bois to the relatively obscure Leonora Sansay. Some of these historical readings are themselves as disturbingly Gothic as any of the tales. Indeed, the boundaries between fiction and nonfiction are tenuous in the Gothic South. It is our contention that Southern Gothic tales are essentially realistic fiction and, even at their most grotesque and haunting, are closely linked to the realities of southern life.

All Gothic writers disturb and sometimes delight us by evoking our fears. The Gothic is a literature of crossing borders, often forbidden borders: between consciousness and nightmare, known and unknown, civilization and savagery, the living and dead … and the list could be extended almost forever. Gothic confronts taboos and universal fears, but it also provides a chart of the fears of a particular culture, at a particular time.

In America, the great fears, taboos and boundaries often concern race. In *Playing in the Dark* Toni Morrison explores the issue of "Africanism" in American culture, by which she means the system of assumptions and fears that white Americans have used to define themselves and black Americans. This system pervades all aspects of American culture. Morrison uses the metaphor of the fishbowl: even though it is transparent and easily overlooked, it shapes and contains the life within.[1] Morrison teaches us to be alert for black characters, often silent, on the margins of American stories. And they may be felt even when they are not physically present. No slaves appear in Poe's "The System of Doctor Tarr and Professor Fether," for example, but the story gestures toward slave rebellion, the greatest fear of the Old South.

Race, through slavery, is intertwined with the history of the South. While the "Peculiar Institution" existed elsewhere in the colonial period and early years of the United States,

---

1 See Toni Morrison, *Playing in the Dark* (New York: Vintage, 1993), p. 17.

it continued longest in the South and was deeply engrained in its culture. The Civil War was a war to defend slavery, despite claims (still made) by Southern apologists that the rebellion was about an abstract principle of states' rights. The period after the war was marked by historical revisionism in the South that sought to justify the old plantation system, and painted Reconstruction as a brutal mistake. As part of this rewriting of the past, there arose a literature of Southern nostalgia, sometimes called the "Plantation School," that romanticized the life of the Old South, depicting happy slaves, paternalistic masters, glamorous balls and elegant manners. This legend was not harmless nostalgia but propaganda in the service of the counterrevolution that began in 1877, following the election of Rutherford B. Hayes. The subsequent period of segregation and denial of rights, enforced by "Jim Crow" laws and lynch law, lasted into the next century. The Gothic, however, is inherently anti-nostalgic, and Southern Gothic provides a counternarrative, exposing the brutalities beneath the myths of the plantation school.

This collection, then, places race—slavery and its aftermath—at the center of Southern Gothic. Such familiar emblems of the Southern Gothic as the swamp and the decaying mansion (seen in several of our tales) are peripheral and reflect the core concern of race. Likewise, this collection insists on the importance of the Caribbean, and especially Haiti, to Southern history and Southern Gothic. European colonization of the Americas began in the Caribbean; the introduction of enslaved Africans began there, as did the plantation system that linked the islands to North America in an economy of sugar cane, rum and slaves. The successful revolt of Haitians against colonial rule (1791–1804) was a defining episode in the history of the Americas, and it became the enduring fear of Southern slave owners. This nightmare was made real by Nat Turner's revolt in Virginia in 1831. Works in this collection reflect both the Haitian Revolution and Turner's rebellion.

The tales in this book are arranged chronologically, as are the historical readings.

The first tale in the collection, Victor Séjour's "The Mulatto," also may be the first short story ever written by an African American. Séjour was a Louisianan of Haitian descent, who wrote in French and spent his professional life in France. (His story is presented here in a new translation.) Written after the Haitian Revolution, but set before it, Séjour's story depicts an act of violence that forecasts events to come. It also introduces another key issue of Southern Gothic. When the story's hero, Georges, kills his master, Alfred, he is killing his own father. Thus Séjour introduces the issue of interracial sex that runs throughout Southern Gothic. The paternity of mixed-race children was usually known, but seldom acknowledged. There is a pattern of hidden or suppressed genealogy in Southern life and literature, a Gothic element that threatens to disrupt the narrative of white purity and the rigid classifications that marginalized large groups of mixed-race people.

The best-known author in this book, Edgar A. Poe, is represented by "The System of Doctor Tarr and Professor Fether" and "The Fall of the House of Usher." The latter is an urtext of Southern Gothic, as the image of the collapsing house (the house in both senses, as a structure and a family) becomes a familiar trope after the Civil War, and it will be seen later in our collection in George Washington Cable's "Belles Demoiselle Plantation." The plantation house is also the setting of Chopin's "Désirée's Baby," M. E.

M. Davis's vampire ghost story "At La Glorieuse" and, in part, E. Levi Brown's "At the Hermitage."

"A Struggle for Life," by the short-lived and seldom remembered Henry Clay Lewis, provides an early example of the swamp as a Southern Gothic setting, and Thomas Nelson Page's "No Haid Pawn" brings the manor house and the swamp together in a tale that clearly is an homage to Poe.

New Orleans, which may be considered the capital of the Gothic South, was home at different times to Séjour, Cable, Hearn, King, Chopin and Davis. Hearn, who lived for several years in New Orleans before moving on to Japan, and is sometimes credited with inventing New Orleans as a literary region, contributes "The Ghostly Kiss," a weird tale in the tradition of supernatural tales by Poe.

Near the end of the fiction section we have tales by Charles Chesnutt and Kate Chopin. Both authors had initial success with short stories but lost their audiences when they began to publish novels. Chesnutt was a mixed-race author who was assumed white by his early readers. In "Po' Sandy" he deconstructs the plantation narrative in a way that anticipates, many decades later, Toni Morrison's *Beloved.*

Similarly disruptive is the story by Kate Chopin, "Désirée's Baby," a Gothic tale of suppressed genealogy that begins in a dark manor house and ends in a swamp. The question of racial heritage is also prominent in Grace King's "The Little Convent Girl" and in E. Levi Brown's "At the Hermitage." These stories reveal the sexual exploitation of enslaved women, and the arbitrariness of the color line. The revelation of racial heritage comes with a shock that destroys the title character of King's tale, while a shameful sexual and racial history is known by the women in Brown's "At the Hermitage." The reader, as outsider, is left to puzzle it out.

M. E. M. Davis's "At La Glorieuse" gives us a glimpse into the world of Creole plantation culture. This tale is less explicitly racial than most in this collection and appears, in many ways, in the tradition of the school of Southern nostalgia. The apparently conventional love story is disrupted, however, by a ghost with a mysterious past that muddles the sequence of generations and brings a hint of incest.

The background materials include pieces published in the early years of the republic by Crèvecoeur and Thomas Jefferson, both demonstrating the importance of slavery to the imagination of the country from its early days. As in the literary texts, the historical selections stress the importance of the Haitian Revolution. Jacques Dessalines's "Proclamation," in which he justifies the massacre of white prisoners, is given in a new translation. A vivid firsthand account of the Haitian Revolution is provided by Leonora Sansay, an American woman who was a friend of Alexander Hamilton. The most famous American novelist of the time, Charles Brockden Brown, contributes an essay in which he struggles with the implications of the events in Haiti.

The final historical reading from the antebellum period is Thomas Ruffin Gray's "The Confessions of Nat Turner." Turner's rebellion in Virginia, though suppressed after only a few days, was a traumatic event in the slave-owning South, threatening that the revolution of Haiti might come to North America, and undercutting the official line that slaves in the American South were well treated and content. We hear Turner's story through the intermediary of Gray, who is not entirely trustworthy. Still, the reader gains a vivid picture of the events that so horrified white Virginians, and perhaps glimpses the personality of the charismatic rebel.

The selections from George Washington Cable's *Strange True Stories of Louisiana*, though written after the Civil War, look back to the period of slavery. "Salomé Müller" gives us the story, strange indeed, of a German child who was sold as a slave; "The Haunted House in Royal Street" tells of a sadistic female slave owner whose behavior toward her slaves was so horrific that the residents of New Orleans rioted and chased her from the city. These stories also undercut the dominant narratives of slavery that the South was asserting after the war. As Cable well knew, in the South, truth is often stranger than fiction.

The selection from Lafcadio Hearn (who, like Cable, also has fiction in this collection) reminds us again of the connections of the African diaspora of the South to that of the Caribbean, with his description of a voudou ceremony on the shores of Lake Pontchartrain.

The readings conclude with W. E. B. Du Bois's tour through Georgia's Black Belt at the turn of the twentieth century. For Du Bois, this is a land drenched in history. Every crossroad, river or hamlet brings with it a tale of the peoples who lived and fought and suffered there. His descriptions of a bleak and impoverished countryside, its tenant shacks and decaying mansions, its struggling farmers and the remnants of its former aristocracy accentuates the tormented circularity of a book that began with Poe's haunted House of Usher.

I

THE TALES

Chapter One

VICTOR SÉJOUR (1817–1874)

Victor Séjour was born in the French Quarter of New Orleans in 1817. His parents were free *gens de couleur*, relatively affluent mixed-race people who nonetheless did not enjoy the same rights as those who were classified as white. They provided him with a solid education, and at the age of 19 he went to Paris. There he came to the attention of Cyrille Bissette, the influential editor of the *Revue des Colonies*, who published Séjour's short story "The Mulatto" ("Le Mulâtre") in 1837.

"The Mulatto" is acknowledged as the first short fiction published by an African American. It makes a compelling argument against slavery, and is set in St. Domingue (present-day Haiti), where enslaved people were treated with extreme brutality. It tells the story of Georges, a mixed-race man, and evokes the complex network of family relationships between enslaved people and their owners, describing the sexual abuse of enslaved women and the unrelenting exploitation of slave labor. The character of Georges embodies the greatest fear of Southern slaveholders, that of armed slave insurrection, which in this case involves not only rebellion but also patricide.

Text: Victor Séjour, "Le Mulâtre," http://french.centenary.edu/textes/mulatre.html, downloaded March 7, 2018, at 11:54. Translated by Susan Castillo Street.

THE MULATTO[1]

I

The first rays of dawn had just begun to illuminate the dark mountain peaks when I left the Cape for Saint-Marc, a small town in St. Domingue,[2] which is now the republic of Haiti. I had seen so many beautiful landscapes and tall deep forests that I had begun to feel indifferent to these stalwart beauties of Creation. However, when I beheld the aspect of this town, with its picturesque vegetation and its bizarre and novel nature, I was dazed and astonished at the sublime diversity of God's works. Upon my arrival, I was accosted by an old Negro, at least seventy years of age. His stride was firm, his head held high, his figure imposing and vigorous; the only thing that revealed his age was the remarkable whiteness of his curly hair. He wore a large straw hat, as is the custom of that country, and coarse grey linen trousers, with a plain batiste[3] jacket.

1 Mulatto is a dated term used to classify people of mixed race, usually with one black and one white parent.

2 A French colony on the island of Hispaniola from 1659 to 1804, now the Republic of Haiti.

3 A light linen or cotton fabric.

"Good morning, Master," he said, tipping his hat.

"Ah! There you are." I reached out my hand, which he shook.

"Master," he said, "you have a noble heart. But you know, do you not, that a Negro is as vile as a dog. Society rejects him; men detest him; the laws curse him … Yes, he's an unhappy creature, without even the consolation of always being virtuous. Though he may have been born good, noble, generous; that God may have granted him a virtuous soul, in spite of this he often goes to his grave with bloodstained hands, and a heart still crying out for vengeance. More than once he has seen his youthful dreams shattered, because experience has taught him that his good actions do not count, that he should not love his wife and his children, because one day the former will be seduced by his master, and his flesh and blood sold far away, despite his despair. What, then, can he be expected to become? Will he smash his own head against the paving stones? Will he kill his tormentor? Or do you believe that the human heart can manage to endure such misfortune?"

The old Negro awaited my response in silence.

"Whoever believes that is mad," he said heatedly. "If he survives, it is for revenge. Soon he will rise up … and the day he shakes off his servility, it would be preferable for his master to encounter a hungry tiger roaring at his side than to meet him face to face." While the old man spoke, his face lit up, his eyes glowed, and his heart beat hard. I would never have expected to encounter so much force and energy under such an elderly exterior. Taking advantage of this moment of high emotion, I said to him, "Antoine, you had promised to tell me the story of your old friend Georges."

"Do you want to hear it now?"

"Absolutely." We sat down, he on my trunk, I on my valise. Here is what he said to me.

"Do you see the building that rises so gracefully toward the sky, that is mirrored in the sea? That unique building that resembles a temple, or rather in its pretense, a palace? That is the house of Saint-M***. In one of the rooms of this building, one could find every day a group of idlers, of men of independent means, and of the owners of large plantations. The two first groups would play billiards, or smoke delicious Havana cigars, while the last group would buy Negroes, that is to say free men, taken by treachery or by force from their homeland, and transformed by violence into the asset, the property, of their fellow human beings. Here, we see the husband without his wife; there, the sister without her brother; there, the mother without her children. Does this make you shudder?" Still, this loathsome trade continues uninterrupted. Soon, the offering is a young Senegalese[4] woman, so lovely that the planters exclaim in unison, "How beautiful!" Every man there wants her for his mistress, but none dares bid against young Alfred, about twenty-two years old and one of the richest planters of this country.

"How much do you want for this woman?"

"Fifteen hundred piasters,"[5] said the auctioneer.

"Fifteen hundred piasters," repeated Alfred drily.

---

4 Many enslaved people were taken to the Americas from Senegal, in West Africa.

5 Silver coinage in use in France's North American and Caribbean colonies.

"Yes, Monsieur."

"Is that your price?"

"Yes, it is."

"That's horribly expensive."

"Expensive?" replied the auctioneer with an air of astonishment. "Do you not see how lovely she is, how fresh her skin is, how firm her flesh is? She is at most eighteen years old." As he spoke, he caressed the voluptuous, semi-naked body of the young African woman.

"Is she guaranteed?" asked Alfred, after a moment of reflection.

"Pure as the morning dew," replied the auctioneer. "But of course you yourself could …"

"No, that's not necessary," Alfred said, interrupting him. "I have confidence in you."

"I have never sold inferior merchandise," replied the auctioneer, with a triumphant gesture. When the bill of sale had been signed and all the formalities carried out, the auctioneer went over to the young slave.

"This man is now your master," he said, pointing to Alfred.

"I know," the Negress replied coldly.

"Are you pleased?"

"What does it matter, whether it is him or someone else?"

"But surely …" stammered the auctioneer, searching for some response.

"But surely what?" the African woman replied, with some irony. "And if he doesn't suit me?"

"My word, that would be unfortunate, for that would be the end of the matter."

"Then I'll keep my thoughts to myself."

Ten minutes later, Alfred's new slave stepped into a carriage that took the road called the Chemin des Guêpes,[6] winding through the beautiful landscapes clustered around St. Marc like young virgins at the foot of the altar. Her soul was drenched in melancholy, and she began to weep.

The driver understood what she was feeling, and tried to distract her. But when he saw Alfred's white house in the distance, he leaned toward her and asked, "Sister, what is your name?"

"Laïsa," she answered, not looking up.

When he heard this name, the driver shivered. Trying to control his emotion, he said, "Your mother?"

"She is dead."

"Your father?"

"He is dead."

"Poor child," he murmured. "What country are you from?"

"Senegal."

His eyes filled with tears. She was a fellow countrywoman.

"Sister," he said, wiping his eyes, "surely you know old Chambo and his daughter?"

6 Literally, Path of the Wasps.

"Why?" the young woman replied, raising her head.

"Why?" repeated the driver in anguish. "Old Chambo is my father, and …"

"My God," cried out the orphan, interrupting the driver before he could finish. "You are? …"

"Jacques Chambo,"

"My brother!"

"Laïsa!"

They fell into each other's arms. They were still in each other's arms when the carriage passed through the main entrance to Alfred's property. The overseer was there. "What's this I see!" he shouted, uncoiling a large whip which he always carried on his belt. "Jacques taking liberties before my very eyes with the new girl. What impertinence!" Lashes rained down on the unfortunate man, and streams of blood spurted from his eyes.

II

Alfred may have been a good humane man, loyal toward his peers, but he was certainly a hard, cruel man toward his slaves. I will not tell you everything he did to possess Laïsa; in the end, she was almost raped. For nearly a year she shared her master's bed, but he began to tire of her: he found her ugly, cold, insolent. Eventually she gave birth to a boy to whom she gave the name Georges. Alfred did not recognize him, and sent his mother away to the most decrepit hut on his lands, despite being aware, as much as he could be, that he was the child's father.

Georges grew up without ever hearing the name of his father. If he tried to pierce the veil that covered his birth, he found his mother inflexible and mute on this subject. Only on one occasion did she tell him, "My son, you will not know his name until you are twenty-five years old, for then you will be a man and will be able to keep such a secret. You do not know that he has forbidden me to speak of him and threatens to harm you if I do … do you see, Georges, that this man's hatred would be deadly for you.

"Who cares!" Georges cried out impetuously. "At least I could reproach him for his despicable conduct!"

"Hush, Georges, hush … walls have ears and even the undergrowth can speak," said the poor mother, trembling.

Some years later this poor woman died, bequeathing to Georges, her only son, a small leather pouch containing a portrait of his father, exacting the promise only to open it when he reached the age of twenty-five. She kissed him and her head fell back against the pillow. She was dead. The other slaves heard the orphan's cry of grief, and they began to weep, beat their breasts and tear their hair in sorrow. After these expressions of grief, they washed the dead woman's body and laid her out on a sort of long table, resting on wooden supports. They placed her lying on her back, facing east as is their custom, hands folded on her breast. At her feet was a bowl of holy water, with a sprig of jasmine floating on its surface. In the four corners around the deathbed were flaming torches. Each of them, after blessing the mortal remains of the deceased, knelt and prayed, for most of the Negro races, despite their fetishes, believe deeply in the existence of God. Once the ceremony came to an end, another one, no less singular, began, with shouts, weeping, chants, and funeral dances!

III

Georges had all the traits necessary to become an upstanding gentleman, but his character was haughty and stubborn, an oriental disposition that, once it strays from the path of virtue, will stride boldly down the road of crime. He would have given ten years of his life to know the name of his father, but he did not dare betray the solemn promise given to his mother on her deathbed. It was as though Nature urged him toward Alfred. He loved him, inasmuch as one can love a man, and Alfred was fond of him, but with that fondness that a horseman feels for the most beautiful and spirited of his racehorses. At the time, a group of bandits were wreaking havoc in the region; more than one settler had been their victim. One night, by what means I do not know, Georges learned of their plot. They had sworn to murder Alfred. The slave raced to his master's side:

"Master! Master!" he cried. "In the name of God, come with me!"

Alfred frowned.

"Oh! Follow me, follow me!" the mulatto said with feeling.

"Good heavens," said Alfred, "I think you are giving me orders."

"Forgive me, master, forgive me. I am beside myself. I don't know what I am saying. But in the name of Heaven, come with me, because …"

"Explain yourself," said Alfred in anger.

The mulatto hesitated.

"I insist. I order you," said Alfred, rising menacingly.

"Master, you're to be murdered tonight."

"By the Virgin, you're lying!"

"Master, they want to take your life."

"Who?"

"The bandits."

"Who told you?

"Master, that is my secret," said the mulatto in a submissive tone.

"Are you armed?" asked Alfred, after a moment of silence.

The mulatto pulled back some of the rags that covered him, revealing an axe and a pair of pistols.

"Good," said Alfred, hastily arming himself.

"Master, are you ready?"

"Let's go."

"Let's go," repeated the mulatto, taking a step toward the door. Alfred held him back by the arm. "Where are we going?" he asked.

"To the closest of your friends, M. Arthur.!"

They were about to leave when there was a loud pounding on the door.

"Hell," said the mulatto. "It's too late."

"What are you saying?"

"They're here," Georges replied, pointing at the door.

"Ah!"

"Master, what is the matter?"

"Nothing. A sudden malaise."

"Fear not, Master. To get to you they'll have to walk over my body," said the slave, with a calm, resigned air.

That calm air, that noble devotion would have been enough to reassure the most cowardly mortal. But on hearing these last words, Alfred trembled even harder, as he was overcome by a terrible idea: he imagined that the generous George was the accomplice of the assassins. Such is the tyrant: he believes all men incapable of elevated sentiments or selfless dedication, for their souls are narrow and perfidious, a terrain where nothing grows but thorns and weeds. The door shook violently. This time Alfred could not conceal his cowardice, when he saw the mulatto smiling. Was it in anger or joy? He knew not, and did not ask himself the question.

"Scoundrel!" he shouted, dashing into the next room. "You are plotting to have me killed, but your plot will not succeed." He disappeared.

Georges bit his lips in fury, but had no time to think. The door flew open, and four men stood on the threshold.

"We want to speak to you face to face," said one, shooting at Georges at close range.

"A fine shot," said Georges, trembling.

The bullet had broken his left arm. Georges fired a shot. The brigand spun around three times and fell stone dead. A second bandit followed. Then, like a furious lion surrounded by hunters, Georges, axe in hand, with a dagger between his teeth, leapt upon his adversaries. A ferocious battle ensued. The adversaries engage, collide as though they are bound together. The axe blade glistens ... blood flows ... the dagger, faithful to the hand that wields it, carves the chest of the enemy. But not a cry, not a word emerges from the mouths of the three men, kicking and brawling amid the corpses as though they were taking part in a drunken orgy. The sight of them, pale and blood-stained, mute and desperate, brought to mind three ghosts striking out at one another, tearing one another apart in the depths of a tomb. Meanwhile, Georges is covered with wounds and can hardly remain standing. Oh! The intrepid mulatto has reached the end of his life: a sharp axe hovers over his head. Suddenly, two shots ring out, and the two brigands fall to the ground, blaspheming against God.

At that moment, Alfred returns, accompanied by a young Negro. The wounded man is carried to his cabin, and Alfred orders that his own doctor attend him. Now you will learn how Georges came to be saved by the same man who accused him of treachery. As he ran away, Alfred heard gunshots, and the clash of steel; blushing at his own cowardice, he woke his manservant, and rushed to the aid of his liberator.

I had forgot to say that Georges had a wife named Zélie whom he loved with every fibre of his being. She was a mulatress aged between eighteen and twenty, tall and graceful, with black hair and a gaze full of love and sensuality. Georges hovered between life and death for twelve days, and Alfred went to visit him often. As luck would have it, he was taken with Zélie, but unfortunately for him, she was not one of those women whose favours are for sale, or use those favours to pay homage to their master. She repelled Alfred's advances, with humble dignity, for she did not forget that he was the master talking to a slave. Rather than being touched by this virtue which is so rare among women, especially among those, who, like Zélie, are slaves and see around them every day shameless women who prostitute themselves to colonists and encourage their libertine behavior, instead of being moved by this, as I have said, Alfred was annoyed. What? He, the Bey,[7] the sultan of the Antilles, to be turned down by a slave? What irony! He vowed he would possess her. Some days before Georges's recovery, Alfred ordered Zélie to come to his room. There, heeding only his own lawless desires, he put his arms around her and planted an ardent kiss on her cheek. The young slave implored, pleaded, resisted, but in vain. Now he leads her towards the bed of shame … Then the young slave, filled with noble indignation, pushes him away as a last resort, but so suddenly and with such strength that Alfred lost his balance and struck his head as he fell. At the sight of this, Zélie tore her hair in despair and wept in rage, for the poor girl realized that death was the fate of anyone who shed the blood of such a vile being. After weeping for some time, she went to her husband. He was no doubt dreaming of her, for on his lips was a smile. "Georges … Georges!" she cried out in anguish.

The mulatto opened his eyes. His first impulse was to smile at his beloved. Zélie told him what had just happened. He could hardly believe it, but soon he was convinced of his misfortune, for men burst into the room and bound his wife, who was sobbing. George attempted to rise, but as he was still too weak, he fell back onto the bed, his eyes sunken, his fists clenched, his open mouth panting for air.

IV

Days later, two white Creole children were playing in the street.

"Charles," said one, "they say the mulatto woman who tried to kill her master will be hanged tomorrow"?

"At eight o'clock,' replied the other.

"Are you going?"

"Of course."

"It will be fun to see her dance between heaven and earth" responded the first child, as they walked away laughing.

It will astonish you to hear two ten-year-old children finding someone's death so wonderfully entertaining. It is a consequence, perhaps inevitably, of their upbringing. From an early age they hear repeatedly that we are born to serve them, created to serve their whims, and that they should have the same consideration for us that they would have for a dog. What does our agony, our sufferings, matter to them? Do they not often see their best horses die? They do not weep, for they are rich and soon will buy others … As these two children were talking, George was kneeling at his master's feet.

"Master, have mercy … mercy," he cried, weeping. "Take pity on Her … Master, save her … .Oh! yes, save her, for you can … Oh! Speak … You have only one word to say, only one, and she will live." Alfred did not reply.

---

[7] "Bey" is the Turkish title for chieftain, traditionally applied to the leaders or rulers of the Ottoman Empire.

"Oh, for pity's sake, Master … for pity's sake tell me that you will pardon her … Oh! Speak … answer me, Master … won't you pardon her." The poor man was bent double in pain.

"I can do nothing," answered Alfred coldly.

The mulatto wiped away his tears and drew himself up to his full height.

"Master," he went on in a hollow voice, "do you remember what you told me when I was on my sickbed writhing in agony?"

"No …"

"Well I can remember. The master said to the slave: "You saved my life. What do you want as a reward? Do you want your freedom?" "Master,' responded the slave, I cannot be free while my son and my wife are enslaved."

Then the master responded, "If you ever ask me, I give you my word that your wishes will be granted." And the slave did not ask, for he was happy that he had saved his master's life. But today, when he knows that in eighteen hours his wife will no longer be alive, he comes to kneel at your feet and cry out, "Master, in the name of God, save my wife." And the mulatto, hands clasped, in an attitude of supplication, knelt down and wept floods of tears.

Alfred turned away.

"Master … master … for pity's sake answer me … Oh! Say that you want for her to live … in the name of God … in your mother's name … mercy … have mercy on us." The mulatto kissed the dust at his master's feet.

Alfred remained silent.

"But at least speak to this poor man who is begging you," the mulatto sobbed. "My God … my God! How miserable I am." He writhed on the floor, tearing his hair in despair.

Alfred then chose to speak: "I have told you that it is no longer up to me to pardon her."

"Master," Georges murmured in tears, "she will probably be condemned, for only you and I know that she is innocent."

On hearing these last words from the mulatto, Alfred's face reddened, and his heart was filled with rage. Georges realized that the moment for begging had passed, for he had raised the veil concealing his master's crime. He rose to his feet with a resolute air.

"Leave! Go away, I say!" shouted Alfred.

Instead of leaving, the mulatto crossed his arms over his chest. With a wild air, he gazed at his master from head to foot.

"Go away! Go away, I tell you!" responded Alfred, whose anger was increasing.

"I am not leaving," replied Georges.

"You are defying me, you wretch." Alfred made a movement to strike him, but his hand remained at his side when he saw the pride and hatred in George's face.

"What! You will leave her to be killed, to have her throat cut, to be murdered," said the mulatto, "when you know that she is innocent … when, like a coward, you tried to seduce her."

"Insolent! What are you saying?"

"I am saying that it would be an infamous act to let her die."

"Georges … Georges …"

"I am saying that you are a scoundrel," Georges shouted, giving full rein to his anger, seizing Alfred's arm …" Ah! She'll die…she will die because she did not prostitute herself to you, because you are white … because you are her master … you corrupt coward!"

"Careful, Georges," replied Alfred, trying to keep his voice under control. "Be careful that, instead of one victim, the hangman does not find two.

"You speak of victim and hangman, you wretch," Georges screamed. "That means she will die … she … my Zélie … but you do not know that your life is linked to hers."

"Georges!"

"You do not know that your head will remain on your shoulders only as long as she is alive."

"Georges … Georges!"

"You do not know that I will kill you … that I will drink your blood if one hair of her head is harmed." During all this time the mulatto was shaking Alfred with all his strength.

"Leave me alone!" shrieked Alfred.

"Ah! She will die … she will die," cried the mulatto in anguish.

"Georges, leave me!"

"Shut up … shut up, wretch … ah! She is dying … well, if the executioner ends my wife's life …" he continued with a dreadful smile. Alfred was so agitated that he did not see Georges leave. Georges went straight to his cabin, where a two-year-old child lay sleeping in a cradle made of lianas.[8] He picked him up and disappeared. To understand what follows, you should be aware that from Alfred's house, one had only to cross a small river to find oneself in the middle of the dense forest, like those who seem to hold the New World in their arms. For six long hours, Georges walked on without stopping to rest. At last he stopped a few steps away from a cabin built in the deepest part of the forest. You will understand the kind of joy that shone in his eyes when you discover that this small isolated cabin was part of the Maroon[9] camp, that is to say of slaves who had fled the tyranny of their masters. At that moment the cabin was filled with rumors, because a rustling noise had been heard in the forest, and the chief could have sworn that the noise had not been made by any animal. He took up his firearm and stepped out. Suddenly the undergrowth parted before him, and he found himself face to face with a stranger.

"By my freedom," he said, looking carefully at the stranger, "you know our hiding-place too well."

"Africa and freedom," replied Georges calmly, pushing the gun barrel to one side. "I'm one of you."

"Your name."

"Georges, Alfred's slave."

They shook hands and embraced.

---

8 A woody climbing plant found in tropical rainforests.

9 Maroons were enslaved people who had escaped from their masters. The term is derived from *cimarrón,* a Spanish word meaning "wild or unruly."

The next a crowd milled around the foot of a scaffold, where the corpse of a young mulatto woman was hanging … Once she was dead, the hangman lowered her body into a pine coffin. Ten minutes later, body and coffin were thrown into a pit which had been dug at the entrance to the forest. Thus this woman, who had been too virtuous, met a death like that meted out to the vilest of criminals. Would this alone not be enough to make the most gentle of men dangerous and bloodthirsty?

V

Three years had gone by since the death of the virtuous Zélie. For a time, Alfred was tormented. By day, he constantly imagined a vengeful hand hovering over his head; by night, he trembled, because of hideous, frightful dreams. Soon, however, he banished from his mind the painful memory of the martyred woman and the terrifying threat made by Georges; he married and became a father. How happy he was when he was told that his prayers had been answered, he who had kissed the paving stones of the temple praying to Our Lady of the Sorrows for a son.

Georges too was content with this child's arrival. For if he had waited for three years to strike against his wife's executioner, if he had spent countless sleepless nights with rage in his heart and his hand on his dagger, it is because he was waiting for Alfred to have, like him, a wife and a son; he only wanted to kill him at the moment these dear and precious bonds linked him to this world …

Georges had always maintained close ties to one of Alfred's slaves, and went to see him every week. This slave hastened to inform him of the newborn's arrival. He immediately set out for the house of his enemy and encountered on the way a Negro woman who was taking a cup of broth to Alfred's wife. He stopped her, exchanged a few insignificant words, and pressed on. After some difficulties, he slipped like a serpent into Alfred's bed-chamber … There, hidden in the space beside the bed, he waited for his master …

Alfred entered the room humming a song. He opened his secretary and took out a superb jewellery box set with diamonds that he had promised his wife if she gave him a son. Full of joy and happiness, he sat down with his head between his hands, like a man who can hardly believe his own unexpected good fortune. But when he raised his head, he saw in front of him a motionless shadow, arms crossed on its chest, its two burning eyes with the ferocity of a tiger about to tear its prey to bits. Alfred attempted to rise, but a strong hand held him in his chair.

"What do you want of me?" asked Alfred, his voice trembling.

"To congratulate you on your son's birth," said a voice that sounded as though it was emerging from a grave.

Alfred shivered from head to foot, and broke into a cold sweat.

"I do not know you," Alfred murmured weakly.

"My name is Georges."

"You …"

"You thought I was dead, didn't you?" said the mulatto, with a grim laugh. "Help! Help!" cried Alfred.

"Who will help you?" replied the mulatto. "Haven't you sent all your servants away and locked all the doors so that you can be alone with your wife? You see, don't you, that your cries are useless. You should commend your soul to God."

Alfred had risen little by little from his chair, but on hearing this he fell back, pale and trembling.

"Oh! Have pity, Georges, do not kill me, not today."

Georges shrugged. "Master, isn't it horrible to die at the moment you are seeing your dearest dreams come true? Isn't it dreadful?" said the mulatto, with a devilish laugh.

"Mercy, Georges …"

"And yet this is your fate … you will die today, this hour, this minute, without telling your wife farewell for the last time."

"Pity … have pity."

"Without holding your newborn son again."

"Oh! Mercy … have mercy."

"My revenge is worthy of yours…I would have sold my soul to Satan if he had promised me this moment."

"Oh! Mercy … have pity," cried Alfred, clinging to the mulatto's knees.

Alfred shrugged and raised his hatchet.

"Oh! Just one more hour of life!" "To embrace your wife, is that it?" "One minute."

"To see your child, isn't it?"

"Oh! Have mercy."

"You might as well ask a hungry tiger to let go of his prey."

"In the name of God, Georges!"

"I no longer believe in Him."

"In the name of your father."

At that word, Georges's fury subsided. "My father … my father," said the mulatto, his eyes overflowing with tears. "You know him … oh! tell me his name. What is he called? Oh! tell me his name. I will bless you … I will pardon you." And the mulatto was about to kneel at his master's feet. But suddenly shrill cries were heard …

"By Heaven, that is my wife's voice!" cried Alfred, dashing toward the corner where the cries were coming from. As though returning to his senses, the mulatto recalled that he had come to his master's house, not to learn the name of his father, but to settle accounts with him for the blood of his wife. Holding Alfred back, he told him with a dreadful sneer, "Stop, Master, it's nothing."

"Jesus and Mary, don't you hear that she's crying out for help?"

"It's nothing, I tell you."

"Let me go … let me go. It is my wife's voice."

"No, it is the death rattle of a woman."

"Wretch, you lie!"

"I have poisoned her."

"Oh!"

"Do you hear these shrieks? They are hers."

"The Devil …"

"Do you hear those cries? They are hers."

"Damnation!"

As this was taking place, Alfred struggled to escape from the hands of the mulatto, but the latter held him tighter and tighter, for his head was exploding, his heart was beating faster as he braced himself for his dreadful task.

"Alfred … help … water … I am suffocating," cried a woman as she staggered into the middle of the room. She was pale and weak, and her eyes seemed to be popping out of her head; her hair was dishevelled.

"Alfred! Alfred, in the name of heaven, help me … water! A little water. My blood is boiling … my heart is clenching … oh! Water! Water!"

Alfred struggled mightily to come to her aid, but Georges held him back with an iron hand. Laughing like one of the damned, he cried, "No, Master, no. I want for this woman to die … right here … before your very eyes, in front of you. Do you understand, master, in front of you, begging for water, for air, without your being able to help her?"

"Damnation! Damn you," howled Alfred, struggling like a madman.

"Curse and blaspheme all you like," answered the mulatto. "This is how it will be."

"Alfred," the dying woman moaned once more. "Farewell, farewell. I am dying."

"Look on, "responded the mulatto, still laughing. "Look … she is gasping for air. Just one drop of this water would bring her back to life." He showed him a small vial.

"My entire fortune for that drop of water," cried Alfred.

"You must be mad, master."

"That water … that water … can't you see she's dying? Give it to me! Please give it to me."

"Here," and the mulatto dashed the vial against the wall.

"Damn you," screamed Alfred, seizing George by the neck. "Oh! My whole life, my soul, for a dagger …"

Georges released Alfred's hands "Now that she is dead, it is your turn, master," he said, lifting the hatchet.

"Strike, executioner … strike … after poisoning her, you might as well kill your own fa—." The hatchet fell, and Alfred's head rolled across the floor, but as it rolled it murmured distinctly the last syllable "—ther." Georges thought he had not heard correctly, but the word "father," tolling like a funeral bell, rang in his ear. To be certain, he opened the fateful pouch. "Ah!" he cried. "I am damned." A shot rang out, and the next day, near the corpse of Alfred, was found the body of the unfortunate Georges.

Chapter Two

EDGAR ALLAN POE (1809–1849)

Poe's fame is universal and his influence on both poetry and prose is immense, and international. He may at first seem an unusual choice for a collection specifically on Southern Gothic. He was born in Boston and spent part of his childhood in England. His landscapes seem projections of dream or nightmare and are usually stripped of local reference. However, he had deep connections with the South, especially Richmond, Virginia, the home of the Allans, his adopted parents. He attended, for a time, the University of Virginia. Recent scholars have stressed Southern and racial themes in his works.

"The Fall of the House of Usher" is a foundational text of the Southern Gothic. The doomed house (in both senses, a physical structure and a family) are found throughout Southern literature, and especially looms after the Civil War, when decaying mansions and a decaying plantation aristocracy could be seen everywhere in the deep South. W. E. B. Du Bois describes these families and houses with a historian's eyes, and they are to be seen in several stories in this collection, as well as in great twentieth-century Gothic novels such as William Faulkner's *Absalom, Absalom!* Over all these houses falls the shadow of the Ushers.

Text: Rufus Wilmot Griswold, *The Works of the Late Edgar Allan Poe*, 4 vols. (New York: Redfield, 1857).

THE FALL OF THE HOUSE OF USHER

Son cœur est un luth suspendu;
Sitôt qu'on le touche il résonne.[1]

De Béranger

During the whole of a dull, dark, and soundless day in the autumn of the year, when the clouds hung oppressively low in the heavens, I had been passing alone, on horseback, through a singularly dreary tract of country; and at length found myself, as the shades of the evening drew on, within view of the melancholy House of Usher. I know not how it was—but, with the first glimpse of the building, a sense of insufferable gloom pervaded my spirit. I say insufferable; for the feeling was unrelieved by any of that half-pleasurable, because poetic, sentiment with which the mind usually receives even the sternest natural images of the desolate or terrible. I looked upon the scene before me—upon the mere

---

1 French: His heart is a lute; touch it, and at once it sounds.

house, and the simple landscape features of the domain—upon the bleak walls—upon the vacant eye-like windows—upon a few rank sedges[2]—and upon a few white trunks of decayed trees—with an utter depression of soul which I can compare to no earthly sensation more properly than to the after-dream of the reveller upon opium—the bitter lapse into everyday life—the hideous dropping off of the veil. There was an iciness, a sinking, a sickening of the heart—an unredeemed dreariness of thought which no goading of the imagination could torture into aught of the sublime. What was it—I paused to think—what was it that so unnerved me in the contemplation of the House of Usher? It was a mystery all insoluble; nor could I grapple with the shadowy fancies that crowded upon me as I pondered. I was forced to fall back upon the unsatisfactory conclusion, that while, beyond doubt, there *are* combinations of very simple natural objects which have the power of thus affecting us, still the analysis of this power lies among considerations beyond our depth.[3] It was possible, I reflected, that a mere different arrangement of the particulars of the scene, of the details of the picture, would be sufficient to modify, or perhaps to annihilate its capacity for sorrowful impression; and, acting upon this idea, I reined my horse to the precipitous brink of a black and lurid tarn[4] that lay in unruffled lustre by the dwelling, and gazed down—but with a shudder even more thrilling than before—upon the remodelled and inverted images of the gray sedge, and the ghastly tree-stems, and the vacant and eye-like windows.

Nevertheless, in this mansion of gloom I now proposed to myself a sojourn of some weeks. Its proprietor, Roderick Usher, had been one of my boon companions in boyhood; but many years had elapsed since our last meeting. A letter, however, had lately reached me in a distant part of the country—a letter from him—which, in its wildly importunate nature, had admitted of no other than a personal reply. The MS. gave evidence of nervous agitation. The writer spoke of acute bodily illness—of a mental disorder which oppressed him—and of an earnest desire to see me, as his best, and indeed his only personal friend, with a view of attempting, by the cheerfulness of my society, some alleviation of his malady. It was the manner in which all this, and much more, was said—it was the apparent *heart* that went with his request—which allowed me no room for hesitation; and I accordingly obeyed forthwith what I still considered a very singular summons.

Although, as boys, we had been even intimate associates, yet I really knew little of my friend. His reserve had been always excessive and habitual. I was aware, however, that his very ancient family had been noted, time out of mind, for a peculiar sensibility of temperament, displaying itself, through long ages, in many works of exalted art, and manifested, of late, in repeated deeds of munificent yet unobtrusive charity, as well as in a passionate devotion to the intricacies, perhaps even more than to the orthodox and easily recognizable beauties, of musical science. I had learned, too, the very remarkable fact, that the stem of the Usher race, all time-honored as it was, had put forth, at no

---

2 Grass-like vegetation.

3 Poe probably did not know of the Chinese system of *fung shui*, which describes the spiritual effects of the placement of objects in landscapes, but this is essentially what he is describing.

4 Term in northern England for a small lake.

period, any enduring branch; in other words, that the entire family lay in the direct line of descent, and had always, with very trifling and very temporary variation, so lain. It was this deficiency, I considered, while running over in thought the perfect keeping of the character of the premises with the accredited character of the people, and while speculating upon the possible influence which the one, in the long lapse of centuries, might have exercised upon the other—it was this deficiency, perhaps, of collateral issue, and the consequent undeviating transmission, from sire to son, of the patrimony with the name, which had, at length, so identified the two as to merge the original title of the estate in the quaint and equivocal appellation of the "House of Usher"—an appellation which seemed to include, in the minds of the peasantry who used it, both the family and the family mansion.

I have said that the sole effect of my somewhat childish experiment—that of looking down within the tarn—had been to deepen the first singular impression. There can be no doubt that the consciousness of the rapid increase of my superstition—for why should I not so term it?—served mainly to accelerate the increase itself. Such, I have long known, is the paradoxical law of all sentiments having terror as a basis. And it might have been for this reason only, that, when I again uplifted my eyes to the house itself, from its image in the pool, there grew in my mind a strange fancy—a fancy so ridiculous, indeed, that I but mention it to show the vivid force of the sensations which oppressed me. I had so worked upon my imagination as really to believe that about the whole mansion and domain there hung an atmosphere peculiar to themselves and their immediate vicinity—an atmosphere which had no affinity with the air of heaven, but which had reeked up from the decayed trees, and the gray wall, and the silent tarn—a pestilent and mystic vapor, dull, sluggish, faintly discernible, and leaden-hued.

Shaking off from my spirit what *must* have been a dream, I scanned more narrowly the real aspect of the building. Its principal feature seemed to be that of an excessive antiquity. The discoloration of ages had been great. Minute fungi overspread the whole exterior, hanging in a fine tangled web-work from the eaves. Yet all this was apart from any extraordinary dilapidation. No portion of the masonry had fallen; and there appeared to be a wild inconsistency between its still perfect adaptation of parts, and the crumbling condition of the individual stones. In this there was much that reminded me of the specious totality of old wood-work which has rotted for long years in some neglected vault, with no disturbance from the breath of the external air. Beyond this indication of extensive decay, however, the fabric gave little token of instability. Perhaps the eye of a scrutinizing observer might have discovered a barely perceptible fissure, which, extending from the roof of the building in front, made its way down the wall in a zig-zag direction, until it became lost in the sullen waters of the tarn.

Noticing these things, I rode over a short causeway to the house. A servant in waiting took my horse, and I entered the Gothic archway of the hall. A valet, of stealthy step, thence conducted me, in silence, through many dark and intricate passages in my progress to the *studio* of his master. Much that I encountered on the way contributed, I know not how, to heighten the vague sentiments of which I have already spoken. While the objects around me—while the carvings of the ceilings, the sombre tapestries of the walls, the ebon blackness of the floors, and the phantasmagoric armorial trophies which rattled as

I strode, were but matters to which, or to such as which, I had been accustomed from my infancy—while I hesitated not to acknowledge how familiar was all this—I still wondered to find how unfamiliar were the fancies which ordinary images were stirring up. On one of the staircases, I met the physician of the family. His countenance, I thought, wore a mingled expression of low cunning and perplexity. He accosted me with trepidation and passed on. The valet now threw open a door and ushered me into the presence of his master.

The room in which I found myself was very large and lofty. The windows were long, narrow, and pointed, and at so vast a distance from the black oaken floor as to be altogether inaccessible from within. Feeble gleams of encrimsoned light made their way through the trellissed panes, and served to render sufficiently distinct the more prominent objects around; the eye, however, struggled in vain to reach the remoter angles of the chamber, or the recesses of the vaulted and fretted ceiling. Dark draperies hung upon the walls. The general furniture was profuse, comfortless, antique, and tattered. Many books and musical instruments lay scattered about, but failed to give any vitality to the scene. I felt that I breathed an atmosphere of sorrow. An air of stern, deep, and irredeemable gloom hung over and pervaded all.

Upon my entrance, Usher arose from a sofa on which he had been lying at full length, and greeted me with a vivacious warmth which had much in it, I at first thought, of an overdone cordiality—of the constrained effort of the *ennuyé* man of the world. A glance, however, at his countenance convinced me of his perfect sincerity. We sat down; and for some moments, while he spoke not, I gazed upon him with a feeling half of pity, half of awe. Surely, man had never before so terribly altered, in so brief a period, as had Roderick Usher! It was with difficulty that I could bring myself to admit the identity of the wan being before me with the companion of my early boyhood. Yet the character of his face had been at all times remarkable. A cadaverousness of complexion; an eye large, liquid, and luminous beyond comparison; lips somewhat thin and very pallid, but of a surpassingly beautiful curve; a nose of a delicate Hebrew model, but with a breadth of nostril unusual in similar formations; a finely moulded chin, speaking, in its want of prominence, of a want of moral energy; hair of a more than weblike softness and tenuity; these features, with an inordinate expansion above the regions of the temple, made up altogether a countenance not easily to be forgotten. And now in the mere exaggeration of the prevailing character of these features, and of the expression they were wont to convey, lay so much of change that I doubted to whom I spoke. The now ghastly pallor of the skin, and the now miraculous lustre of the eye, above all things startled and even awed me. The silken hair, too, had been suffered to grow all unheeded, and as, in its wild gossamer texture, it floated rather than fell about the face, I could not, even with effort, connect its Arabesque expression with any idea of simple humanity.

In the manner of my friend I was at once struck with an incoherence—an inconsistency; and I soon found this to arise from a series of feeble and futile struggles to overcome an habitual trepidancy—an excessive nervous agitation. For something of this nature I had indeed been prepared, no less by his letter, than by reminiscences of certain boyish traits, and by conclusions deduced from his peculiar physical conformation and temperament. His action was alternately vivacious and sullen. His voice varied rapidly

from a tremulous indecision (when the animal spirits seemed utterly in abeyance) to that species of energetic concision—that abrupt, weighty, unhurried, and hollow-sounding enunciation—that leaden, self-balanced, and perfectly modulated guttural utterance, which may be observed in the lost drunkard, or the irreclaimable eater of opium, during the periods of his most intense excitement.

It was thus that he spoke of the object of my visit, of his earnest desire to see me, and of the solace he expected me to afford him. He entered, at some length, into what he conceived to be the nature of his malady. It was, he said, a constitutional and a family evil, and one for which he despaired to find a remedy—a mere nervous affection, he immediately added, which would undoubtedly soon pass off. It displayed itself in a host of unnatural sensations. Some of these, as he detailed them, interested and bewildered me; although, perhaps, the terms, and the general manner of their narration had their weight. He suffered much from a morbid acuteness of the senses; the most insipid food was alone endurable; he could wear only garments of certain texture; the odors of all flowers were oppressive; his eyes were tortured by even a faint light; and there were but peculiar sounds, and these from stringed instruments, which did not inspire him with horror.

To an anomalous species of terror I found him a bounden slave. "I shall perish," said he, "I *must* perish in this deplorable folly. Thus, thus, and not otherwise, shall I be lost. I dread the events of the future, not in themselves, but in their results. I shudder at the thought of any, even the most trivial, incident, which may operate upon this intolerable agitation of soul. I have, indeed, no abhorrence of danger, except in its absolute effect—in terror. In this unnerved, in this pitiable, condition I feel that the period will sooner or later arrive when I must abandon life and reason together, in some struggle with the grim phantasm, FEAR."

I learned, moreover, at intervals, and through broken and equivocal hints, another singular feature of his mental condition. He was enchained by certain superstitious impressions in regard to the dwelling which he tenanted, and whence, for many years, he had never ventured forth—in regard to an influence whose supposititious force was conveyed in terms too shadowy here to be re-stated—an influence which some peculiarities in the mere form and substance of his family mansion had, by dint of long sufferance, he said, obtained over his spirit—an effect which the *physique* of the gray walls and turrets, and of the dim tarn into which they all looked down, had, at length, brought about upon the *morale* of his existence.

He admitted, however, although with hesitation, that much of the peculiar gloom which thus afflicted him could be traced to a more natural and far more palpable origin—to the severe and long-continued illness—indeed to the evidently approaching dissolution—of a tenderly beloved sister, his sole companion for long years, his last and only relative on earth. "Her decease," he said, with a bitterness which I can never forget, "would leave him (him, the hopeless and the frail) the last of the ancient race of the Ushers." While he spoke, the lady Madeline (for so was she called) passed through a remote portion of the apartment, and, without having noticed my presence, disappeared. I regarded her with an utter astonishment not unmingled with dread; and yet I found it impossible to account for such feelings. A sensation of stupor oppressed me as my eyes followed her retreating steps. When a door, at length, closed upon her, my glance sought instinctively and eagerly the countenance of the brother—but he had buried his face in his hands, and I could only perceive that a far more than ordinary wanness had overspread the emaciated fingers through which trickled many passionate tears.

The disease of the lady Madeline had long baffled the skill of her physicians. A settled apathy, a gradual wasting away of the person, and frequent although transient affections of a partially cataleptical character were the unusual diagnosis. Hitherto she had steadily borne up against the pressure of her malady, and had not betaken herself finally to bed; but on the closing in of the evening of my arrival at the house, she succumbed (as her brother told me at night with inexpressible agitation) to the prostrating power of the destroyer; and I learned that the glimpse I had obtained of her person would thus probably be the last I should obtain—that the lady, at least while living, would be seen by me no more.

For several days ensuing, her name was unmentioned by either Usher or myself: and during this period I was busied in earnest endeavors to alleviate the melancholy of my friend. We painted and read together; or I listened, as if in a dream, to the wild improvisations of his speaking guitar. And thus, as a closer and still closer intimacy admitted me more unreservedly into the recesses of his spirit, the more bitterly did I perceive the futility of all attempts at cheering a mind from which darkness, as if an inherent positive quality, poured forth upon all objects of the moral and physical universe in one unceasing radiation of gloom.

I shall ever bear about me a memory of the many solemn hours I thus spent alone with the master of the House of Usher. Yet I should fail in any attempt to convey an idea of the exact character of the studies, or of the occupations, in which he involved me, or led me the way. An excited and highly distempered ideality threw a sulphureous lustre over all. His long improvised dirges will ring forever in my ears. Among other things, I hold painfully in mind a certain singular perversion and amplification of the wild air of the last waltz of Von Weber. From the paintings over which his elaborate fancy brooded, and which grew, touch by touch, into vaguenesses at which I shuddered the more thrillingly, because I shuddered knowing not why;—from these paintings (vivid as their images now are before me) I would in vain endeavor to educe more than a small portion which should lie within the compass of merely written words. By the utter simplicity, by the nakedness of his designs, he arrested and overawed attention. If ever mortal painted an idea, that mortal was Roderick Usher. For me at least, in the circumstances then surrounding me, there arose out of the pure abstractions which the hypochondriac contrived to throw upon his canvas, an intensity of intolerable awe, no shadow of which felt I ever yet in the contemplation of the certainly glowing yet too concrete reveries of Fuseli.

One of the phantasmagoric conceptions of my friend, partaking not so rigidly of the spirit of abstraction, may be shadowed forth, although feebly, in words. A small picture presented the interior of an immensely long and rectangular vault or tunnel, with low walls, smooth, white, and without interruption or device. Certain accessory points of the design served well to convey the idea that this excavation lay at an exceeding depth below the surface of the earth. No outlet was observed in any portion of its vast extent, and no torch or other artificial source of light was discernible; yet a flood of intense rays rolled throughout, and bathed the whole in a ghastly and inappropriate splendor.

I have just spoken of that morbid condition of the auditory nerve which rendered all music intolerable to the sufferer, with the exception of certain effects of stringed instruments. It was, perhaps, the narrow limits to which he thus confined himself upon the guitar which gave birth, in great measure, to the fantastic character of his performances. But the fervid *facility* of his *impromptus* could not be so accounted for. They must have been, and were, in the notes, as well as in the words of his wild fantasias (for he not unfrequently accompanied himself with rhymed verbal improvisations), the result of that intense mental collectedness and concentration to which I have previously alluded as observable only in particular moments of the highest artificial excitement. The words of one of these rhapsodies I have easily remembered. I was, perhaps, the more forcibly impressed with it as he gave it, because, in the under or mystic current of its meaning, I fancied that I perceived, and for the first time, a full consciousness on the part of Usher of the tottering of his lofty reason upon her throne. The verses, which were entitled "The Haunted Palace," ran very nearly, if not accurately, thus:

I.
In the greenest of our valleys,
   By good angels tenanted,
Once a fair and stately palace—
   Radiant palace—reared its head.
In the monarch Thought's dominion—
   It stood there!
Never seraph spread a pinion
   Over fabric half so fair.

II.
Banners yellow, glorious, golden,
   On its roof did float and flow;
(This—all this—was in the olden
   Time long ago)
And every gentle air that dallied,
   In that sweet day,
Along the ramparts plumed and pallid,
   A winged odor went away.

III.
Wanderers in that happy valley
   Through two luminous windows saw
Spirits moving musically
   To a lute's well-tunèd law;
Round about a throne, where sitting

(Porphyrogene!)[5]
In state his glory well befitting,
The ruler of the realm was seen.

IV.
And all with pearl and ruby glowing
Was the fair palace door,
Through which came flowing, flowing, flowing
And sparkling evermore,
A troop of Echoes whose sweet duty
Was but to sing,
In voices of surpassing beauty,
The wit and wisdom of their king.

V.
But evil things, in robes of sorrow,
Assailed the monarch's high estate;
(Ah, let us mourn, for never morrow
Shall dawn upon him, desolate!)
And, round about his home, the glory
That blushed and bloomed
Is but a dim-remembered story
Of the old time entombed.

VI.
And travellers now within that valley,
Through the red-litten windows see
Vast forms that move fantastically
To a discordant melody;
While, like a rapid ghastly river,
Through the pale door;
A hideous throng rush out forever,
And laugh—but smile no more.

I well remember that suggestions arising from this ballad led us into a train of thought wherein there became manifest an opinion of Usher's which I mention not so much on account of its novelty (for other men[6] have thought thus), as on account of the pertinacity with which he maintained it. This opinion, in its general form, was that of the sentience of all vegetable things. But, in his disordered fancy, the idea had assumed

5 Apparently Poe's invention: "born to the purple," i.e., royal.

6 Poe's note: Watson, Dr. Percival, Spallanzini, and especially the Bishop of Landaff—See "Chemical Essays," vol. v.

a more daring character, and trespassed, under certain conditions, upon the kingdom of inorganization. I lack words to express the full extent, or the earnest *abandon* of his persuasion. The belief, however, was connected (as I have previously hinted) with the gray stones of the home of his forefathers. The conditions of the sentience had been here, he imagined, fulfilled in the method of collocation of these stones—in the order of their arrangement, as well as in that of the many *fungi* which overspread them, and of the decayed trees which stood around—above all, in the long undisturbed endurance of this arrangement, and in its reduplication in the still waters of the tarn. Its evidence—the evidence of the sentience—was to be seen, he said (and I here started as he spoke), in the gradual yet certain condensation of an atmosphere of their own about the waters and the walls. The result was discoverable, he added, in that silent yet importunate and terrible influence which for centuries had moulded the destinies of his family, and which made him what I now saw him—what he was. Such opinions need no comment, and I will make none.

Our books—the books which, for years, had formed no small portion of the mental existence of the invalid—were, as might be supposed, in strict keeping with this character of phantasm. We pored together over such works as the Ververt et Chartreuse of Gresset; the Belphegor of Machiavelli; the Heaven and Hell of Swedenborg; the Subterranean Voyage of Nicholas Klimm by Holberg; the Chiromancy of Robert Flud, of Jean D'Indaginé, and of Dela Chambre; the Journey into the Blue Distance of Tieck; and the City of the Sun of Campanella. One favorite volume was a small octavo edition of the *Directorium Inquisitorium*, by the Dominican Eymeric de Gironne; and there were passages in Pomponius Mela, about the old African Satyrs and Œgipans, over which Usher would sit dreaming for hours. His chief delight, however, was found in the perusal of an exceedingly rare and curious book in quarto Gothic—the manual of a forgotten church—the *Vigiliae Mortuorum secundum Chorum Ecclesiae Maguntinae.*

I could not help thinking of the wild ritual of this work, and of its probable influence upon the hypochondriac, when, one evening, having informed me abruptly that the lady Madeline was no more, he stated his intention of preserving her corpse for a fortnight (previously to its final interment,) in one of the numerous vaults within the main walls of the building. The worldly reason, however, assigned for this singular proceeding, was one which I did not feel at liberty to dispute. The brother had been led to his resolution (so he told me) by consideration of the unusual character of the malady of the deceased, of certain obtrusive and eager inquiries on the part of her medical men, and of the remote and exposed situation of the burial-ground of the family. I will not deny that when I called to mind the sinister countenance of the person whom I met upon the staircase, on the day of my arrival at the house, I had no desire to oppose what I regarded as at best but a harmless, and by no means an unnatural, precaution.

At the request of Usher, I personally aided him in the arrangements for the temporary entombment. The body having been encoffined, we two alone bore it to its rest. The vault in which we placed it (and which had been so long unopened that our torches, half smothered in its oppressive atmosphere, gave us little opportunity for investigation) was small, damp, and entirely without means of admission for light; lying, at great depth, immediately beneath that portion of the building in which was my own sleeping apartment. It had been used, apparently, in remote feudal times, for the worst purposes of a donjon-keep, and, in later days, as a place of deposit for powder, or some other highly combustible substance, as a portion of its floor, and the whole interior of a long archway through which we reached it, were carefully sheathed with copper. The door, of massive iron, had been, also, similarly protected. Its immense weight caused an unusually sharp, grating sound, as it moved upon its hinges.

Having deposited our mournful burden upon tressels within this region of horror, we partially turned aside the yet unscrewed lid of the coffin, and looked upon the face of the tenant. A striking similitude between the brother and sister now first arrested my attention; and Usher, divining, perhaps, my thoughts, murmured out some few words from which I learned that the deceased and himself had been twins, and that sympathies of a scarcely intelligible nature had always existed between them. Our glances, however, rested not long upon the dead—for we could not regard her unawed. The disease which had thus entombed the lady in the maturity of youth, had left, as usual in all maladies of a strictly cataleptical character, the mockery of a faint blush upon the bosom and the face, and that suspiciously lingering smile upon the lip which is so terrible in death. We replaced and screwed down the lid, and, having secured the door of iron, made our way, with toil, into the scarcely less gloomy apartments of the upper portion of the house.

And now, some days of bitter grief having elapsed, an observable change came over the features of the mental disorder of my friend. His ordinary manner had vanished. His ordinary occupations were neglected or forgotten. He roamed from chamber to chamber with hurried, unequal, and objectless step. The pallor of his countenance had assumed, if possible, a more ghastly hue—but the luminousness of his eye had utterly gone out. The once occasional huskiness of his tone was heard no more; and a tremendous quaver, as if of extreme terror, habitually characterized his utterance. There were times, indeed, when I thought his unceasingly agitated mind was laboring with some oppressive secret, to divulge which he struggled for the necessary courage. At times, again, I was obliged to resolve all into the mere inexplicable vagaries of madness, for I beheld him gazing upon vacancy for long hours, in an attitude of the profoundest attention, as if listening to some imaginary sound. It was no wonder that his condition terrified—that it infected me. I felt creeping upon me, by slow yet certain degrees, the wild influences of his own fantastic yet impressive superstitions.

It was, especially, upon retiring to bed late in the night of the seventh or eighth day after the placing of the lady Madeline within the donjon, that I experienced the full power of such feelings. Sleep came not near my couch—while the hours waned and waned away. I struggled to reason off the nervousness which had dominion over me. I endeavored to believe that much, if not all of what I felt, was due to the bewildering influence of the gloomy furniture of the room—of the dark and tattered draperies, which, tortured into motion by the breath of a rising tempest, swayed fitfully to and fro upon the walls, and rustled uneasily about the decorations of the bed. But my efforts were fruitless. An irrepressible tremor gradually pervaded my frame; and, at length, there sat upon my very heart an incubus of utterly causeless alarm. Shaking this off with a gasp and a struggle, I uplifted myself upon the pillows, and, peering earnestly within the intense darkness of the chamber, hearkened—I know not why, except that an instinctive spirit prompted

me—to certain low and indefinite sounds which came, through the pauses of the storm, at long intervals, I knew not whence. Overpowered by an intense sentiment of horror, unaccountable yet unendurable, I threw on my clothes with haste (for I felt that I should sleep no more during the night), and endeavored to arouse myself from the pitiable condition into which I had fallen, by pacing rapidly to and fro through the apartment.

I had taken but few turns in this manner, when a light step on an adjoining staircase arrested my attention. I presently recognized it as that of Usher. In an instant afterward he rapped, with a gentle touch, at my door, and entered, bearing a lamp. His countenance was, as usual, cadaverously wan—but, moreover, there was a species of mad hilarity in his eyes an evidently restrained *hysteria* in his whole demeanor. His air appalled me—but any thing was preferable to the solitude which I had so long endured, and I even welcomed his presence as a relief.

"And you have not seen it?" he said abruptly, after having stared about him for some moments in silence—"you have not then seen it?—but, stay! you shall." Thus speaking, and having carefully shaded his lamp, he hurried to one of the casements, and threw it freely open to the storm.

The impetuous fury of the entering gust nearly lifted us from our feet. It was, indeed, a tempestuous yet sternly beautiful night, and one wildly singular in its terror and its beauty. A whirlwind had apparently collected its force in our vicinity; for there were frequent and violent alterations in the direction of the wind; and the exceeding density of the clouds (which hung so low as to press upon the turrets of the house) did not prevent our perceiving the lifelike velocity with which they flew careering from all points against each other, without passing away into the distance. I say that even their exceeding density did not prevent our perceiving this—yet we had no glimpse of the moon or stars, nor was there any flashing forth of the lightning. But the under surfaces of the huge masses of agitated vapor, as well as all terrestrial objects immediately around us, were glowing in the unnatural light of a faintly luminous and distinctly visible gaseous exhalation which hung about and enshrouded the mansion.

"You must not—you shall not behold this!" said I, shuddering, to Usher, as I led him, with a gentle violence, from the window to a seat. "These appearances, which bewilder you, are merely electrical phenomena not uncommon—or it may be that they have their ghastly origin in the rank miasma of the tarn. Let us close this casement;—the air is chilling and dangerous to your frame. Here is one of your favorite romances. I will read, and you shall listen;—and so we will pass away this terrible night together."

The antique volume which I had taken up was the "Mad Trist" of Sir Launcelot Canning; but I had called it a favorite of Usher's more in sad jest than in earnest; for, in truth, there is little in its uncouth and unimaginative prolixity which could have had interest for the lofty and spiritual ideality of my friend. It was, however, the only book immediately at hand; and I indulged a vague hope that the excitement which now agitated the hypochondriac, might find relief (for the history of mental disorder is full of similar anomalies) even in the extremeness of the folly which I should read. Could I have judged, indeed, by the wild overstrained air of vivacity with which he hearkened, or apparently hearkened, to the words of the tale, I might well have congratulated myself upon the success of my design.

I had arrived at that well-known portion of the story where Ethelred, the hero of the Trist, having sought in vain for peaceable admission into the dwelling of the hermit, proceeds to make good an entrance by force. Here, it will be remembered, the words of the narrative run thus:

"And Ethelred, who was by nature of a doughty heart, and who was now mighty withal, on account of the powerfulness of the wine which he had drunken, waited no longer to hold parley with the hermit, who, in sooth, was of an obstinate and maliceful turn, but, feeling the rain upon his shoulders, and fearing the rising of the tempest, uplifted his mace outright, and, with blows, made quickly room in the plankings of the door for his gauntleted hand; and now pulling therewith sturdily, he so cracked, and ripped, and tore all asunder, that the noise of the dry and hollow-sounding wood alarummed and reverberated throughout the forest."

At the termination of this sentence I started and, for a moment, paused; for it appeared to me (although I at once concluded that my excited fancy had deceived me)—it appeared to me that, from some very remote portion of the mansion, there came, indistinctly, to my ears, what might have been, in its exact similarity of character, the echo (but a stifled and dull one certainly) of the very cracking and ripping sound which Sir Launcelot had so particularly described. It was, beyond doubt, the coincidence alone which had arrested my attention; for, amid the rattling of the sashes of the casements, and the ordinary commingled noises of the still increasing storm, the sound, in itself, had nothing, surely, which should have interested or disturbed me. I continued the story:

"But the good champion Ethelred, now entering within the door, was sore enraged and amazed to perceive no signal of the maliceful hermit; but, in the stead thereof, a dragon of a scaly and prodigious demeanor, and of a fiery tongue, which sate in guard before a palace of gold, with a floor of silver; and upon the wall there hung a shield of shining brass with this legend enwritten—

Who entereth herein, a conqueror hath bin;
Who slayeth the dragon, the shield he shall win;

And Ethelred uplifted his mace, and struck upon the head of the dragon, which fell before him, and gave up his pesty breath, with a shriek so horrid and harsh, and withal so piercing, that Ethelred had fain to close his ears with his hands against the dreadful noise of it, the like whereof was never before heard."

Here again I paused abruptly, and now with a feeling of wild amazement—for there could be no doubt whatever that, in this instance, I did actually hear (although from what direction it proceeded I found it impossible to say) a low and apparently distant, but harsh, protracted, and most unusual screaming or grating sound—the exact counterpart of what my fancy had already conjured up for the dragon's unnatural shriek as described by the romancer.

Oppressed, as I certainly was, upon the occurrence of this second and most extraordinary coincidence, by a thousand conflicting sensations, in which wonder and extreme terror were predominant, I still retained sufficient presence of mind to avoid exciting, by any observation, the sensitive nervousness of my companion. I was by no means certain that he had noticed the sounds in question; although, assuredly, a strange alteration had, during the last few minutes, taken place in his demeanor. From a position fronting my own, he had gradually brought round his chair, so as to sit with his face to the door of the chamber; and thus I could but partially perceive his features, although I saw that his lips trembled as if he were murmuring inaudibly. His head had dropped upon his breast—yet I knew that he was not asleep, from the wide and rigid opening of the eye as I caught a glance of it in profile. The motion of his body, too, was at variance with this idea—for he rocked from side to side with a gentle yet constant and uniform sway. Having rapidly taken notice of all this, I resumed the narrative of Sir Launcelot, which thus proceeded:

"And now, the champion, having escaped from the terrible fury of the dragon, bethinking himself of the brazen shield, and of the breaking up of the enchantment which was upon it, removed the carcass from out of the way before him, and approached valorously over the silver pavement of the castle to where the shield was upon the wall; which in sooth tarried not for his full coming, but fell down at his feet upon the silver floor, with a mighty great and terrible ringing sound."

No sooner had these syllables passed my lips, than—as if a shield of brass had indeed, at the moment, fallen heavily upon a floor of silver—I became aware of a distinct, hollow, metallic, and clangorous, yet apparently muffled, reverberation. Completely unnerved, I leaped to my feet; but the measured rocking movement of Usher was undisturbed. I rushed to the chair in which he sat. His eyes were bent fixedly before him, and throughout his whole countenance there reigned a stony rigidity. But, as I placed my hand upon his shoulder, there came a strong shudder over his whole person; a sickly smile quivered about his lips; and I saw that he spoke in a low, hurried, and gibbering murmur, as if unconscious of my presence. Bending closely over him, I at length drank in the hideous import of his words.

"Not hear it?—yes, I hear it, and *have* heard it. Long—long—long—many minutes, many hours, many days, have I heard it—yet I dared not—oh, pity me, miserable wretch that I am!—I dared not—I *dared* not speak! *We have put her living in the tomb!* Said I not that my senses were acute? I now tell you that I heard her first feeble movements in the hollow coffin. I heard them—many, many days ago—yet I dared not—*I dared not speak!* And now—to-night—Ethelred—ha! ha!—the breaking of the hermit's door, and the death-cry of the dragon, and the clangor of the shield—say, rather, the rending of her coffin, and the grating of the iron hinges of her prison, and her struggles within the coppered archway of the vault! Oh whither shall I fly? Will she not be here anon? Is she not hurrying to upbraid me for my haste? Have I not heard her footstep on the stair? Do I not distinguish that heavy and horrible beating of her heart? Madman!"—here he sprang furiously to his feet, and shrieked out his syllables, as if in the effort he were giving up his soul—"*Madman! I tell you that she now stands without the door!*"

As if in the superhuman energy of his utterance there had been found the potency of a spell—the huge antique pannels to which the speaker pointed, threw slowly back, upon the instant, their ponderous and ebony jaws. It was the work of the rushing gust—but then without those doors there *did* stand the lofty and enshrouded figure of the lady Madeline of Usher. There was blood upon her white robes, and the evidence of some bitter struggle upon every portion of her emaciated frame. For a moment she remained trembling and reeling to and fro upon the threshold—then, with a low moaning cry fell heavily inward upon the person of her brother, and in her violent and now final death-agonies, bore him to the floor a corpse, and a victim to the terrors he had anticipated.

From that chamber, and from that mansion, I fled aghast. The storm was still abroad in all its wrath as I found myself crossing the old causeway. Suddenly there shot along the path a wild light, and I turned to see whence a gleam so unusual could have issued; for the vast house and its shadows were alone behind me. The radiance was that of the full, setting and blood-red moon, which now shone vividly through that once barely discernible fissure, of which I have before spoken as extending from the roof of the building, in a zig-zag direction, to the base. While I gazed, this fissure rapidly widened—there came a fierce breath of the whirlwind—the entire orb of the satellite burst at once upon my sight—my brain reeled as I saw the mighty walls rushing asunder—there was a long tumultuous shouting sound like the voice of a thousand waters—and the deep and dank tarn at my feet closed sullenly and silently over the fragments of the "*House of Usher.*"

Chapter Three

EDGAR ALLAN POE (1809–1849)

Poe's disturbing story "The System of Doctor Tarr and Professor Fether" describes a visit to a madhouse, ostensibly in the South of France, by a traveler who wishes to examine what is called the "soothing system" by which its inmates are treated. As the story progresses, the reader becomes aware that the lunatics have literally taken over the asylum, and that the system of "soothing" or appeasement has resulted in anarchy and racialized violence.

Text: Rufus Wilmot Griswold, *The Works of the Late Edgar Allan Poe*, 4 vols. (New York: Redfield, 1857).

THE SYSTEM OF DOCTOR TARR AND PROFESSOR FETHER

DURING the autumn of 18—, while on a tour through the extreme Southern provinces of France, my route led me within a few miles of a certain *Maison de Santé*[1] or private mad-house, about which I had heard much in Paris from my medical friends. As I had never visited a place of the kind, I thought the opportunity too good to be lost; and so proposed to my travelling companion (a gentleman with whom I had made casual acquaintance a few days before) that we should turn aside, for an hour or so, and look through the establishment. To this he objected—pleading haste in the first place, and, in the second, a very usual horror at the sight of a lunatic.[2] He begged me, however, not to let any mere courtesy towards himself interfere with the gratification of my curiosity, and said that he would ride on leisurely, so that I might overtake him during the day, or, at all events, during the next. As he bade me good-bye, I bethought me that there might be some difficulty in obtaining access to the premises, and mentioned my fears on this point. He replied that, in fact, unless I had personal knowledge of the superintendent, Monsieur Maillard, or some credential in the way of a letter, a difficulty might be found to exist, as the regulations of these private mad-houses were more rigid than the public hospital laws. For himself, he added, he had, some years since, made the acquaintance of Maillard, and would so far assist me as to ride up to the door and introduce me; although his feelings on the subject of lunacy would not permit of his entering the house.

---

1 Sanitarium.

2 Antiquated term once commonly used in law to refer to a person considered mentally ill, dangerous, foolish or unpredictable—conditions once attributed to *lunacy*, a word derived from *lunaticus*,"of the moon" or "moonstruck."

I thanked him, and, turning from the mainroad, we entered a grass-grown by-path, which, in half an hour, nearly lost itself in a dense forest, clothing the base of a mountain. Through this dank and gloomy wood we rode some two miles, when the *Maison de Santé* came in view. It was a fantastic *chateau*,[3] much dilapidated, and indeed scarcely tenantable through age and neglect. Its aspect inspired me with absolute dread, and, checking my horse, I half resolved to turn back. I soon, however, grew ashamed of my weakness, and proceeded.

As we rode up to the gate-way, I perceived it slightly open, and the visage of a man peering through. In an instant afterward, this man came forth, accosted my companion by name, shook him cordially by the hand, and begged him to alight. It was Monsieur Maillard himself. He was a portly, fine-looking gentleman of the old school, with a polished manner, and a certain air of gravity, dignity, and authority which was very impressive.

My friend, having presented me, mentioned my desire to inspect the establishment, and received Monsieur Maillard's assurance that he would show me all attention, now took leave, and I saw him no more.

When he had gone, the superintendent ushered me into a small and exceedingly neat parlor, containing, among other indications of refined taste, many books, drawings, pots of flowers, and musical instruments. A cheerful fire blazed upon the hearth. At a piano, singing an aria from Bellini,[4] sat a young and very beautiful woman, who, at my entrance, paused in her song, and received me with graceful courtesy. Her voice was low, and her whole manner subdued. I thought, too, that I perceived the traces of sorrow in her countenance, which was excessively, although to my taste, not unpleasingly, pale. She was attired in deep mourning, and excited in my bosom a feeling of mingled respect, interest, and admiration.

I had heard, at Paris, that the institution of Monsieur Maillard was managed upon what is vulgarly termed the "system of soothing"—that all punishments were avoided—that even confinement was seldom resorted to—that the patients, while secretly watched, were left much apparent liberty, and that most of them were permitted to roam about the house and grounds in the ordinary apparel of persons in right mind.

Keeping these impressions in view, I was cautious in what I said before the young lady; for I could not be sure that she was sane; and, in fact, there was a certain restless brilliancy about her eyes which half led me to imagine she was not. I confined my remarks, therefore, to general topics, and to such as I thought would not be displeasing or exciting even to a lunatic. She replied in a perfectly rational manner to all that I said; and even her original observations were marked with the soundest good sense, but a long acquaintance with the metaphysics of *mania*,[5] had taught me to put no faith in such evidence of sanity, and I continued to practise, throughout the interview, the caution with which I commenced it.

---

[3] Castle.

[4] Vicenzo Bellini, Italian opera composer, 1801–1835.

[5] Mental illness marked by periods of great excitement or euphoria, delusions and overactivity.

Presently a smart footman in livery brought in a tray with fruit, wine, and other refreshments, of which I partook, the lady soon afterward leaving the room. As she departed I turned my eyes in an inquiring manner toward my host.

"No," he said, "oh, no—a member of my family—my niece, and a most accomplished woman."

"I beg a thousand pardons for the suspicion," I replied, "but of course you will know how to excuse me. The excellent administration of your affairs here is well understood in Paris, and I thought it just possible, you know—"

"Yes, yes—say no more—or rather it is myself who should thank you for the commendable prudence you have displayed. We seldom find so much of forethought in young men; and, more than once, some unhappy *contre-temps*[6] has occurred in consequence of thoughtlessness on the part of our visitors. While my former system was in operation, and my patients were permitted the privilege of roaming to and fro at will, they were often aroused to a dangerous frenzy by injudicious persons who called to inspect the house. Hence I was obliged to enforce a rigid system of exclusion; and none obtained access to the premises upon whose discretion I could not rely."

"While your *former* system was in operation!" I said, repeating his words—"do I understand you, then, to say that the 'soothing system' of which I have heard so much is no longer in force?"

"It is now," he replied, "several weeks since we have concluded to renounce it forever."

"Indeed! you astonish me!"

"We found it, sir," he said, with a sigh, "absolutely necessary to return to the old usages. The *danger* of the soothing system was, at all times, appalling; and its advantages have been much overrated. I believe, sir, that in this house it has been given a fair trial, if ever in any. We did every thing that rational humanity could suggest. I am sorry that you could not have paid us a visit at an earlier period, that you might have judged for yourself. But I presume you are conversant with the soothing practice—with its details."

"Not altogether. What I have heard has been at third or fourth hand."

"I may state the system, then, in general terms, as one in which the patients were *menagés*,[7] humored. We contradicted *no* fancies which entered the brains of the mad. On the contrary, we not only indulged but encouraged them; and many of our most permanent cures have been thus effected. There is no argument which so touches the feeble reason of the madman as the *reductio ad absurdum*[8]. We have had men, for example, who fancied themselves chickens. The cure was, to insist upon the thing as a fact—to accuse the patient of stupidity in not sufficiently perceiving it to be a fact—and thus to refuse him any other diet for a week than that which properly appertains to a chicken. In this manner a little corn and gravel were made to perform wonders."

"But was this species of acquiescence all?"

6 Difficulty or setback.

7 Cosseted or humored.

8 A method of proving the falsity of a premise by showing that its logical consequence is absurd or contradictory.

"By no means. We put much faith in amusements of a simple kind, such as music, dancing, gymnastic exercises generally, cards, certain classes of books, and so forth. We affected to treat each individual as if for some ordinary physical disorder, and the word 'lunacy' was never employed. A great point was to set each lunatic to guard the actions of all the others. To repose confidence in the understanding or discretion of a madman, is to gain him body and soul. In this way we were enabled to dispense with an expensive body of keepers."

"And you had no punishments of any kind?"

"None."

"And you never confined your patients?"

"Very rarely. Now and then, the malady of some individual growing to a crisis, or taking a sudden turn of fury, we conveyed him to a secret cell, lest his disorder should infect the rest, and there kept him until we could dismiss him to his friends—for with the raging maniac we have nothing to do. He is usually removed to the public hospitals."

"And you have now changed all this—and you think for the better?"

"Decidedly. The system had its disadvantages, and even its dangers. It is now, happily, exploded throughout all the *Maisons de Santé* of France."

"I am very much surprised," I said, "at what you tell me; for I made sure that, at this moment, no other method of treatment for mania existed in any portion of the country."

"You are young yet, my friend," replied my host, "but the time will arrive when you will learn to judge for yourself of what is going on in the world, without trusting to the gossip of others. Believe nothing you hear, and only one-half that you see. Now about our *Maisons de Santé*, it is clear that some ignoramus has misled you. After dinner, however, when you have sufficiently recovered from the fatigue of your ride, I will be happy to take you over the house, and introduce to you a system which, in my opinion, and in that of every one who has witnessed its operation, is incomparably the most effectual as yet devised."

"Your own?" I inquired—"one of your own invention?"

"I am proud," he replied, "to acknowledge that it is—at least in some measure."

In this manner I conversed with Monsieur Maillard for an hour or two, during which he showed me the gardens and conservatories of the place.

"I cannot let you see my patients," he said, "just at present. To a sensitive mind there is always more or less of the shocking in such exhibitions; and I do not wish to spoil your appetite for dinner. We will dine. I can give you some veal *à la Menehoult*,[9] with cauliflowers in *velouté*[10] sauce—after that a glass of Clos de Vougeot—then your nerves will be sufficiently steadied."

At six, dinner was announced; and my host conducted me into a large *salle à manger*,[11] where a very numerous company were assembled—twenty-five or thirty in all. They were, apparently, people of rank—certainly of high breeding—although their

[9] A way of cooking pig's feet or veal.

[10] A savoury sauce, made from a roux (browned flour) and a light stock.

[11] Dining room.

habiliments, I thought, were extravagantly rich, partaking somewhat too much of the ostentatious finery of the *vielle cour.*[12] I noticed that at least two-thirds of these guests were ladies; and some of the latter were by no means accoutred in what a Parisian would consider good taste at the present day. Many females, for example, whose age could not have been less than seventy were bedecked with a profusion of jewelry, such as rings, bracelets, and earrings, and wore their bosoms and arms shamefully bare. I observed, too, that very few of the dresses were well made—or, at least, that very few of them fitted the wearers. In looking about, I discovered the interesting girl to whom Monsieur Maillard had presented me in the little parlor; but my surprise was great to see her wearing a hoop and farthingale,[13] with high-heeled shoes, and a dirty cap of Brussels lace, so much too large for her that it gave her face a ridiculously diminutive expression. When I had first seen her, she was attired, most becomingly, in deep mourning. There was an air of oddity, in short, about the dress of the whole party, which, at first, caused me to recur to my original idea of the "soothing system," and to fancy that Monsieur Maillard had been willing to deceive me until after dinner, that I might experience no uncomfortable feelings during the repast, at finding myself dining with lunatics; but I remembered having been informed, in Paris, that the southern provincialists were a peculiarly eccentric people, with a vast number of antiquated notions; and then, too, upon conversing with several members of the company, my apprehensions were immediately and fully dispelled.

The dining-room itself, although perhaps sufficiently comfortable and of good dimensions, had nothing too much of elegance about it. For example, the floor was uncarpeted; in France, however, a carpet is frequently dispensed with. The windows, too, were without curtains; the shutters, being shut, were securely fastened with iron bars, applied diagonally, after the fashion of our ordinary shop-shutters. The apartment, I observed, formed, in itself, a wing of the *chateau*, and thus the windows were on three sides of the parallelogram, the door being at the other. There were no less than ten windows in all.

The table was superbly set out. It was loaded with plate,[14] and more than loaded with delicacies. The profusion was absolutely barbaric. There were meats enough to have feasted the Anakim.[15] Never, in all my life, had I witnessed so lavish, so wasteful an expenditure of the good things of life. There seemed very little taste, however, in the arrangements; and my eyes, accustomed to quiet lights, were sadly offended by the prodigious glare of a multitude of wax candles, which, in silver *candelabra*, were deposited upon the table, and all about the room, wherever it was possible to find a place. There were several active servants in attendance; and, upon a large table, at the farther end of the apartment, were seated seven or eight people with fiddles, fifes, trombones, and a drum. These fellows annoyed me very much, at intervals, during the repast, by an infinite

---

[12] The pre-Napoleonic royal Bourbon court.

[13] Petticoat.

[14] Silver plate.

[15] A race of giants said to have lived in the southern part of the land of Canaan.

variety of noises, which were intended for music, and which appeared to afford much entertainment to all present, with the exception of myself.

Upon the whole, I could not help thinking that there was much of the *bizarre* about every thing I saw—but then the world is made up of all kinds of persons, with all modes of thought, and all sorts of conventional customs. I had travelled, too, so much, as to be quite an adept at the *nil admirari*;[16] so I took my seat very coolly at the right hand of my host, and, having an excellent appetite, did justice to the good cheer set before me.

The conversation, in the meantime, was spirited and general. The ladies, as usual, talked a great deal. I soon found that nearly all the company were well educated; and my host was a world of good-humored anecdote in himself. He seemed quite willing to speak of his position as superintendent of a *Maison de Santé*; and, indeed, the topic of lunacy was, much to my surprise, a favorite one with all present. A great many amusing stories were told, having reference to the *whims* of the patients.

"We had a fellow here once," said a fat little gentleman, who sat at my right—"a fellow that fancied himself a tea-pot; and by the way, is it not especially singular how often this particular crotchet has entered the brain of the lunatic? There is scarcely an insane asylum in France which cannot supply a human tea-pot. Our gentleman was a Britannia-ware[17] tea-pot, and was careful to polish himself every morning with buckskin and whiting."

"And then," said a tall man just opposite, "we had here, not long ago, a person who had taken it into his head that he was a donkey—which allegorically speaking, you will say, was quite true. He was a troublesome patient; and we had much ado to keep him within bounds. For a long time he would eat nothing but thistles; but of this idea we soon cured him by insisting upon his eating nothing else. Then he was perpetually kicking out his heels—so—so—"

"Mr. De Kock! I will thank you to behave yourself!" here interrupted an old lady, who sat next to the speaker. "Please keep your feet to yourself! You have spoiled my brocade! Is it necessary, pray, to illustrate a remark in so practical a style? Our friend here can surely comprehend you without all this. Upon my word, you are nearly as great a donkey as the poor unfortunate imagined himself. Your acting is very natural, as I live."

"Mille pardons! Ma'm'selle!"[18] replied Monsieur De Kock, thus addressed—"a thousand pardons! I had no intention of offending. Ma'm'selle Laplace—Monsieur De Kock will do himself the honor of taking wine with you."

Here Monsieur De Kock bowed low, kissed his hand with much ceremony, and took wine with Ma'm'selle Laplace.

"Allow me, *mon ami*,"[19] now said Monsieur Maillard, addressing myself, "allow me to send you a morsel of this veal *à la St. Menhoult*—you will find it particularly fine."

---

[16] Loosely translated, "nothing would surprise me."

[17] Britannia ware was made of pewter alloy, favoured for its silvery appearance and smooth surface.

[18] A thousand pardons, Miss.

[19] My friend.

At this instant three sturdy waiters had just succeeded in depositing safely upon the table an enormous dish, or trencher, containing what I supposed to be the *"monstrum horrendum, informe, ingens, cui lumen ademptum."*[20] A closer scrutiny assured me, however, that it was only a small calf roasted whole, and set upon its knees, with an apple in its mouth, as is the English fashion of dressing a hare.

"Thank you, no," I replied; "to say the truth, I am not particularly partial to veal *à la St.*—what is it?—for I do not find that it altogether agrees with me. I will change my plate, however, and try some of the rabbit."

There were several side-dishes on the table, containing what appeared to be the ordinary French rabbit—a very delicious *morceau*,[21] which I can recommend.

"Pierre," cried the host, "change this gentleman's plate, and give him a side-piece of this rabbit *au-chát*."[22]

"This what?" said I.

"This rabbit *au-chát*."

"Why, thank you—upon second thoughts, no. I will just help myself to some of the ham."

There is no knowing what one eats, thought I to myself, at the tables of these people of the province. I will have none of their rabbit *au-chát*—and, for the matter of that, none of their *cat-au-rabbit* either.

"And then," said a cadaverous looking personage, near the foot of the table, taking up the thread of the conversation where it had been broken off, — "and then, among other oddities, we had a patient, once upon a time, who very pertinaciously maintained himself to be a Cordova[23] cheese, and went about, with a knife in his hand, soliciting his friends to try a small slice from the middle of his leg."

"He was a great fool, beyond doubt," interposed some one, "but not to be compared with a certain individual whom we all know, with the exception of this strange gentleman. I mean the man who took himself for a bottle of champagne, and always went off with a pop and a fizz, in this fashion."

Here the speaker, very rudely, as I thought, put his right thumb in his left cheek, withdrew it with a sound resembling the popping of a cork, and then, by a dexterous movement of the tongue upon the teeth, created a sharp hissing and fizzing, which lasted for several minutes, in imitation of the frothing of champagne. This behavior, I saw plainly, was not very pleasing to Monsieur Maillard; but that gentleman said nothing, and the conversation was resumed by a very lean little man in a big wig.

"And then there was an ignoramus," said he, "who mistook himself for a frog, which, by the way, he resembled in no little degree. I wish you could have seen him, sir,"—here the speaker addressed myself—"it would have done your heart good to see the natural

---

[20] A reference from Virgil to the blinded Cyclops: "monster horrendous, hideous, and vast, deprived of sight."

[21] Tidbit.

[22] Rabbit cat-style.

[23] Cordoba, a city in Southern Spain.

airs that he put on. Sir, if that man was *not* a frog, I can only observe that it is a pity he was not. His croak thus—o-o-o-o-gh—o-o-o-o-gh! was the finest note in the world—B flat; and when he put his elbows upon the table thus—after taking a glass or two of wine—and distended his mouth, thus, and rolled up his eyes, thus, and winked them with excessive rapidity, thus, why then, sir, I take it upon myself to say, positively, that you would have been lost in admiration of the genius of the man."

"I have no doubt of it," I said.

"And then," said somebody else, "then there was Petit Gaillard, who thought himself a pinch of snuff, and was truly distressed because he could not take himself between his own finger and thumb."

"And then there was Jules Desouliéres, who was a very singular genius, indeed, and went mad with the idea that he was a pumpkin. He persecuted the cook to make him up into pies—a thing which the cook indignantly refused to do. For my part, I am by no means sure that a pumpkin pie *a la Desouliéres* would not have been very capital eating indeed!"

"You astonish me!" said I; and I looked inquisitively at Monsieur Maillard.

"Ha! ha! ha!" said that gentleman—"he! he! he!—hi! hi! hi!—ho! ho! ho!—hu! hu! hu! hu!—very good indeed! You must not be astonished, *mon ami*; our friend here is a wit—a *drôle*—you must not understand him to the letter."

"And then," said some other one of the party,—"then there was Bouffon Le Grand—another extraordinary personage in his way. He grew deranged through love, and fancied himself possessed of two heads. One of these he maintained to be the head of Cicero;[24] the other he imagined a composite one, being Demosthenes' from the top of the forehead to the mouth, and Lord Brougham's from the mouth to the chin. It is not impossible that he was wrong; but he would have convinced you of his being in the right; for he was a man of great eloquence. He had an absolute passion for oratory, and could not refrain from display. For example, he used to leap upon the dinner-table thus, and—and—."

Here a friend, at the side of the speaker, put a hand upon his shoulder and whispered a few words in his ear, upon which he ceased talking with great suddenness, and sank back within his chair.

"And then," said the friend who had whispered, "there was Boullard, the tee-totum. I call him the tee-totum because, in fact, he was seized with the droll but not altogether irrational crotchet, that he had been converted into a tee-totum. You would have roared with laughter to see him spin. He would turn round upon one heel by the hour, in this manner—so—"

Here the friend whom he had just interrupted by a whisper, performed an exactly similar office for himself.

"But then," cried the old lady, at the top of her voice, "your Monsieur Boullard was a madman, and a very silly madman at best; for who, allow me to ask you, ever heard of a human tee-totum? The thing is absurd. Madame Joyeuse was a more sensible person, as

---

24 Marcus Tullius Cicero (106 BC–7 December 43 BC): Roman statesman, orator, lawyer and philosopher.

you know. She had a crotchet, but it was instinct with common sense, and gave pleasure to all who had the honor of her acquaintance. She found, upon mature deliberation, that, by some accident, she had been turned into a chicken-cock; but, as such, she behaved with propriety. She flapped her wings with prodigious effect—so—so—and, as for her crow, it was delicious! Cock-a-doodle-doo!—cock-a-doodle-doo!—cock-a-doodle-de-doo-dooo-do-o-o-o-o-o-o!"

"Madame Joyeuse, I will thank you to behave yourself!" here interrupted our host, very angrily. "You can either conduct yourself as a lady should do, or you can quit the table forthwith—take your choice."

The lady (whom I was much astonished to hear addressed as Madame Joyeuse, after the description of Madame Joyeuse she had just given) blushed up to the eyebrows, and seemed exceedingly abashed at the reproof. She hung down her head, and said not a syllable in reply. But another and younger lady resumed the theme. It was my beautiful girl of the little parlor!

"Oh, Madame Joyeuse *was* a fool!" she exclaimed, "but there was really much sound sense, after all, in the opinion of Eugénie Salsafette. She was a very beautiful and painfully modest young lady, who thought the ordinary mode of habiliment indecent, and wished to dress herself, always, by getting outside instead of inside of her clothes. It is a thing very easily done, after all. You have only to do so—and then so—so—so—and then so—so ci—so—and then so—so—and then—"

"Mon dieu! Mam'selle Salsafette!" here cried a dozen voices at once. "What *are* you about?—forbear!—that is sufficient!—we see, very plainly, how it is done!—hold! hold!" and several persons were already leaping from their seats to withhold Mam'selle Salsafette from putting herself upon a par with the Medicean Venus,[25] when the point was very effectually and suddenly accomplished by a series of loud screams, or yells, from some portion of the main body of the *chateau*.

My nerves were very much affected, indeed, by these yells; but the rest of the company I really pitied. I never saw any set of reasonable people so thoroughly frightened in my life. They all grew as pale as so many corpses, and, shrinking within their seats, sat quivering and gibbering with terror, and listening for a repetition of the sound. It came again—louder and seemingly nearer—and then a third time *very* loud, and then a fourth time with a vigor evidently diminished. At this apparent dying away of the noise, the spirits of the company were immediately regained, and all was life and anecdote as before. I now ventured to inquire the cause of the disturbance.

"A mere *bagatelle*," said Monsieur Maillard. "We are used to these things, and care really very little about them. The lunatics, every now and then, get up a howl in concert; one starting another, as is sometimes the case with a bevy of dogs at night. It occasionally happens, however, that the *concerto* yells are succeeded by a simultaneous effort at breaking loose, when, of course, some little danger is to be apprehended."

"And how many have you in charge?"

"At present we have not more than ten, altogether."

[25] The Medici Venus is a Hellenistic marble nude depicting the Greek goddess of love Aphrodite.

"Principally females, I presume?"

"Oh, no—every one of them men, and stout fellows, too, I can tell you."

"Indeed! I have always understood that the majority of lunatics were of the gentler sex."

"It is generally so, but not always. Some time ago, there were about twenty-seven patients here; and, of that number, no less than eighteen were women; but, lately, matters have changed very much, as you see."

"Yes—have changed very much, as you see," here interrupted the gentleman who had broken the shins of Ma'mselle Laplace.

"Yes—have changed very much, as you see!" chimed in the whole company at once.

"Hold your tongues, every one of you!" said my host, in a great rage. Whereupon the whole company maintained a dead silence for nearly a minute. As for one lady, she obeyed Monsieur Maillard to the letter, and thrusting out her tongue, which was an excessively long one, held it very resignedly, with both hands, until the end of the entertainment.

"And this gentlewoman," said I, to Monsieur Maillard, bending over and addressing him in a whisper—"this good lady who has just spoken, and who gives us the cock-a-doodle-de-doo—she, I presume, is harmless—quite harmless, eh?"

"Harmless!" ejaculated he, in unfeigned surprise, "why—why, what can you mean?"

"Only slightly touched?" said I, touching my head. "I take it for granted that she is not particularly not dangerously affected, eh?"

"*Mon dieu!*[26] what is it you imagine? This lady, my particular old friend Madame Joyeuse, is as absolutely sane as myself. She has her little eccentricities, to be sure—but then, you know, all old women—all *very* old women are more or less eccentric!"

"To be sure," said I,—"to be sure—and then the rest of these ladies and gentlemen—"

"Are my friends and keepers," interrupted Monsieur Maillard, drawing himself up with *hauteur*,[27]—"my very good friends and assistants."

"What! all of them?" I asked,—"the women and all?"

"Assuredly," he said,—"we could not do at all without the women; they are the best lunatic nurses in the world; they have a way of their own, you know; their bright eyes have a marvellous effect;—something like the fascination of the snake, you know."

"To be sure," said I,—"to be sure! They behave a little odd, eh?—they are a little *queer*, eh?—don't you think so?"

"Odd!—queer!—why, do you *really* think so? We are not very prudish, to be sure, here in the South—do pretty much as we please—enjoy life, and all that sort of thing, you know—"

"To be sure," said I,—"to be sure."

And then, perhaps, this *Clos de Vougeôt*[28]is a little heady, you know—a little *strong*—you understand, eh?"

---

[26] My God!

[27] Pride, arrogance.

[28] A vintage Burgundy.

"To be sure," said I,—"to be sure. By-the-bye, Monsieur, did I understand you to say that the system you have adopted, in place of the celebrated soothing system, was one of very rigorous severity?"

"By no means. Our confinement is necessarily close; but the treatment—the medical treatment, I mean—is rather agreeable to the patients than otherwise."

"And the new system is one of your own invention?"

"Not altogether. Some portions of it are referable to Professor Tarr, of whom you have, necessarily, heard; and, again, there are modifications in my plan which I am happy to acknowledge as belonging of right to the celebrated Fether, with whom, if I mistake not, you have the honor of an intimate acquaintance."

"I am quite ashamed to confess," I replied, "that I have never even heard the names of either gentleman before."

"Good heavens!" ejaculated my host, drawing back his chair abruptly, and uplifting his hands. "I surely do not hear you aright! You did not intend to say, eh? that you had never *heard* either of the learned Doctor Tarr, or of the celebrated Professor Fether?"

"I am forced to acknowledge my ignorance," I replied; "but the truth should be held inviolate above all things. Nevertheless, I feel humbled to the dust, not to be acquainted with the works of these, no doubt, extraordinary men. I will seek out their writings forthwith, and peruse them with deliberate care. Monsieur Maillard, you have really—I must confess it—you have really—made me ashamed of myself!"

And this was the fact.

"Say no more, my good young friend," he said kindly, pressing my hand,—"join me now in a glass of Sauterne."[29]

We drank. The company followed our example without stint. They chatted—they jested—they laughed—they perpetrated a thousand absurdities—the fiddles shrieked—the drum row-de-dowed—the trombones bellowed like so many brazen bulls of Phalaris—and the whole scene, growing gradually worse and worse, as the wines gained the ascendancy, became at length a sort of pandemonium *in petto*. In the meantime, Monsieur Maillard and myself, with some bottles of Sauterne and Vougeôt between us, continued our conversation at the top of the voice. A word spoken in an ordinary key stood no more chance of being heard than the voice of a fish from the bottom of Niagara Falls.

"And, sir," said I, screaming in his ear, "you mentioned something before dinner about the danger incurred in the old system of soothing. How is that?"

"Yes," he replied, "there was, occasionally, very great danger indeed. There is no accounting for the caprices of madmen; and, in my opinion as well as in that of Dr. Tarr and Professor Fether, it is *never* safe to permit them to run at large unattended. A lunatic may be 'soothed,' as it is called, for a time, but, in the end, he is very apt to become obstreperous. His cunning, too, is proverbial and great. If he has a project in view, he conceals his design with a marvellous wisdom; and the dexterity with which he counterfeits sanity, presents, to the metaphysician, one of the most singular problems in

[29] A French wine from the Bordeaux region.

the study of mind. When a madman appears *thoroughly* sane, indeed, it is high time to put him in a straitjacket."

"But the *danger*, my dear sir, of which you were speaking, in your own experience—during your control of this house—have you had practical reason to think liberty hazardous in the case of a lunatic?"

"Here?—in my own experience?—why, I may say, yes. For example:—no *very* long while ago, a singular circumstance occurred in this very house. The 'soothing system,' you know, was then in operation, and the patients were at large. They behaved remarkably well—especially so, any one of sense might have known that some devilish scheme was brewing from that particular fact, that the fellows behaved so *remarkably* well. And, sure enough, one fine morning the keepers found themselves pinioned hand and foot, and thrown into the cells, where they were attended, as if *they* were the lunatics, by the lunatics themselves, who had usurped the offices of the keepers."

"You don't tell me so! I never heard of any thing so absurd in my life!"

"Fact—it all came to pass by means of a stupid fellow—a lunatic—who, by some means, had taken it into his head that he had invented a better system of government than any ever heard of before—of lunatic government, I mean. He wished to give his invention a trial, I suppose, and so he persuaded the rest of the patients to join him in a conspiracy for the overthrow of the reigning powers."

"And he really succeeded?"

"No doubt of it. The keepers and kept were soon made to exchange places. Not that exactly either—for the madmen had been free, but the keepers were shut up in cells forthwith, and treated, I am sorry to say, in a very cavalier manner."

"But I presume a counter-revolution was soon effected. This condition of things could not have long existed. The country people in the neighborhood-visitors coming to see the establishment—would have given the alarm."

"There you are out. The head rebel was too cunning for that. He admitted no visitors at all—with the exception, one day, of a very stupid-looking young gentleman of whom he had no reason to be afraid. He let him in to see the place—just by way of variety,—to have a little fun with him. As soon as he had gammoned him sufficiently, he let him out, and sent him about his business."

"And *how* long, then, did the madmen reign?"

"Oh, a very long time, indeed—a month certainly—how much longer I can't precisely say. In the meantime, the lunatics had a jolly season of it—that you may swear. They doffed their own shabby clothes, and made free with the family wardrobe and jewels. The cellars of the *chateau* were well stocked with wine; and these madmen are just the devils that know how to drink it. They lived well, I can tell you."

"And the treatment—what was the particular species of treatment which the leader of the rebels put into operation?"

"Why, as for that, a madman is not necessarily a fool, as I have already observed; and it is my honest opinion that his treatment was a much better treatment than that which it superseded. It was a very capital system indeed—simple—neat—no trouble at all—in fact it was delicious—it was—"

Here my host's observations were cut short by another series of yells, of the same character as those which had previously disconcerted us. This time, however, they seemed to proceed from persons rapidly approaching.

"Gracious Heavens!" I ejaculated—"the lunatics have most undoubtedly broken loose."

"I very much fear it is so," replied Monsieur Maillard, now becoming excessively pale. He had scarcely finished the sentence, before loud shouts and imprecations were heard beneath the windows; and, immediately afterward, it became evident that some persons outside were endeavoring to gain entrance into the room. The door was beaten with what appeared to be a sledge-hammer, and the shutters were wrenched and shaken with prodigious violence.

A scene of the most terrible confusion ensued. Monsieur Maillard, to my excessive astonishment threw himself under the side-board. I had expected more resolution at his hands. The members of the orchestra, who, for the last fifteen minutes, had been seemingly too much intoxicated to do duty, now sprang all at once to their feet and to their instruments, and, scrambling upon their table, broke out, with one accord, into, "Yankee Doodle," which they performed, if not exactly in tune, at least with an energy superhuman, during the whole of the uproar.

Meantime, upon the main dining-table, among the bottles and glasses, leaped the gentleman who, with such difficulty, had been restrained from leaping there before. As soon as he fairly settled himself, he commenced an oration, which, no doubt, was a very capital one, if it could only have been heard. At the same moment, the man with the tee-totum predilection, set himself to spinning around the apartment, with immense energy, and with arms outstretched at right angles with his body; so that he had all the air of a tee-totum in fact, and knocked everybody down that happened to get in his way. And now, too, hearing an incredible popping and fizzing of champagne, I discovered at length, that it proceeded from the person who performed the bottle of that delicate drink during dinner. And then, again, the frog-man croaked away as if the salvation of his soul depended upon every note that he uttered. And, in the midst of all this, the continuous braying of a donkey arose over all. As for my old friend, Madame Joyeuse, I really could have wept for the poor lady, she appeared so terribly perplexed. All she did, however, was to stand up in a corner, by the fireplace, and sing out incessantly at the top of her voice, "Cock-a-doodle-de-dooooooh!"

And now came the climax—the catastrophe of the drama. As no resistance, beyond whooping and yelling and cock-a-doodling, was offered to the encroachments of the party without, the ten windows were very speedily, and almost simultaneously, broken in. But I shall never forget the emotions of wonder and horror with which I gazed, when, leaping through these windows, and down among us *pêle-mêle*,[30] fighting, stamping, scratching, and howling, there rushed a perfect army of what I took to be Chimpanzees, Ourang-Outangs,[31] or big black baboons of the Cape of Good Hope.

---

[30] Chaotically.

[31] Orangutans.

I received a terrible beating—after which I rolled under a sofa and lay still. After lying there some fifteen minutes, during which time I listened with all my ears to what was going on in the room, I came to same satisfactory *dénouement*[32] of this tragedy. Monsieur Maillard, it appeared, in giving me the account of the lunatic who had excited his fellows to rebellion, had been merely relating his own exploits. This gentleman had, indeed, some two or three years before, been the superintendent of the establishment, but grew crazy himself, and so became a patient. This fact was unknown to the travelling companion who introduced me. The keepers, ten in number, having been suddenly overpowered, were first well tarred, then—carefully feathered, and then shut up in underground cells. They had been so imprisoned for more than a month, during which period Monsieur Maillard had generously allowed them not only the tar and feathers (which constituted his "system"), but some bread and abundance of water. The latter was pumped on them daily. At length, one escaping through a sewer, gave freedom to all the rest.

The "soothing system," with important modifications, has been resumed at the *chateau*; yet I cannot help agreeing with Monsieur Maillard, that his own "treatment" was a very capital one of its kind. As he justly observed, it was "simple—neat—and gave no trouble at all—not the least."

I have only to add that, although I have searched every library in Europe for the works of Doctor *Tarr* and Professor *Fether*, I have, up to the present day, utterly failed in my endeavors at procuring an edition.

[32] Understanding, interpretation.

Chapter Four

HENRY CLAY LEWIS (1825–1850)

Henry Clay Lewis (1825–1850) published one collection of sketches and stories, *Odd Leaves from the Life of a Louisiana Swamp Doctor* (1850) under the pseudonym Madison Tensas. He was writing in a tradition inadequately called "Old Southwest Humor," rough stories of frontier life, often in dialect, usually published in a New York men's magazine called *The Spirit of the Times*. Often written by professional men—lawyers, politicians, journalists or doctors—these stories, freed from the usual constraints of Victorian-era publication, had a crude energy that made them influential on writers from Melville to Mark Twain to Faulkner—whose novella *The Bear* derives from T. B. Thorpe's "The Big Bear of Arkansas."

Even by standards of Old Southwest Humor, Lewis's work is brutal and offensive. "A Struggle for Life" is a fantasy that exposes the South's deepest nightmare, the slave rebellion. It is a Gothic tale in the familiar pattern of a journey into the wilderness and an encounter with the Other—who seems to have sprung directly from the narrator's racial anxiety and repressed guilt.

Henry Clay Lewis was only 25 when he drowned, while trying to cross a swamp.

Text: Madison Tensas [Henry Clay Lewis], *Odd Leaves from the Life of a Louisiana Swamp Doctor* (Philadelphia, PA: A. Hart, 1850).

A STRUGGLE FOR LIFE

It was the spring of 183--, the water from the Mississippi had commenced overflowing the low swamps, and rendering travelling on horseback very disagreeable. The water had got to that troublesome height, when it was rather too high for a horse, and not high enough for a canoe or skiff to pass easily over the submerged grounds.

I was sitting out under my favourite oak, congratulating myself that I had no travelling to do just then,—it was very healthy—when my joy was suddenly nipped in the bud by a loud hello from the opposite side of the bayou. Looking over, and answering the hail, I discerned first a mule, and then something which so closely resembled an ape or an ourang outang, that I was in doubt whether the voice had proceeded from it, until a repetition of the hail, this time coming unmistakeably from it, assured me that it was a human.

"Massa doctor at home?" yelled the voice.

"Yes, I am the doctor; what do you want?"

"Massa sent me with a letter to you."

Jumping in the skiff, a few vigorous strokes sent me to the opposite shore, where the singular being awaited my coming.

He was a negro dwarf of the most frightful appearance; his diminutive body was garnished with legs and arms of enormously disproportionate length; his face was hideous: a pair of tushes[1] projected from either side of a double hare-lip; and taking him altogether, he was the nearest resemblance to the ourang outang mixed with the devil that human eyes ever dwelt upon. I could not look at him without feeling disgust.

"Massa Bill sent me with a letter," was his reply to my asking him his business.

Opening it, I found a summons to see a patient, the mother of a man named Disney, living some twenty miles distant by the usual road. It was in no good humour that I told the dwarf to wait until I could swim my horse over, and I would accompany him.

By the time I had concluded my preparations, and put a large bottle of brandy in my pocket, my steed was awaiting me upon the opposite shore.

"Massa tole me to tell you ef you didn't mine swimming a little you had better kum de nere way."

"Do you have to swim much?"

"Oh no, massa, onely swim Plurisy Lake, and wade de back water a few mile, you'll save haf de way at leste."

I looked at the sun. It was only about two hours high, and the roads were in such miserable condition that six miles an hour would be making fine speed, so I determined to go the near way, and swim "Pleurisy Slough."

"You are certain you know the road, boy?"

"Oh, yes, massa, me know um ebery inch ob de groun'; hunted possum an' coon ober him many a night. Massa, you ain't got any 'baccy, is you?"

"There's a chaw—and here's a drink of brandy. I'll give you another if you pilot me safe through, and a good pounding if you get lost."

"Dank you, Massa, um's good. No fere I lose you, know ebery inch of de groun'."

I had poured him out a dram, not considering his diminutive stature, sufficient to unsettle the nerves of a stout man, but he drank it off with great apparent relish; and by this time, everything being ready, we commenced ploughing our way through the muddy roads.

We made but slow progress. I would dash on, and then have to wait for the dwarf, who, belabouring his mule with a cudgel almost as large as himself, strove in vain to keep up.

The road was directly down the bayou, for some miles. There were few settlers on it then, and the extent of their clearing consisted of a corn-patch. They were the pre-emptioners or squatters; men who settled upon government land before its survey, and awaited the incoming of planters with several negroes to buy their claims, themselves to be bought out by more affluent emigrants. To one of the first-mentioned class—the pre-emptioners—my visit was directed, or rather to his mother, who occupied an intermediate grade between the squatter and the small planter, inasmuch as she possessed one negro, the delectable morsel for whom I was waiting every few hundred yards.

---

1 Tusks.

It wanted but an hour to sundown when we reached the place where it was optional with me, either to go the longer route by the bayou, or save several miles by cutting across the bend of the stream, having, however, to swim "Pleurisy Slough" if I did so.

The path across was quite obscure, and it would be dark by the time we crossed; but the negro declared he knew every inch of the way, and as saving distance was a serious consideration, I determined to try it and "Pleurisy Slough."

Taking a drink to warm me, for the dew that had commenced to fall was quite chilling, I gave one to the negro, not noticing the wild sparkle of his eye or the exhilaration of his manner.

We pressed on eagerly, I ahead as long as the path lasted; but it giving out at the edge of the back water, it became necessary for the negro to precede and pilot the way.

I followed him mechanically for some distance, relying on his intimate knowledge of the swamp, our steeds making but slow progress through the mud and water.

When we entered the swamp I had remarked that the sun was in our faces; and great was my astonishment, when we had travelled some time, on glancing my eye upwards to see if it had left the tree-tops, to perceive its last beams directly at my back, the very reverse of what it should have been. Thinking perhaps that it was some optical illusion, I consulted the moss on the trees, and its indication was that we were taking the back track. I addressed the negro very sharply for having misled me, when, instead of excusing himself, he turned on me his hideous countenance and chuckled the low laugh of drunkenness. I saw that I had given him too much brandy for his weak brain, and that he was too far gone to be of any assistance to me in finding the way.

Mine was a pleasant situation truly. To return home would be as bad as to endeavour to go on; it would be night at any rate before I could get out of the swamp; and after it fell, as there was no moon, it would be dangerous to travel, as the whole country was full of lakes and sloughs, and we might be precipitated suddenly into one of them, losing our animals if not being drowned ourselves.

It was evident that I would have to pass the night in the swamp, my only companion the drunken dwarf. I had nothing to eat, and no weapons to protect myself if assailed by wild beasts; but the swamp was high enough to preclude the attack of anything but an alligator, and their bellow was resounding in too close proximity to be agreeable.

Fortunately, being a cigar-smoker, I had a box of matches in my pocket, so I would have a fire at least. My next care was to find a ridge sufficiently above the water to furnish a dry place for building a fire and camp. After considerable search, just at night-fall the welcome prospect of a cane ridge above the overflow met my gaze; hurrying up the negro, who by this time was maudlin drunk, I reached the cane, and forcing my way with considerable difficulty through it until I got out of the reach of the water, dismounted, and tying my horse, took the negro down and performed the same office for his mule.

My next care was to gather materials for a fire before impenetrable darkness closed over the swamp; fortunately for me, a fallen oak presented itself not ten steps from where I stood. To have a cheerful blazing fire was the work of a few minutes. Breaking off sufficient cane-tops to last the steeds till morning, I stripped my horse—the mule had nothing on but a bridle—and with the saddle and cane-leaves made me a couch that a monarch, had he been as tired as I was, would have found no fault with. As the negro was perfectly helpless, and nearly naked, I gave him my saddle blanket, and making him a bed at a respectful distance, bade him go to sleep.

Replenishing the fire with sufficient fuel to last till morning, I lit a cigar, and throwing myself down upon my fragrant couch, gave myself up to reflections upon the peculiarity of my situation. Had it been a voluntary bivouac with a set of chosen companions, it would not have awakened half the interest in my mind that it did, for the attending circumstances imparted to it much of the romantic.

There, far from human habitation, my only companion a hideous dwarf, surrounded with water, the night draperied darkly around, I lay, the cane-leaves for my bed, the saddle for my pillow; the huge fire lighting up the darkness for a space around, and giving natural objects a strange, distorted appearance, bringing the two steeds into high relief against the dark background of waving cane, which nodded over, discoursing a wild, peculiar melody of its own. Occasionally a loud explosion would be heard as the fire communicated with a green reed; the wild hoot of an owl was heard, and directly I almost felt the sweep of his wings as he went sailing by, and alighted upon an old tree just where the light sank mingling with the darkness. I followed him with my eye, and as he settled himself, he turned his gaze towards me; I moved one of the logs, and his huge eyes fairly glistened with light, as the flames shot up with increased vigour; the swamp moss was flowing around him in long, tangled masses, and as a more vivid gleam uprose, I gazed and started involuntarily. Had I not known it was an owl surrounded with moss that sat upon that stricken tree, I would have sworn it was the form of an old man, clad in a sombre flowing mantle, his arm raised in an attitude of warning, that I gazed upon. A cane exploding, startled the owl, and with a loud "tu whit, tu whoo," he went sailing away in the darkness. The unmelodious bellow of the alligator, and the jarring cry of the heron, arose from a lake on the opposite side of the cane; whilst the voices of a myriad of frogs, and the many undistinguishable sounds of the swamp, made the night vocal with discordancy.

My cigar being by this time exhausted, I took the bottle from my pocket, and taking a hearty drink to keep the night air from chilling me when asleep, was about to restore it to its place, and commend myself to slumber, when, glancing at the dwarf, I saw his eyes fixed upon me with a demoniac expression that I shall never forget.

"Give me a dram," he said very abruptly, not prefacing the request by those deferential words never omitted by the slave when in his proper mind.

"No, sir, you have already taken too much; I will give you no more," I replied.

"Give me a dram," he again said, more fiercely than before.

Breaking off a cane, I told him that if he spoke to me in that manner again I would give him a severe flogging.

But to my surprise he retorted, "D—n you, white man, I will kill you ef you don't give me more brandy!" his eyes flashing and sparkling with electric light.

I rose to correct him, but a comparison of my well developed frame with his stunted deformed proportions, and the reflection that his drunkenness was attributable to my giving him the brandy, deterred me.

"I will kill you," he again screamed, his fangs clashing, and the foam flying from his mouth, his long arms extended as if to clutch me, and the fingers quivering nervously.

I took a hasty glance of my condition. I was lost in the midst of the swamp, an unknown watery expanse surrounding me; remote from any possible assistance; the swamps were rapidly filling with water, and if we did not get out to-morrow or next day, we would in all probability be starved or drowned; the negro was my only dependence, to pilot me to the settlements, and he was threatening my life if I did not give him more brandy; should I do it or not? Judging from the effects of the two drinks I had given him, if he got possession of the bottle it might destroy him, or at least render him incapable of travelling, until starvation and exposure would destroy us. My mind was resolved upon that subject; I would give him no more. There was no alternative, I would have to stand his assault; considering I was three times his size, a fearful adventure, truly, thought I, not doubting a moment but that my greater size would give me proportionate strength; I must not hurt him, but will tie him until he recovers.

The dwarf, now aroused to maniacal fury by the persistence in my refusal, slowly approached me to carry his threat into execution. The idea of such a diminutive object destroying without weapons a man of my size, presented something ludicrous, and I laughingly awaited his attack, ready to tie his hands before he could bite or scratch me. Wofully I underrated his powers!

With a yell like a wild beast's, he precipitated himself upon me; evading my blow, he clutched with his long fingers at my throat, burying his talons in my flesh, and writhing his little body around mine, strove to bear me to earth.

I summoned my whole strength, and endeavoured to shake him off; but, possessing the proverbial power of the dwarf, increased by his drunken mania to an immense degree, I found all my efforts unavailing, and, oh God! horrors of horrors, what awful anguish was mine, when I found him bearing me slowly to earth, and his piercing talons buried in my throat, cutting off my breath! My eyes met his with a more horrid gleam than that he glared upon me: his was the fire of brutal nature, aroused by desire to intense malignancy; and mine the gaze of despair and death. Closer and firmer his grip closed upon my throat, barring out the sweet life's breath. I strove to shriek for help, but could not. How shall I describe the racking agony that tortured me? A mountain, heavier than any earth's bosom holds, was pressing upon my breast, slowly crushing me to fragments. All kinds of colours first floated before my eyes, and then everything wore a settled, intensely fiery red. I felt my jaw slowly dropping, and my tongue protruding, till it rested on the hellish fangs that encircled my throat. I could hear distinctly every pulsation of even the minutest artery in my frame. Its wild singing was in my ears like the ocean wave playing over the shell-clad shore. I remember it all perfectly, for the mind, through all this awful struggle, still remained full of thought and clearness. Closer grew the gripe of those talons around my throat, and I knew that I could live but a few moments more. I did not pray. I did not commend my soul to God. I had not a fear of death. But oh! awful were my thoughts at dying in such a way—suffocated by a hellish negro in the midst of the noisome swamp, my flesh to be devoured by the carrion crow, my bones to whiten where they lay for long years, and then startle the settler, when civilization had strode into the wilderness, and the cane that would conceal my bones would be falling before the knife of the cane-cutter. I ceased to breathe. I was dead. I had suffered the last pangs of that awful hour, and either it was the soul not yet resigned to leave its human tenement, or else immortal mind triumphing over death, but I still retained the sentient principle within my corpse. I remember distinctly when the demon relaxed his clutch, and shaking me to see if I were really dead, broke into a hellish laugh. I remember distinctly when tearing the bottle from me, he pulled my limber body off my couch, and stretched himself upon it. And what were my thoughts? I was dead, yet am living now. Ay, dead as human ever becomes. My lungs had ceased to play; my heart was still; my muscles were inactive; even my skin had the dead clammy touch. Had men been there, they would have placed me in a coffin, and buried me deep in the ground, and the worm would have eaten me, and the death-rats made nests in my heart, and what was lately a strong man would have become a loathsome mass. But still in that coffin amidst those writhing worms, would have been the immortal mind, and still would it have thought and pondered on till the last day was come. For such is the course of soul and death, as my interpretation has it. I was dead, all but my mind, and that still thought on as vividly, as ramblingly, as during life. My body lay dead in that murderer's swamp, my mind roamed far away in thought, reviewing my carnal life. I stood, as when a boy, by my mother's grave. The tall grass was waving over it, the green sod smiled at my feet. "Mother," I whispered, "your child is weary—the world looks harsh upon him—coldness comes from those who should shelter the orphan. Mother, open your large black eyes and smile upon your child." Again, I stood upon the steamer, a childish fugitive, giving a last look upon my fleeing home, and mingling my tears with the foaming wave beneath. I dragged my exhausted frame through the cotton-fields of the south. My back was wearied with stooping—we were picking the first opening—and as dreams of future distinction would break upon my soul, the strap of the cotton-sack, galling my shoulder, recalled me to myself. All the phases of my life were repeated, until they ended where I lay dead!—dead as mortal ever becomes. I thought, What will my friends say when they hear that on a visit to the sick, I disappeared in the swamp, and was never heard of more?—drowned or starved to death? Will they weep for me? for me?—Not many, I ween, will be the tears that will be shed for me. Then, after the lapse of long years, my bones will be found. I wonder who will get my skull? Perhaps an humble doctor like myself, who, meditating upon it, will not think that it holds the mind of a creature of his own ambition—his own lofty instincts. He will deem it but an empty skull, and little dream that it held a sentient principle. But I know that the mind will still tenant it. Ha, ha! how that foul ape is gurgling his blood-bought pleasure. I would move if I could, and wrench the bottle from him; but mine is thought, not action. Hark! there is a storm arising. I hear with my ear, that is pressed on the earth, the thunder of the hurricane. How the trees crash beneath it! Will it prostrate those above me? Hark! what awful thunder! Ah me! what fierce pang is that piercing my very vitals? There is a glimmering of light before my eyes. Can it be that I the dead am being restored to human life? Another thunder peal! 'tis the second stroke of my heart—my blood is red-hot—it comes with fire through my veins—the earth quakes—the mountain is rolling off my chest—I live!—I breathe!—I see!—I hear!—Where am I? Who brought me here? I hear other sounds, but cannot my own voice. Where am I? Ah! I remember the dwarf strangled me. Hark! where is he? Is that the sunbeam playing over the trees? What noisome odour like consuming flesh is that which poisons the gale? Great God! can that disfigured half-consumed mass be my evil genius?

I rose up, and staggering, fell again; my strength was nearly gone. I lay until I thought myself sufficiently recruited to stand, and then got up and surveyed the scene. The animals were tied as I left them, and were eating their cane unconcernedly; but fearfully my well-nigh murderer had paid for his crime, and awful was the retribution. Maddened by the spirits, he had rushed into the flames, and, in the charred and loathsome mass, nothing of the human remained; he had died the murderer's death and been buried in his grave,—a tomb of fire.

To remain longer in the horrid place was impossible; my throat pained me excessively where the talons had penetrated the flesh, and I could not speak above a whisper. I turned the mule loose, thinking that it would return home, and conduct me out of the swamp. I was not incorrect in my supposition; the creature led me to his owner's cabin. The patient had died during the night.

My account of the dwarf's attack did not surprise the family; he had once, when in a similar condition, made an attack upon his mistress, and would have strangled her, had assistance not been near.

His bones were left to bleach where they lay. I would not for the universe have looked again upon the place; and his mistress being dead, there were none to care for giving him the rites of sepulture.

THE END.

Chapter Five

GEORGE WASHINGTON CABLE (1844–1925)

George Washington Cable was born in New Orleans in 1844. After serving in the Confederate Army during the Civil War, he became a journalist, contributing articles to the *New Orleans Picayune*. His activities as a reporter exposed him to the complexities of racial and social structures in the South and provided a rich vein of material which would later serve as inspiration for his historical fiction. His short stories were initially published by Scribner's Monthly as local color fiction, and subsequently as part of a collection, *Old Creole Days*. In his fiction, Cable depicts the collision between the rigid racial classifications of the Anglo-Americans who poured into New Orleans after 1803 and the intricate webs of family allegiances in Francophone New Orleans.

In "Belles Demoiselles Plantation," we encounter Coronel de Charleu, a member of the old New Orleans Creole elite, and his mixed-race Choctaw relation, Injin' Charlie. The story is notable for its depiction of the ethical dilemmas arising from the convoluted nature of interracial sexuality as it collides with the arbitrary racial categories of nineteenth-century Louisiana.

Text: George Washington Cable, *Old Creole Days* (New York: C. Scribner's Sons, 1879).

BELLES DEMOISELLES PLANTATION

THE original grantee was Count—, assume the name to be De Charleu; the old Creoles never forgive a public mention. He was the French king's commissary. One day, called to France to explain the lucky accident of the commissariat having burned down with the account-books inside, he left his wife, a Choctaw[1] Comtesse,[2] behind.

Arrived at court, his excuses were accepted, and that tract granted him where afterwards stood Belles Demoiselles Plantation. A man cannot remember every thing! In a fit of forgetfulness he married a French gentlewoman, rich and beautiful, and "brought her out." However, "All's well that ends well"; a famine had been in the colony, and the Choctaw Comtesse had starved, leaving nought but a half-caste orphan family lurking on the edge of the settlement, bearing our French gentlewoman's own new name, and being mentioned in Monsieur's will.

And the new Comtesse—she tarried but a twelvemonth, left Monsieur a lovely son, and departed, led out of this vain world by the swamp fever.[3]

1 The Choctaw are a Native American group who originally occupied land in what is now the Southeastern United States.

2 Countess.

3 Probably malaria or yellow fever.

From this son sprang the proud Creole family of De Charleu. It rose straight up, up, up, generation after generation, tall, branchless, slender, palm-like; and finally, in the time of which I am to tell, flowered with all the rare beauty of a century-plant, in Artémise, Innocente, Felicité, the twins Marie and Martha, Leontine and little Septima; the seven beautiful daughters for whom their home had been fitly named Belles Demoiselles.

The Count's grant had once been a long Pointe,[4] round which the Mississippi used to whirl, and seethe, and foam, that it was horrid to behold. Big whirlpools would open and wheel about in the savage eddies under the low bank, and close up again, and others open, and spin, and disappear. Great circles of muddy surface would boil up from hundreds of feet below, and gloss over, and seem to float away,—sink, come back again under water, and with only a soft hiss surge up again, and again drift off, and vanish. Every few minutes the loamy bank would tip down a great load of earth upon its besieger, and fall back a foot,—sometimes a yard,—and the writhing river would press after, until at last the Pointe was quite swallowed up, and the great river glided by in a majestic curve, and asked no more; the bank stood fast, the "caving" became a forgotten misfortune, and the diminished grant was a long, sweeping, willowy bend, rustling with miles of sugar-cane.

Coming up the Mississippi in the sailing craft of those early days, about the time one first could descry the white spires of the old St. Louis Cathedral,[5] you would be pretty sure to spy, just over to your right under the levee, Belles Demoiselles Mansion, with its broad veranda and red painted cypress roof, peering over the embankment, like a bird in the nest, half hid by the avenue of willows which one of the departed De Charleus,—he that married a Marot,—had planted on the levee's crown.

The house stood unusually near the river, facing eastward, and standing four-square, with an immense veranda about its sides, and a flight of steps in front spreading broadly downward, as we open arms to a child. From the veranda nine miles of river were seen; and in their compass, near at hand, the shady garden full of rare and beautiful flowers; farther away broad fields of cane and rice, and the distant quarters of the slaves, and on the horizon everywhere a dark belt of cypress forest.

The master was old Colonel De Charleu,—Jean Albert Henri Joseph De Charleu-Marot, and "Colonel" by the grace of the first American governor. Monsieur,—he would not speak to any one who called him "Colonel,"—was a hoary-headed[6] patriarch. His step was firm, his form erect, his intellect strong and clear, his countenance classic, serene, dignified, commanding, his manners courtly, his voice musical,—fascinating. He had had his vices,—all his life; but had borne them, as his race do, with a serenity of conscience and a cleanness of mouth that left no outward blemish on the surface of the gentleman. He had gambled in Royal Street, drank hard in Orleans Street, run his adversary through in the duelling-ground at Slaughter-house Point, and danced and quarrelled at the St.

4 Peninsula.

5 The oldest cathedral in what is now the United States. A first church was built on the site in 1718. A later building, built in 1789, was given cathedral status in 1793.

6 With grayish-white hair.

Philippe-street-theatre quadroon[7] balls. Even now, with all his courtesy and bounty, and a hospitality which seemed to be entertaining angels, he was bitter-proud and penurious, and deep down in his hard-finished heart loved nothing but himself, his name, and his motherless children. But these!—their ravishing beauty was all but excuse enough for the unbounded idolatry of their father. Against these seven goddesses he never rebelled. Had they even required him to defraud old De Carlos—

I can hardly say.

Old De Carlos was his extremely distant relative on the Choctaw side. With this single exception, the narrow thread-like line of descent from the Indian wife, diminished to a mere strand by injudicious alliances, and deaths in the gutters of old New Orleans, was extinct. The name, by Spanish contact, had become De Carlos; but this one surviving bearer of it was known to all, and known only, as Injin Charlie.

One thing I never knew a Creole to do. He will not utterly go back on the ties of blood, no matter what sort of knots those ties may be. For one reason, he is never ashamed of his or his father's sins; and for another,—he will tell you—he is "all heart!"

So the different heirs of the De Charleu estate had always strictly regarded the rights and interests of the De Carloses, especially their ownership of a block of dilapidated buildings in a part of the city, which had once been very poor property, but was beginning to be valuable. This block had much more than maintained the last De Carlos through a long and lazy lifetime, and, as his household consisted only of himself, and an aged and crippled negress, the inference was irresistible that he "had money." Old Charlie, though by *alias* an "Injin," was plainly a dark white man, about as old as Colonel De Charleu, sunk in the bliss of deep ignorance, shrewd, deaf, and, by repute at least, unmerciful.

The Colonel and he always conversed in English. This rare accomplishment, which the former had learned from his Scotch wife,—the latter from upriver traders,—they found an admirable medium of communication, answering, better than French could, a similar purpose to that of the stick which we fasten to the bit of one horse and breast-gear of another, whereby each keeps his distance. Once in a while, too, by way of jest, English found its way among the ladies of Belles Demoiselles, always signifying that their sire was about to have business with old Charlie.

Now a long-standing wish to buy out Charlie troubled the Colonel. He had no desire to oust him unfairly; he was proud of being always fair; yet he did long to engross the whole estate under one title. Out of his luxurious idleness he had conceived this desire, and thought little of so slight an obstacle as being already somewhat in debt to old Charlie for money borrowed, and for which Belles Demoiselles was, of course, good, ten times over. Lots, buildings, rents, all, might as well be his, he thought, to give, keep, or destroy. "Had he but the old man's heritage. Ah! he might bring that into existence which his *belles demoiselles* had been begging for, 'since many years;' a home,—and such a home,—in the gay city. Here he should tear down this row of cottages, and make his garden wall; there that long rope-walk should give place to vine-covered arbors; the bakery yonder should make way for a costly conservatory; that wine warehouse should

[7] An archaic term used to designate people who are one-quarter black.

come down, and the mansion go up. It should be the finest in the State. Men should never pass it, but they should say—'the palace of the De Charleus; a family of grand descent, a people of elegance and bounty, a line as old as France, a fine old man, and seven daughters as beautiful as happy; whoever dare attempt to marry there must leave his own name behind him!'

"The house should be of stones fitly set, brought down in ships from the land of 'les Yankees,'[8] and it should have an airy belvedere, with a gilded image tip-toeing and shining on its peak, and from it you should see, far across the gleaming folds of the river, the red roof of Belles Demoiselles, the country-seat. At the big stone gate there should be a porter's lodge, and it should be a privilege even to see the ground."

Truly they were a family fine enough, and fancy-free enough to have fine wishes, yet happy enough where they were, to have had no wish but to live there always.

To those, who, by whatever fortune, wandered into the garden of Belles Demoiselles some summer afternoon as the sky was reddening towards evening, it was lovely to see the family gathered out upon the tiled pavement at the foot of the broad front steps, gayly chatting and jesting, with that ripple of laughter that comes so pleasingly from a bevy of girls. The father would be found seated in their midst, the centre of attention and compliment, witness, arbiter, umpire, critic, by his beautiful children's unanimous appointment, but the single vassal, too, of seven absolute sovereigns.

Now they would draw their chairs near together in eager discussion of some new step in the dance, or the adjustment of some rich adornment. Now they would start about him with excited comments to see the eldest fix a bunch of violets in his button-hole. Now the twins would move down a walk after some unusual flower, and be greeted on their return with the high pitched notes of delighted feminine surprise.

As evening came on they would draw more quietly about their paternal centre. Often their chairs were forsaken, and they grouped themselves on the lower steps, one above another, and surrendered themselves to the tender influences of the approaching night. At such an hour the passer on the river, already attracted by the dark figures of the broad-roofed mansion, and its woody garden standing against the glowing sunset, would hear the voices of the hidden group rise from the spot in the soft harmonies of an evening song; swelling clearer and clearer as the thrill of music warmed them into feeling, and presently joined by the deeper tones of the father's voice; then, as the daylight passed quite away, all would be still, and he would know that the beautiful home had gathered its nestlings under its wings.

And yet, for mere vagary, it pleased them not to be pleased.

"Arti!" called one sister to another in the broad hall, one morning,—mock amazement in her distended eyes,—"something is goin' to took place!"

"*Comm-e-n-t?*"—long-drawn perplexity.

"Papa is goin' to town!"

The news passed up stairs.

"Inno!"—one to another meeting in a doorway,—"something is goin' to took place!"

[8] English-speaking settlers of American origin.

"*Qu'est-ce-que c'est?*"[9]—vain attempt at gruffness.

"Papa is goin' to town!"

The unusual tidings were true. It was afternoon of the same day that the Colonel tossed his horse's bridle to his groom, and stepped up to old Charlie, who was sitting on his bench under a China-tree, his head, as was his fashion, bound in a Madras handkerchief. The "old man" was plainly under the effect of spirits, and smiled a deferential salutation without trusting himself to his feet.

"Eh, well Charlie!"—the Colonel raised his voice to suit his kinsman's deafness,—"how is those times with my friend Charlie?"

"Eh?" said Charlie, distractedly.

"Is that goin' well with my friend Charlie?"

"In de house,—call her,"—making a pretence of rising.

"*Non, non!* I don't want,"—the speaker paused to breathe—"ow is collection?"

"Oh!" said Charlie, "every day he make me more poorer!"

"What do you hask for it?" asked the planter indifferently, designating the house by a wave of his whip.

"Ask for w'at?" said Injin Charlie.

"De *house*! What you ask for it?"

"I don't believe," said Charlie.

"What you would *take* for it!" cried the planter.

"Wait for w'at?"

"What you would *take* for the whole block?"

"I don't want to sell him!"

"I'll give you *ten thousand dollah* for it."

"Ten t'ousand dollah for dis house? Oh, no, dat is no price. He is blame good old house,—dat old house." (Old Charlie and the Colonel never swore in presence of each other.) "Forty years dat old house didn't had to be paint! I easy can get fifty t'ousand dollah for dat old house."

"Fifty thousand picayunes; yes," said the Colonel.

"She's a good house. Can make plenty money," pursued the deaf man.

"That's what make you so rich, eh, Charlie?"

"*Non*, I don't make nothing. Too blame clever, me, dat's de troub'. She's a good house,—make money fast like a steamboat,—make a barrel full in a week! Me, I lose money all de days. Too blame clever."

"Charlie!"

"Eh?"

"Tell me what you'll take."

"Make? I don't make *nothing*. Too blame clever."

"What will you *take?*"

"Oh! I got enough already,—half drunk now."

"What will you take for the 'ouse?"

---

[9] "What is that?"

"You want to buy her?"

"I don't know,"—(shrug),—"may*be*,—if you sell it cheap."

"She's a bully old house."

There was a long silence. By and by old Charlie commenced—

"Old Injin Charlie is a low-down dog."

"*C'est vrai, oui!*"[10] retorted the Colonel in an undertone.

"He's got Injin blood in him."

The Colonel nodded assent.

"But he's got some blame good blood, too, ain't it?"

The Colonel nodded impatiently.

"*Bien!* Old Charlie's Injin blood says, 'sell de house, Charlie, you blame old fool!' *Mais*, old Charlie's good blood says, 'Charlie! if you sell dat old house, Charlie, you low-down old dog, Charlie, what de Compte De Charleu make for you grace-gran'-muzzer, de dev' can eat you, Charlie, I don't care.' "

"But you'll sell it anyhow, won't you, old man?"

"No!" And the *no* rumbled off in muttered oaths like thunder out on the Gulf. The incensed old Colonel wheeled and started off.

"Curl!" (Colonel) said Charlie, standing up unsteadily.

The planter turned with an inquiring frown.

"I'll trade with you!" said Charlie.

The Colonel was tempted. " 'Ow'l you trade?" he asked.

"My house for yours!"

The old Colonel turned pale with anger. He walked very quickly back, and came close up to his kinsman.

"Charlie!" he said.

"Injin Charlie,"—with a tipsy nod.

But by this time self-control was returning. "Sell Belles Demoiselles to you?" he said in a high key, and then laughed "Ho, ho, ho!" and rode away.

A cloud, but not a dark one, overshadowed the spirits of Belles Demoiselles' plantation. The old master, whose beaming presence had always made him a shining Saturn, spinning and sparkling within the bright circle of his daughters, fell into musing fits, started out of frowning reveries, walked often by himself, and heard business from his overseer fretfully.

No wonder. The daughters knew his closeness in trade, and attributed to it his failure to negotiate for the Old Charlie buildings,—so to call them. They began to depreciate Belles Demoiselles. If a north wind blew, it was too cold to ride. If a shower had fallen, it was too muddy to drive. In the morning the garden was wet. In the evening the grasshopper was a burden. *Ennui*[11] was turned into capital; every headache was interpreted a premonition of ague; and when the native exuberance of a flock of ladies without a want or a care burst out in laughter in the father's face, they spread their French eyes,

[10] "This is true, yes."

[11] Boredom.

rolled up their little hands, and with rigid wrists and mock vehemence vowed and vowed again that they only laughed at their misery, and should pine to death unless they could move to the sweet city. "Oh! the theatre! Oh! Orleans Street! Oh! the masquerade! the Place d'Armes![12] the ball!" and they would call upon Heaven with French irreverence, and fall into each other's arms, and whirl down the hall singing a waltz, end with a grand collision and fall, and, their eyes streaming merriment, lay the blame on the slippery floor, that would some day be the death of the whole seven.

Three times more the fond father, thus goaded, managed, by accident,—business accident,—to see old Charlie and increase his offer; but in vain. He finally went to him formally.

"Eh?" said the deaf and distant relative. "For what you want him, eh? Why you don't stay where you halways be 'appy? Dis is a blame old rat-hole,—good for old Injin Charlie,—da's all. Why you don't stay where you be halways 'appy? Why you don't buy somewheres else?"

"That's none of your business," snapped the planter. Truth was, his reasons were unsatisfactory even to himself.

A sullen silence followed. Then Charlie spoke:

"Well, now, look here; I sell you old Charlie's house."

"*Bien!* and the whole block," said the Colonel.

"Hold on," said Charlie. "I sell you de 'ouse and de block. Den I go and git drunk, and go to sleep; de dev' comes along and says, 'Charlie! old Charlie, you blame low-down old dog, wake up! What you doin' here? Where's de 'ouse what Monsieur le Compte give your grace-gran-muzzer? Don't you see dat fine gentyman, De Charleu, done gone and tore him down and make him over new, you blame old fool, Charlie, you low-down old Injin dog!' "

"I'll give you forty thousand dollars," said the Colonel.

"For de 'ouse?"

"For all."

The deaf man shook his head.

"Forty-five!" said the Colonel.

"What a lie? For what you tell me 'What a lie?' I don't tell you no lie."

"*Non, non!* I give you *forty-five!*" shouted the Colonel.

Charlie shook his head again.

"Fifty!"

He shook it again.

The figures rose and rose to—

"Seventy-five!"

The answer was an invitation to go away and let the owner alone, as he was, in certain specified respects, the vilest of living creatures, and no company for a fine gentyman.

The "fine gentyman" longed to blaspheme,—but before old Charlie!—in the name of pride, how could he? He mounted and started away.

---

[12] A historic park in the French Quarter, now known as Jackson Square.

"Tell you what I'll make wid you," said Charlie.

The other, guessing aright, turned back without dismounting, smiling.

"How much Belles Demoiselles hoes me now?" asked the deaf one.

"One hundred and eighty thousand dollars," said the Colonel, firmly.

"Yass," said Charlie. "I don't want Belles Demoiselles."

The old Colonel's quiet laugh intimated it made no difference either way.

"But me," continued Charlie, "me,—I'm got le Compte De Charleu's blood in me, any'ow,—a litt' bit, any'ow, ain't it?"

The Colonel nodded that it was.

"*Bien!* If I go out of dis place and don't go to Belles Demoiselles, de peoples will say,—dey will say, 'Old Charlie he been all doze time tell a blame *lie!* He ain't no kin to his old grace-gran-muzzer, not a blame bit! He don't got nary drop of De Charleu blood to save his blame low-down old Injin soul!' No, sare! What I want wid money, den? No, sare! My place for yours!"

He turned to go into the house, just too soon to see the Colonel make an ugly whisk at him with his riding-whip. Then the Colonel, too, moved off.

Two or three times over, as he ambled homeward, laughter broke through his annoyance, as he recalled old Charlie's family pride and the presumption of his offer. Yet each time he could but think better of—not the offer to swap, but the preposterous ancestral loyalty. It was so much better than he could have expected from his "low-down" relative, and not unlike his own whim withal—the proposition which went with it was forgiven.

This last defeat bore so harshly on the master of Belles Demoiselles, that the daughters, reading chagrin in his face, began to repent. They loved their father as daughters can, and when they saw their pretended dejection harassing him seriously they restrained their complaints, displayed more than ordinary tenderness, and heroically and ostentatiously concluded there was no place like Belles Demoiselles. But the new mood touched him more than the old, and only refined his discontent. Here was a man, rich without the care of riches, free from any real trouble, happiness as native to his house as perfume to his garden, deliberately, as it were with premeditated malice, taking joy by the shoulder and bidding her be gone to town, whither he might easily have followed, only that the very same ancestral nonsense that kept Injin Charlie from selling the old place for twice its value prevented him from choosing any other spot for a city home.

But by and by the charm of nature and the merry hearts around him prevailed; the fit of exalted sulks passed off, and after a while the year flared up at Christmas, flickered, and went out.

New Year came and passed; the beautiful garden of Belles Demoiselles put on its spring attire; the seven fair sisters moved from rose to rose; the cloud of discontent had warmed into invisible vapor in the rich sunlight of family affection, and on the common memory the only scar of last year's wound was old Charlie's sheer impertinence in crossing the caprice of the De Charleus. The cup of gladness seemed to fill with the filling of the river.

How high that river was! Its tremendous current rolled and tumbled and spun along, hustling the long funeral flotillas of drift,—and how near shore it came! Men were out day and night, watching the levee. On windy nights even the old Colonel took part, and grew light-hearted with occupation and excitement, as every minute the river threw a white arm over the levee's top, as though it would vault over. But all held fast, and, as the summer drifted in, the water sunk down into its banks and looked quite incapable of harm.

On a summer afternoon of uncommon mildness, old Colonel Jean Albert Henri Joseph De Charleu-Marot, being in a mood for revery, slipped the custody of his feminine rulers and sought the crown of the levee, where it was his wont to promenade. Presently he sat upon a stone bench,—a favorite seat. Before him lay his broad-spread fields; near by, his lordly mansion; and being still,—perhaps by female contact,—somewhat sentimental, he fell to musing on his past. It was hardly worthy to be proud of. All its morning was reddened with mad frolic, and far toward the meridian it was marred with elegant rioting. Pride had kept him well-nigh useless, and despised the honors won by valor; gaming had dimmed prosperity; death had taken his heavenly wife; voluptuous ease had mortgaged his lands; and yet his house still stood, his sweet-smelling fields were still fruitful, his name was fame enough; and yonder and yonder, among the trees and flowers, like angels walking in Eden, were the seven goddesses of his only worship.

Just then a slight sound behind him brought him to his feet. He cast his eyes anxiously to the outer edge of the little strip of bank between the levee's base and the river. There was nothing visible. He paused, with his ear toward the water, his face full of frightened expectation. Ha! There came a single plashing sound, like some great beast slipping into the river, and little waves in a wide semi-circle came out from under the bank and spread over the water!

"My God!"

He plunged down the levee and bounded through the low weeds to the edge of the bank. It was sheer, and the water about four feet below. He did not stand quite on the edge, but fell upon his knees a couple of yards away, wringing his hands, moaning and weeping, and staring through his watery eyes at a fine, long crevice just discernible under the matted grass, and curving outward on either hand toward the river.

"My God!" he sobbed aloud; "my God!" and even while he called, his God answered: the tough Bermuda grass stretched and snapped, the crevice slowly became a gape, and softly, gradually, with no sound but the closing of the water at last, a ton or more of earth settled into the boiling eddy and disappeared.

At the same instant a pulse of the breeze brought from the garden behind, the joyous, thoughtless laughter of the fair mistresses of Belles Demoiselles.

The old Colonel sprang up and clambered over the levee. Then forcing himself to a more composed movement, he hastened into the house and ordered his horse.

"Tell my children to make merry while I am gone," he left word. "I shall be back to-night," and the horse's hoofs clattered down a by-road leading to the city.

"Charlie," said the planter, riding up to a window, from which the old man's nightcap was thrust out, "what you say, Charlie,—my house for yours, eh, Charlie—what you say?"

"Ello!" said Charlie; "from where you come from dis time of to-night?"

"I come from the Exchange in St. Louis Street." (A small fraction of the truth.)

"What you want?" said matter-of-fact Charlie.

"I come to trade."

The low-down relative drew the worsted off his ears. "Oh! yass," he said with an uncertain air.

"Well, old man Charlie, what you say: my house for yours,—like you said,—eh, Charlie?"

"I dunno," said Charlie; "it's nearly mine now. Why you don't stay dare youse'f?"

"*Because I don't want!*" said the Colonel savagely. "Is dat reason enough for you? You better take me in de notion, old man, I tell you,—yes!"

Charlie never winced; but how his answer delighted the Colonel! Quoth Charlie:

"I don't care—I take him—*mais*, possession give right off."

"Not the whole plantation, Charlie; only"—

"I don't care," said Charlie; "we easy can fix dat. *Mais*, what for you don't want to keep him? I don't want him. You better keep him."

"Don't you try to make no fool of me, old man," cried the planter.

"Oh, no!" said the other. "Oh, no! but you make a fool of yourself, ain't it?"

The dumbfounded Colonel stared; Charlie went on:

"Yass! Belles Demoiselles is more wort' dan tree block like dis one. I pass by dare since two weeks. Oh, pritty Belles Demoiselles! De cane was wave in de wind, de garden smell like a bouquet, de white-cap was jump up and down on de river; seven *belles demoiselles* was ridin' on horses.'Pritty, pritty, pritty!' says old Charlie. Ah! *Monsieur le père*, 'ow 'appy, 'appy, 'appy!"

"Yass!" he continued—the Colonel still staring—"le Compte De Charleu have two familie. One was low-down Choctaw, one was high up *noblesse*. He gave the low-down Choctaw dis old rat-hole; he give Belles Demoiselles to you gran-fozzer; and now you don't be *satisfait*. What I'll do wid Belles Demoiselles? She'll break me in two years, yass. And what you'll do wid old Charlie's house, eh? You'll tear her down and make you'se'f a blame old fool. I rather wouldn't trade!"

The planter caught a big breathful of anger, but Charlie went straight on:

"I rather wouldn't, *mais* I will do it for you;—just the same, like Monsieur le Compte would say, 'Charlie, you old fool, I want to shange houses wid you.'"

So long as the Colonel suspected irony he was angry, but as Charlie seemed, after all, to be certainly in earnest, he began to feel conscience-stricken. He was by no means a tender man, but his lately-discovered misfortune had unhinged him, and this strange, undeserved, disinterested family fealty on the part of Charlie touched his heart. And should he still try to lead him into the pitfall he had dug? He hesitated;—no, he would show him the place by broad daylight, and if he chose to overlook the "caving bank," it would be his own fault;—a trade's a trade.

"Come," said the planter, "come at my house tonight; to-morrow we look at the place before breakfast, and finish the trade."

"For what?" said Charlie.

"Oh, because I got to come in town in the morning."

"I don't want," said Charlie. "How I'm goin' to come dere?"

"I git you a horse at the liberty stable."

"Well—anyhow—I don't care—I'll go." And they went.

When they had ridden a long time, and were on the road darkened by hedges of Cherokee rose, the Colonel called behind him to the "low-down" scion:

"Keep the road, old man."

"Eh?"

"Keep the road."

"Oh, yes; all right; I keep my word; we don't goin' to play no tricks, eh?"

But the Colonel seemed not to hear. His ungenerous design was beginning to be hateful to him. Not only old Charlie's unprovoked goodness was prevailing; the eulogy on Belles Demoiselles had stirred the depths of an intense love for his beautiful home. True, if he held to it, the caving of the bank, at its present fearful speed, would let the house into the river within three months; but were it not better to lose it so, than sell his birthright? Again,—coming back to the first thought,—to betray his own blood! It was only Injin Charlie; but had not the De Charleu blood just spoken out in him? Unconsciously he groaned.

After a time they struck a path approaching the plantation in the rear, and a little after, passing from behind a clump of live-oaks, they came in sight of the villa. It looked so like a gem, shining through its dark grove, so like a great glow-worm in the dense foliage, so significant of luxury and gayety, that the poor master, from an overflowing heart, groaned again.

"What?" asked Charlie.

The Colonel only drew his rein, and, dismounting mechanically, contemplated the sight before him. The high, arched doors and windows were thrown wide to the summer air; from every opening the bright light of numerous candelabra darted out upon the sparkling foliage of magnolia and bay, and here and there in the spacious verandas a colored lantern swayed in the gentle breeze. A sound of revel fell on the ear, the music of harps; and across one window, brighter than the rest, flitted, once or twice, the shadows of dancers. But oh! the shadows flitting across the heart of the fair mansion's master!

"Old Charlie," said he, gazing fondly at his house, "You and me is both old, eh?"

"Yaas," said the stolid Charlie.

"And we has both been bad enough in our time, eh, Charlie?"

Charlie, surprised at the tender tone, repeated "Yaas."

"And you and me is mighty close?"

"Blame close, yaas."

"But you never know me to cheat, old man!"

"No,"—impassively.

"And do you think I would cheat you now?"

"I dunno," said Charlie. "I don't believe."

"Well, old man, old man,"—his voice began to quiver,—"I sha'n't cheat you now. My God!—old man, I tell you—you better not make the trade!"

"Because for what?" asked Charlie in plain anger; but both looked quickly toward the house! The Colonel tossed his hands wildly in the air, rushed forward a step or two, and giving one fearful scream of agony and fright, fell forward on his face in the path. Old Charlie stood transfixed with horror. Belles Demoiselles, the realm of maiden beauty, the home of merriment, the house of dancing, all in the tremor and glow of pleasure, suddenly sunk, with one short, wild wail of terror—sunk, sunk, down, down, down, into the merciless, unfathomable flood of the Mississippi.

Twelve long months were midnight to the mind of the childless father; when they were only half gone, he took his bed; and every day, and every night, old Charlie, the "low-down," the "fool," watched him tenderly, tended him lovingly, for the sake of his name, his misfortunes, and his broken heart. No woman's step crossed the floor of the sick-chamber, whose western dormer-windows overpeered the dingy architecture of old Charlie's block; Charlie and a skilled physician, the one all interest, the other all gentleness, hope, and patience—these only entered by the door; but by the window came in a sweet-scented evergreen vine, transplanted from the caving bank of Belles Demoiselles. It caught the rays of sunset in its flowery net and let then softly in upon the sick man's bed; gathered the glancing beams of the moon at midnight, and often wakened the sleeper to look, with his mindless eyes, upon their pretty silver fragments strewn upon the floor.

By and by there seemed—there was—a twinkling dawn of returning reason. Slowly, peacefully, with an increase unseen from day to day, the light of reason came into the eyes, and speech became coherent; but withal there came a failing of the wrecked body, and the doctor said that monsieur was both better and worse.

One evening, as Charlie sat by the vine-clad window with his fireless pipe in his hand, the old Colonel's eyes fell full upon his own, and rested there.

"Charl—," he said with an effort, and his delighted nurse hastened to the bedside and bowed his best ear. There was an unsuccessful effort or two, and then he whispered, smiling with sweet sadness,—

"We didn't trade."

The truth, in this case, was a secondary matter to Charlie; the main point was to give a pleasing answer. So he nodded his head decidedly, as who should say—"Oh yes, we did, it was a bonafide swap!" but when he saw the smile vanish, he tried the other expedient and shook his head with still more vigor, to signify that they had not so much as approached a bargain; and the smile returned.

Charlie wanted to see the vine recognized. He stepped backward to the window with a broad smile, shook the foliage, nodded and looked smart.

"I know," said the Colonel, with beaming eyes, "—many weeks."

The next day—

"Charl—"

The best ear went down.

"Send for a priest."

The priest came, and was alone with him a whole afternoon. When he left, the patient was very haggard and exhausted, but smiled and would not suffer the crucifix to be removed from his breast.

One more morning came. Just before dawn Charlie, lying on a pallet in the room, thought he was called, and came to the bedside.

"Old man," whispered the failing invalid, "is it caving yet?"

Charlie nodded.

"It won't pay you out."

"Oh, dat makes not'ing," said Charlie. Two big tears rolled down his brown face. "Dat makes not'in."

The Colonel whispered once more:

"*Mes belles demoiselles!* in paradise;—in the garden—I shall be with them at sunrise;" and so it was.

Chapter Six

LAFCADIO HEARN (1850–1904)

Hearn considered himself an American writer, though he was born on an island in the Ionian Sea to Greek and Irish parents, was raised in France and England and died a citizen of Japan. He lived for several years in New Orleans and explored its culture in fiction, journalism and even a cookbook. It is sometimes claimed that he invented New Orleans as a literary subject. This distinction would have to be shared with Cable, King and Chopin, but he did popularize a vision of the Crescent City as beautiful, haunted and exotic. His fascination with the weird and supernatural would continue in his writings about Japan and China.

Among Hearn's writings about New Orleans are several ghost stories, some set against a realistic background, others, like "The Ghostly Kiss," written in a fantastic style that recalls Poe's.

Text: Lafcadio Hearn, *Fantastics and Other Fancies* (Boston, MA: Houghton Mifflin, 1914).

THE GHOSTLY KISS

The theatre was full. I cannot remember what they were playing. I did not have time to observe the actors. I only remember how vast the building seemed. Looking back, I saw an ocean of faces stretching away almost beyond the eye's power of definition to the far circles where the seats rose tier above tier in lines of illumination. The ceiling was blue, and in the midst a great mellow lamp hung suspended like a moon, at a height so lofty that I could not see the suspending chain. I fancied that the theatre was hung with hangings of black velvet, bordered with a silver trim fringe that glimmered like tears. The audience were all in white.

All in white!—I asked myself whether I was not in some theatre or tropical city—why all in white? I could not guess. I fancied at moments that I could perceive a moonlight landscape through far distant oriel windows, and the crests of palms casting moving shadows like gigantic spiders. The air was sweet with a strange and a new perfume; it was a drowsy air—a poppied air, in which the waving of innumerable white fans made no rustle, no sound.

There was a strange stillness and a strange silence. All eyes were turned toward the stage, except my own. I gazed in every direction but that of the stage! I cannot imagine why it was that I rarely looked toward the stage. No one noticed me; no one appeared to perceive that I was the only person in all that vast assembly clad in black—a tiny dark speck in a sea of white light.

Gradually the voices of the actors seemed to me to become fainter and fainter—thin sounds like whispers from another world—a world of ghosts!—and the music seemed not music, but only an echo in the mind of the hearer, like a memory of songs heard and forgotten in forgotten years.

There were faces that I thought strangely familiar—faces I fancied I had seen somewhere else in some other time. But none recognized me.

A woman sat before me—a fair woman with hair as brightly golden as the locks of Aphrodite. I asked my heart why it beat so strangely when I turned my eyes upon her. I felt as if it sought to leap from my breast and fling itself all palpitating under her feet. I watched the delicate movements of her neck, where a few loose bright curls were straying, like strands of gold clinging to a column of ivory;—the soft curve of the cheek flushed by a faint ruddiness like the velvet surface of a half-ripe peach;—the grace of the curving lips—lips sweet as those of the Cnidian Venus,[1] which even after two thousand years still seem humid, as with the kisses of the last lover. But the eyes I could not see.

And a strange desire rose within me—an intense wish to kiss those lips. My heart said, Yes;—my reason whispered, No. I thought of the ten thousand thousand eyes that might suddenly be turned upon me. I looked back; and it seemed to me as if the whole theatre had grown vaster! The circles of seats had receded;—the great centre lamp seemed to have mounted higher;—the audience seemed vast as that we dream of in visions of the Last Judgment. And my heart beat so violently that I heard its passionate pulsation, louder than the voices of the actors and I feared lest it should betray me to all the host of white-clad men and women above me. But none seemed to hear or to see me. I trembled as I thought of the consequences of obeying the mad impulse that became every moment more overpowering and uncontrollable.

And my heart answered, "One kiss of those lips were worth the pain of ten thousand deaths."

I do not remember that I arose. I only remember finding myself beside her, close to her, breathing her perfumed breath, and gazing into eyes deep as the amethystine heaven of a tropical night. I pressed my lips passionately to hers;—I felt a thrill of inexpressible delight and triumph;—I felt the warm soft lips curl back to meet mine, and give me back my kiss!

And a great fear suddenly came upon me. And all the multitude of white-clad men and women arose in silence; and ten thousand thousand eyes looked upon me.

I heard a voice, faint, sweet,—such a voice as we hear when dead loves visit us in dreams.

"Thou hast kissed me: the compact is sealed forever."

And raising my eyes once more I saw that all the seats were graves and all the white dresses shrouds. Above me a light still shone in the blue roof, but only the light of a white moon in the eternal azure of heaven. White tombs stretched away in weird file to the verge of the horizon;—where it had seemed to me that I beheld a play, I saw only a lofty mausoleum;—and I knew that the perfume of the night was but the breath of flowers dying upon the tombs!

---

1 Nude statue by the Praxiteles of Athens.

Chapter Seven

THOMAS NELSON PAGE (1853–1922)

Thomas Nelson Page is usually remembered for stories like "Marse Chan" that place him in the "Plantation School" of Southern writing. But "No Haid Pawn" is something else entirely. Rather than nostalgia for an era of elegant mansions tended by faithful servants, Page shows the human cost of creating the white-columned great houses and acknowledges the brutality that could lead slaves to rebel or flee into the swamps.

"No Haid Pawn" gestures back toward Poe's "The Fall of the House of Usher," as both the Usher mansion and the empty mansion of Page's tale disappear at the end into a marsh. Page also employs a familiar Gothic plot device, the character forced to spend a night in a haunted house. While the ghosts that seem to menace the narrator may be rationally explained, far deeper horrors of the history of the house are revealed.

Text: *In Ole Virginia* (New York: Scribners, 1895).

NO HAID PAWN[1]

It was a ghostly place in broad daylight, if the glimmer that stole in through the dense forest that surrounded it when the sun was directly overhead deserved this delusive name. At any other time it was—why, we were afraid even to talk about it! and as to venturing within its gloomy borders, it was currently believed among us that to do so was to bring upon the intruder certain death. I knew every foot of ground, wet and dry, within five miles of my father's house, except this plantation, for I had hunted by day and night every field, forest, and marsh within that radius; but the swamp and "ma'shes" that surrounded this place I had never invaded. The boldest hunter on the plantation would call off his dogs and go home if they struck a trail that crossed the sobby[2] boundary-line of "No Haid Pawn."

"Jack 'my lanterns" and "evil sperits" only infested those woods, and the earnest advice of those whom we children acknowledged to know most about them was, "Don't you never go nigh dyah honey; hit's de evil-speritest place in dis wull."

Had not Big William and Cephas and Poliam followed their dogs in there one night, and cut down a tree in which they had with their own eyes seen the coon, and lo! when it fell "de warn no mo' coon dyah 'n a dog!" and the next tree they had "treed in" not only had no coon in it, but when it was cut down it had fallen on Poliam and broken his leg.

---

1 Dialect: No Head Pond.

2 Dialect: soggy.

So the very woods were haunted. From this time they were abandoned to the "jack 'my lanterns" and ghosts, and another shadow was added to No Haid Pawn.

The place was as much cut off from the rest of the country as if a sea had divided it. The river, with marshy banks, swept around it in a wide horseshoe on three sides, and when the hammocks[3] dammed it up it washed its way straight across and scoured out a new bed for itself, completely isolating the whole plantation.

The owners of it, if there were any, which was doubtful, were aliens, and in my time it had not been occupied for forty years. The negroes declared that it was "gin up" to the "ha'nts an' evil sperits," and that no living being could live there. It had grown up in forest and had wholly reverted to original marsh. The road that once ran through the swamp had long since been choked up, and the trees were as thick and the jungle as dense now, in its track, as in the adjacent "ma'sh." Only one path remained. That, it was currently believed by the entire portion of the population who speculated on the subject, was kept open by the evil spirits. Certain it was that no human foot ever trod the narrow, tortuous line that ran through the brakes[4] as deviously as the noiseless, stagnant ditches that curved through the jungle, where the musk-rats played and the moccasin slept unmolested. Yet there it lay, plain and well-defined, month after month and year after year, as No Haid Pawn itself stood, amid its surrounding swamps, all undisturbed and unchanging.

Even the runaway slaves who occasionally left their homes and took to the swamps and woods, impelled by the cruelty of their overseers, or by a desire for a vain counterfeit of freedom, never tried this swamp, but preferred to be caught and returned home to invading its awful shades.

We were brought up to believe in ghosts. Our fathers and mothers laughed at us, and endeavored to reason us out of such a superstition—the fathers with much of ridicule and satire, the mothers giving sweet religious reasons for their argument—but what could they avail against the actual testimony and the blood-curdling experiences of a score of witnesses, who recounted their personal observations with a degree of thrilling realism and a vividness that overbore any arguments our childish reason could grasp! The old mammies and uncles who were our companions and comrades believed in the existence of evil spirits as truly as in the existence of hell or heaven, as to which at that time no question had ever been raised, so far as was known, in that slumberous world. (The Bible was the standard, and all disputes were resolved into an appeal to that authority, the single question as to any point being simply, "Is it in the Bible?") Had not Lazarus, and Mam' Celia, and William, and Twis'-foot-Bob, and Aunt Sukie Brown, and others *seen* with their own eyes the evil spirits, again and again, in the bodily shape of cats, headless dogs, white cows, and other less palpable forms! And was not their experience, who lived in remote cabins, or wandered night after night through the loneliest woods, stronger evidence than the cold reasoning of those who hardly ever stirred abroad except in daylight? It certainly was more conclusive to us; for no one could have listened to those

---

3 Variation of "hummock," an area of solid ground with vegetation in a marsh.

4 Thickets.

narrators without being impressed with the fact that they were recounting what they had actually seen with their bodily eyes. The result of it all was, so far as we were concerned, the triumph of faith over reason, and the fixed belief, on our part, in the actual visible existence of the departed, in the sinister form of apparition known as "evil sperits." Every graveyard was tenanted by them; every old house and every peculiarly desolate spot was known to be their rendezvous; but all spots and places sank into insignificance compared with No Haid Pawn.

The very name was uncanny. Originally it had designated a long, stagnant pool of water lying in the centre of the tract, which marked the spot from which the soil had been dug to raise the elevation on which to set the house. More modernly the place, by reason of the filling up of ditches and the sinking of dikes, had become again simple swamp and jungle, or, to use the local expression, "had turned to ma'sh," and the name applied to the whole plantation.

The origin of the name of the pond had no source; but there was a better explanation than that. Any how, the very name inspired dread, and the place was our terror.

The house had been built many generations before by a stranger in this section, and the owners never made it their permanent home. Thus, no tie either of blood or friendship were formed with their neighbors, who were certainly open-hearted and open-doored enough to overcome anything but the most persistent unneighborliness. Why this spot was selected for a mansion was always a mystery, unless it was that the new-comer desired to isolate himself completely. Instead of following the custom of those who were native and to the manner born, who always chose some eminence for their seats, he had selected for his a spot in the middle of the wide flat which lay in the horseshoe of the river. The low ground, probably owing to the abundance of land in that country, had never been "taken up," and up to the time of his occupation was in a condition of primeval swamp. He had to begin by making an artificial mound for his mansion. Even then, it was said, he dug so deep that he laid the corner-stone in water. The foundation was of stone, which was brought from a distance. Fabulous stories were told of it. The negroes declared that under the old house were solid rock chambers, which had been built for dungeons, and had served for purposes which were none the less awful because they were vague and indefinite. The huge structure itself was of wood, and was alleged to contain many mysterious rooms and underground passages. One of the latter was said to connect with the No Haid Pawn itself, whose dark waters, according to the negroes' traditions, were some day, by some process not wholly consistent with the laws of physics, to overwhelm the fated pile. An evil destiny had seemed to overshadow the place from the very beginning. One of the negro builders had been caught and decapitated between two of the immense foundation stones. The tradition was handed down that he was sacrificed in some awful and occult rite connected with the laying of the corner-stone. The scaffolding had given way and had precipitated several men to the ground, most of whom had been fatally hurt. This also was alleged to be by hideous design. Then the plantation, in the process of being reclaimed, had proved unhealthy beyond all experience, and the negroes employed in the work of diking and reclaiming the great swamp had sickened and died by dozens. The extension of the dangerous fever to the adjoining plantations had left a reputation for typhus malaria from which the whole section suffered for a time. But this did not prevent the colored population from recounting year after year the horrors of the pestilence of No Haid Pawn as a peculiar visitation, nor from relating with blood-curdling details the burial by scores, in a thicket just beside the pond, of the stricken "befo' dee *daid*, honey, befo' dee *daid!*" The bodies, it was said, used to float about in the guts[5] of the swamp and on the haunted pond; and at night they might be seen, if any one were so hardy as to venture there, rowing about in their coffins as if they were boats.

Thus the place from the beginning had an evil name, and when, year after year, the river rose and washed the levees away, or the musk-rats burrowed through and let the water in, and the strange masters cursed not only the elements but Heaven itself, the continued mortality of their negroes was not wholly unexpected nor unaccounted for by certain classes of their neighbors.

At length the property had fallen to one more gloomy, more strange, and more sinister than any who had gone before him—a man whose personal characteristics and habits were unique in that country. He was of gigantic stature and superhuman strength, and possessed appetites and vices in proportion to his size. He could fell an ox with a blow of his fist, or in a fit of anger could tear down the branch of a tree, or bend a bar of iron like a reed. He, either from caprice or ignorance, spoke only a *patois* not unlike the Creole French of the Louisiana parishes. But he was a West Indian. His brutal temper and habits cut him off from even the small measure of intercourse which had existed between his predecessors and their neighbors, and he lived at No Haid Pawn completely isolated. All the stories and traditions of the place at once centred on him, and fabulous tales were told of his prowess and of his life. It was said, among other things, that he preserved his wonderful strength by drinking human blood, a tale which in a certain sense I have never seen reason to question. Making all allowances, his life was a blot upon civilization. At length it culminated. A brutal temper, inflamed by unbridled passions, after a long period of license and debauchery came to a climax in a final orgy of ferocity and fury, in which he was guilty of an act whose fiendishness surpassed belief, and he was brought to judgment.

In modern times the very inhumanity of the crime would probably have proved his security, and as he had destroyed his own property while he was perpetrating a crime of appalling and unparalleled horror, he might have found a defence in that standing refuge of extraordinary scoundrelism—insanity. This defence, indeed, was put in, and was pressed with much ability by his counsel, one of whom was my father, who had just then been admitted to the bar; but, fortunately for the cause of justice, neither courts nor juries were then so sentimental as they have become of late years, and the last occupant of No Haid Pawn paid under the law the full penalty of his hideous crime. It was one of the curious incidents of the trial that his negroes all lamented his death, and declared that

[5] Channels.

he was a good master when he was not drunk. He was hanged just at the rear of his own house, within sight of the spot where his awful crime was committed.

At his execution, which, according to the custom of the country, was public, a horrible coincidence occurred which furnished the text of many a sermon on retributive justice among the negroes.

The body was interred near the pond, close by the thicket where the negroes were buried; but the negroes declared that it preferred one of the stone chambers under the mansion, where it made its home, and that it might be seen at any time of the day or night stalking headless about the place. They used to dwell with peculiar zest on the most agonizing details of this wretch's dreadful crime, the whole culminating in the final act of maniacal fury, when the gigantic monster dragged the hacked and headless corpse of his victim up the staircase and stood it up before the open window in his hall, in the full view of the terrified slaves. After these narrations, the continued reappearance of the murderer and his headless victim was as natural to us as it was to the negroes themselves; and, as night after night we would hurry up to the great house through the darkness, we were ever on the watch lest he should appear to our frighted vision from the shades of the shrubbery-filled yard.

Thus it was that of all ghostly places No Haid Pawn had the distinction of being invested, to us, with unparalleled horror; and thus to us, no less than because the dikes had given way and the overflowed flats had turned again to swamp and jungle, it was explicable that No Haid Pawn was abandoned, and was now untrodden by any foot but that of its ghostly tenants.

The time of my story was 185-. The spring previous continuous rains had kept the river full, and had flooded the low grounds, and this had been followed by an exceptionally dense growth in the summer. Then, public feeling was greatly excited at the time of which I write, over the discovery in the neighborhood of several emissaries of the underground railway, or—as they were universally considered in that country—of the devil. They had been run off or had disappeared suddenly but had left behind them some little excitement on the part of the slaves, and a great deal on the part of their masters, and more than the usual number of negroes had run away. All, however, had been caught, or had returned home after a sufficient interval of freedom, except one who had escaped permanently, and who was supposed to have accompanied his instigators on their flight.

This man was a well-known character. He belonged to one of our neighbors, and had been bought and brought there from an estate on the Lower Mississippi. He was the most brutal negro I ever knew. He was of a type rarely found among our negroes, who, judging from their physiognomy and general characteristics, came principally from the coast of Africa. They are of moderate stature, with dull but amiable faces. This man, however, was of immense size, and he possessed the features and expression of a Congo desperado. In character also he differed essentially from all the other slaves in our country. He was alike without their amiability and their docility, and was as fearless as he was brutal. He was the only negro I ever knew who was without either superstition or reverence. Indeed, he differed so widely from the rest of the slaves in that section that there existed some feeling against him almost akin to a race feeling. At the same time that he exercised considerable influence over them they were dreadfully afraid of him, and were always in terror that he would trick[6] them, to which awful power he laid well-known claim. His curses in his strange dialect used to terrify them beyond measure, and they would do anything to conciliate him. He had been a continual source of trouble and an object of suspicion in the neighborhood from the time of his first appearance; and more than one hog that the negroes declared had wandered into the marshes of No Haid Pawn, and had "cut his thote jes' swinin' aroun' an' aroun' in de ma'sh," had been suspected of finding its way to this man's cabin. His master had often been urged to get rid of him, but he was kept, I think, probably because he was valuable on the plantation. He was a fine butcher, a good work-hand, and a first-class boatman. Moreover, ours was a conservative population, in which every man minded his own business and let his neighbor's alone.

At the time of the visits of those secret agents to which I have referred, this negro was discovered to be the leader in the secret meetings held under their auspices, and he would doubtless have been taken up and shipped off at once; but when the intruders fled, as I have related, their convert disappeared also. It was a subject of general felicitation in the neighborhood that he was gotten rid of, and his master, instead of being commiserated on the loss of his slave, was congratulated that he had not cut his throat.

No idea can be given at this date of the excitement occasioned in a quiet neighborhood in old times by the discovery of the mere presence of such characters as Abolitionists. It was as if the foundations of the whole social fabric were undermined. It was the sudden darkening of a shadow that always hung in the horizon. The slaves were in a large majority, and had they risen, though the final issue could not be doubted, the lives of every white on the plantations must have paid the forfeit. Whatever the right and wrong of slavery might have been, its existence demanded that no outside interference with it should be tolerated. So much was certain; self-preservation required this.

I was, at the time of which I speak, a well-grown lad, and had been for two sessions to a boarding school, where I had gotten rid of some portion—I will not say of all—of the superstition of my boyhood. The spirit of adventure was beginning to assert itself in me, and I had begun to feel a sense of enjoyment in overcoming the fears which once mastered me, though, I must confess, I had not entirely shaken off my belief in the existence of ghosts—that is, I did not believe in them at all in the day-time, but when night came I was not so certain about it.

Duck-hunting was my favorite sport, and the marshes on the river were fine ground for them usually, but this season the weather had been so singularly warm that the sport had been poor, and though I had scoured every canal in the marsh and every bend in the river as far as No Haid Pawn Hammock, as the stretch of drifted timber and treacherous marsh was called that marked the boundary-line of that plantation, I had had bad luck. Beyond that point I had never penetrated; partly, no doubt, because of the training of my earlier years, and partly because the marsh on either side of the hammock would have mired a cat. Often, as I watched with envious eyes the wild duck rise up over the

6 Place a curse or spell.

dense trees that surrounded the place and cut straight for the deserted marshes in the horseshoe, I had had a longing to invade the mysterious domain, and crawl to the edge of No Haid Pawn and get a shot at the fowl that floated on its black surface; but something had always deterred me, and the long reaches of No Haid Pawn were left to the wild-fowl and the ghostly rowers. Finally, however, after a spell whose high temperature was rather suited to August than April, in desperation at my ill-luck I determined to gratify my curiosity and try No Haid Pawn. So one afternoon, without telling any one of my intention, I crossed the mysterious boundary and struck through the swamp for the unknown land.

The marsh was far worse than I had anticipated, and no one but a duck-hunter as experienced and zealous as myself, and as indifferent to ditches, briers, mire, and all that make a swamp, could have penetrated it at all. Even I could never have gotten on if I had not followed the one path that led into the marsh, the reputed "parf" of the evil spirits, and, as it was, my progress was both tedious and dangerous.

The track was a mysterious one, for though I knew it had not been trodden by a human foot in many years, yet there, a veritable "parf" it lay. In some places it was almost completely lost, and I would fear I should have to turn back, but an overhanging branch or a vine swinging from one tree to another would furnish a way to some spot where the narrow trail began again. In other spots old logs thrown across the miry canals gave me an uncomfortable feeling as I reflected what feet had last crossed on them. On both sides of this trail the marsh was either an impenetrable jungle or a mire apparently bottomless.

I shall never forget my sensations as I finally emerged from the woods into the clearing, if that desolate waste of willows, cane, and swamp growth could be so termed. About me stretched the jungle, over which a greenish lurid atmosphere brooded, and straight ahead towered the gaunt mansion, a rambling pile of sombre white, with numberless vacant windows staring at me from the leafless trees about it. Only one other clump of trees appeared above the canes and brush, and that I knew by intuition was the graveyard.

I think I should have turned back had not shame impelled me forward.

My progress from this point was even more difficult than it had been hitherto, for the trail at the end of the wood terminated abruptly in a gut of the swamp; however, I managed to keep on by walking on hammocks, pushing through clumps of bushes, and wading as best I could. It was slow and hot work, though.

It never once struck me that it must be getting late. I had become so accustomed to the gloom of the woods that the more open ground appeared quite light to me, and I had not paid any attention to the black cloud that had been for some time gathering overhead, or to the darkening atmosphere.

I suddenly became sensible that it was going to rain. However, I was so much engrossed in the endeavor to get on that even then I took little note of it. The nearer I came to the house the more it arrested my attention, and the more weird and uncanny it looked. Canes and bushes grew up to the very door; the window-shutters hung from the hinges; the broken windows glared like eyeless sockets; the portico had fallen away from the wall, while the wide door stood slightly ajar, giving to the place a singularly ghastly appearance, somewhat akin to the color which sometimes lingers on the face of a corpse. In my progress wading through the swamp I had gone around rather to the side of the house toward where I supposed the "pawn" itself to lie.

I was now quite near to it, and striking a little less miry ground, as I pushed my way through the bushes and canes, which were higher than my head, I became aware that I was very near the thicket that marked the graveyard, just beyond which I knew the pond itself lay. I was somewhat startled, for the cloud made it quite dusky, and, stepping on a long piece of rotten timber lying on the ground, I parted the bushes to look down the pond. As I did so the rattle of a chain grated on me, and glancing up through the cane, before me appeared a heavy upright timber with an arm or cross-beam stretching from it, from which dangled a long chain, almost rusted away. I knew by instinct that I stood under the gallows where the murderer of No Haid Pawn had expiated his dreadful crime. His corpse must have fallen just where I stood. I started back appalled.

Just then the black cloud above me was parted by a vivid flame, and a peal of thunder seemed to rive the earth.

I turned in terror, but before I had gone fifty yards the storm was upon me, and instinctively I made for the only refuge that was at hand. It was a dreadful alternative, but I did not hesitate. Outside I was not even sure that my life was safe. And with extraordinary swiftness I had made my way through the broken iron fence that lay rusting in the swamp, had traversed the yard, all grown up as it was to the very threshold, had ascended the sunken steps, crossed the rotted portico, and entered the open door.

A long dark hall stretched before me, extending, as well as I could judge in the gloom, entirely across the house. A number of doors, some shut, some ajar, opened on the hall on one side; and a broad dark stairway ascended on the other to the upper story. The walls were black with mould. At the far end a large bow window, with all the glass gone, looked out on the waste of swamp, unbroken save by the clump of trees in the graveyard, and just beside this window was a break where the dark staircase descended to the apartments below. The whole place was in a state of advanced decay; almost the entire plastering had fallen with the damp, and the hall presented a scene of desolation that beggars description.

I was at last in the haunted house!

The rain, driven by the wind, poured in at the broken windows in such a deluge that I was forced in self-defence to seek shelter in one of the rooms. I tried several, but the doors were swollen or fastened, I found one, however, on the leeward side of the house, and, pushing the door, which opened easily, I entered. Inside I found something like an old bed; and the great open fireplace had evidently been used at some earlier time, for the ashes were still banked up in the cavernous hearth, and the charred ends of the logs of wood were lying in the chimney corners. To see, still as fresh and natural as though the fire had but just died out, these remnants of domestic life that had survived all else of a similar period struck me as unspeakably ghastly. The bedstead, however, though rude, was convenient as a seat, and I utilized it accordingly, propping myself up against one of the rough posts. From my position I commanded through the open door the entire length of the vacant hall, and could look straight out of the great bow-window at the head of the stairs, through which appeared, against the dull sky, the black mass of the graveyard trees, and a stretch of one of the canals or guts of the swamp curving around it, which gleamed white in the glare of the lightning.

I had expected that the storm would, like most thunder-storms in the latitude, shortly exhaust itself, or, as we say, "blow over;" but I was mistaken, and as the time passed, its violence, instead of diminishing, increased. It grew darker and darker, and presently the startling truth dawned on me that the gloom which I had supposed simply the effect of the overshadowing cloud had been really nightfall. I was shut up alone in No Head Pawn for the night.

I hastened to the door with the intention of braving the storm and getting away; but I was almost blown off my feet. A glance without showed me that the guts with which the swamp was traversed in every direction were now full to the brim, and to attempt to find my way home in the darkness would be sheer madness; so, after a wistful survey, I returned to my wretched perch. I thought I would try and light a fire, but to my consternation I had not a match, and I finally abandoned myself to my fate. It was a desolate, if not despairing, feeling that I experienced. My mind was filled, not only with my own unhappiness, but with the thought of the distress my absence would occasion them at home; and for a little while I had a fleeting hope that a party would be sent out to search for me. This, however, was untenable, for they would not know where I was. The last place in which they would ever think of looking for me was No Haid Pawn, and even if they knew I was there they could no more get to me in the darkness and storm than I could escape from it.

I accordingly propped myself up on my bed and gave myself up to my reflections. I said my prayers very fervently. I thought I would try and get to sleep, but sleep was far from my eyes.

My surroundings were too vivid to my apprehension. The awful traditions of the place, do what I might to banish them, would come to mind. The original building of the house, and its blood-stained foundation stones; the dead who had died of the pestilence that had raged afterward; the bodies carted by scores and buried in the sobby earth of the graveyard, whose trees loomed up through the broken window; the dreadful story of the dead paddling about the swamp in their coffins; and, above all, the gigantic maniac whose ferocity even murder could not satiate, and who had added to murder awful mutilation: he had dragged the mangled corpse of his victim up those very steps and flung it out of the very window which gaped just beyond me in the glare of the lightning. It all passed through my mind as I sat there in the darkness, and no effort of my will could keep my thoughts from dwelling on it. The terrific thunder, outcrashing a thousand batteries,[7] at times engrossed my attention; but it always reverted to that scene of horror; and if I dozed, the slamming of the loose blinds, or the terrific fury of the storm, would suddenly startle me. Once, as the sounds subsided for a moment, or else I having become familiar with them, as I was sinking into a sleepy state, a door at the other end of the hall creaked and then slammed with violence, bringing me bolt upright on the bed, clutching my gun. I could have sworn that I heard footsteps; but the wind was blowing a hurricane, and, after another period of wakefulness and dreadful recollection, nature succumbed, and I fell asleep.

I do not know that I can be said to have lost consciousness even then, for my mind was still enchained by the horrors of my situation, and went on clinging to them and dwelling upon them even in my slumber.

---

[7] Artillery emplacements.

I was, however, certainly asleep; for the storm must have died temporarily away about this hour without my knowing it, and I subsequently heard that it did.

I must have slept several hours, for I was quite stiff from my constrained posture when I became fully aroused.

I was awakened by a very peculiar sound; it was like a distant call or halloo. Although I had been fast asleep a moment before, it startled me into a state of the highest attention. In a second I was wide awake. There was not a sound except the rumble and roll of the thunder, as the storm once more began to renew itself, and in the segment of the circle that I could see along the hall through my door, and, indeed, out through the yawning window at the end, as far as the black clump of trees in the graveyard just at the bend of the canal, which I commanded from my seat whenever there was a flash of lightning, there was only the swaying of the bushes in the swamp and of the trees in the graveyard. Yet there I sat bolt upright on my bed, in the darkness, with every nerve strained to its utmost tension, and that unearthly cry still sounding in my ears. I was endeavoring to reason myself into the belief that I had dreamed it, when a flash of lightning lit up the whole field of my vision as if it had been in the focus of a sun-glass, and out on the canal, where it curved around the graveyard, was a boat—a something—small, black, with square ends, and with a man in it, standing upright, and something lying in a lump or mass at the bow.

I knew I could not be mistaken, for the lightning, by a process of its own, photographs everything on the retina in minutest detail, and I had a vivid impression of everything from the foot of the bed, on which I crouched, to the gaunt arms of those black trees in the graveyard just over that ghostly boatman and his dreadful freight. I was wide awake.

The story of the dead rowing in their coffins was verified!

I am unable to state what passed in the next few minutes.

The storm had burst again with renewed violence and was once more expending itself on the house; the thunder was again rolling overhead; the broken blinds were swinging and slamming madly; and the dreadful memories of the place were once more besetting me.

I shifted my position to relieve the cramp it had occasioned, still keeping my face toward that fatal window. As I did so, I heard above, or perhaps I should say under, the storm a sound more terrible to me—the repetition of that weird halloo, this time almost under the great window. Immediately succeeding this was the sound of something scraping under the wall, and I was sensible when a door on the ground-floor was struck with a heavy thud. It was pitch-dark, but I heard the door pushed wide open, and as a string of fierce oaths, part English and part Creole French, floated up the dark stairway, muffled as if sworn through clinched teeth, I held my breath. I recalled the unknown tongue the ghostly murderer employed; and I knew that the murderer of No Haid Pawn had left his grave, and that his ghost was coming up that stair. I heard his step as it fell on the first stair heavily yet almost noiselessly. It was an unearthly sound—dull, like the tread of a bared foot, accompanied by the scraping sound of a body dragging. Step by step he came up the black stairway in the pitch darkness as steadily as if it were daytime, and he knew every step, accompanied by that sickening sound of dragging. There was a final pull up the last step, and a dull, heavy thud, as, with a strange, wild laugh, he flung his burden on the floor.

For a moment there was not a sound, and then the awful silence and blackness were broken by a crash of thunder that seemed to tear the foundations asunder like a mighty earthquake, and the whole house, and the great swamp outside, were filled with a glare of vivid, blinding light. Directly in front of me, clutching in his upraised hand a long, keen, glittering knife, on whose blade a ball of fire seemed to play, stood a gigantic figure in the very flame of the lightning, and stretched at his feet lay, ghastly and bloody, a black and headless trunk.

I staggered to the door and, tripping, fell prostrate over the sill.

When we could get there, nothing was left but the foundation. The haunted house, when struck, had literally burned to the water's edge. The changed current had washed its way close to the place, and in strange verification of the negroes' traditions. No Haid Pawn had reclaimed its own, and the spot with all its secrets lay buried under its dark waters.

Chapter Eight

CHARLES W. CHESNUTT (1858–1932)

Many early readers of the stories Charles Chesnutt collected in *The Conjure Woman* (1899) would have assumed that Chesnutt was a white man like Joel Chandler Harris, author of *Uncle Remus* (1881). Chesnutt seems to be writing in Harris's tradition of African American tales reimagined for a white audience. Indeed, the stories in *The Conjure Woman* dramatize that assumption: the former slave Julius tells the stories to his white employer John, who frames them and tells them to us.

Chesnutt, however, is more subtle and elusive than he may at first seem. A mixed-race African American who could pass for white, his life and art were complicated negotiations across what he called "the color line." A careful reader will recognize that John, the entitled white Northerner, is not as perceptive as he thinks, and that Julius is more canny than he appears. Julius is a historian, an artist, a teacher—and a trickster.

Chesnutt wrote stories that are more obviously Gothic than "Po' Sandy." These are especially his stories involving the sexual exploitation of enslaved women, and its consequences. See, for example, "The Sheriff's Children," "The Marked Tree" and "The Dumb Witness." In "Po' Sandy" John dismisses Julius's haunted house story as a transparent ploy, an attempt to manipulate him. But if the tale is not Gothic to Julius, it is absolutely Gothic to Annie, John's wife, and has a profound effect on her. We should read the tale with Annie's sensitivity and insight.

Text: Charles Chesnutt, *The Conjure Woman* (New York: Houghton Mifflin, 1899).

PO' SANDY

On the northeast corner of my vineyard in central North Carolina, and fronting on the Lumberton plank-road, there stood a small frame house, of the simplest construction. It was built of pine lumber, and contained but one room, to which one window gave light and one door admission. Its weather-beaten sides revealed a virgin innocence of paint. Against one end of the house, and occupying half its width, there stood a huge brick chimney: the crumbling mortar had left large cracks between the bricks; the bricks themselves had begun to scale off in large flakes, leaving the chimney sprinkled with unsightly blotches. These evidences of decay were but partially concealed by a creeping vine, which extended its slender branches hither and thither in an ambitious but futile attempt to cover the whole chimney. The wooden shutter, which had once protected the unglazed window, had fallen from its hinges, and lay rotting in the rank grass and jimsonweeds beneath. This building, I learned when I bought the place, had been used as a schoolhouse for several years prior to the breaking out of the war, since which time it had remained unoccupied, save when some stray cow or vagrant hog had sought shelter within its walls from the chill rains and nipping winds of winter.

One day my wife requested me to build her a new kitchen. The house erected by us, when we first came to live upon the vineyard, contained a very conveniently arranged kitchen; but for some occult reason my wife wanted a kitchen in the back yard, apart from the dwelling-house, after the usual Southern fashion. Of course I had to build it.

To save expense, I decided to tear down the old schoolhouse, and use the lumber, which was in a good state of preservation, in the construction of the new kitchen. Before demolishing the old house, however, I made an estimate of the amount of material contained in it, and found that I would have to buy several hundred feet of lumber additional, in order to build the new kitchen according to my wife's plan.

One morning old Julius McAdoo, our colored coachman, harnessed the gray mare to the rockaway, and drove my wife and me over to the sawmill from which I meant to order the new lumber. We drove down the long lane which led from our house to the plank-road; following the plank-road for about a mile, we turned into a road running through the forest and across the swamp to the sawmill beyond. Our carriage jolted over the half-rotted corduroy road[1] which traversed the swamp, and then climbed the long hill leading to the sawmill. When we reached the mill, the foreman had gone over to a neighboring farmhouse, probably to smoke or gossip, and we were compelled to await his return before we could transact our business. We remained seated in the carriage, a few rods from the mill, and watched the leisurely movements of the mill-hands. We had not waited long before a huge pine log was placed in position, the machinery of the mill was set in motion, and the circular saw began to eat its way through the log, with a loud whir which resounded throughout the vicinity of the mill. The sound rose and fell in a sort of rhythmic cadence, which, heard from where we sat, was not unpleasing, and not loud enough to prevent conversation. When the saw started on its second journey through the log, Julius observed, in a lugubrious tone, and with a perceptible shudder:—

"Ugh! but dat des do cuddle my blood!"

"What's the matter, Uncle Julius?" inquired my wife, who is of a very sympathetic turn of mind. "Does the noise affect your nerves?"

"No, Mis' Annie," replied the old man, with emotion, "I ain' narvous; but dat saw, a-cuttin' en grindin' thoo dat stick er timber, en moanin', en groanin,' en sweekin', kyars my 'memb'ance back ter ole times, en 'min's me er po' Sandy." The pathetic intonation with which he lengthened out the "po' Sandy" touched a responsive chord in our own hearts.

"And who was poor Sandy?" asked my wife, who takes a deep interest in the stories of plantation life which she hears from the lips of the older colored people. Some of these stories are quaintly humorous; others wildly extravagant, revealing the Oriental cast of the negro's imagination; while others, poured freely into the sympathetic ear of a Northern-bred woman, disclose many a tragic incident of the darker side of slavery.

---

1 A road built with logs sunk across it.

"Sandy," said Julius, in reply to my wife's question, "was a nigger w'at useter b'long ter ole Mars Marrabo McSwayne. Mars Marrabo's place wuz on de yuther side'n de swamp, right nex' ter yo' place. Sandy wuz a monst'us good nigger, en could do so many things erbout a plantation, en alluz 'ten' ter his wuk so well, dat w'en Mars Marrabo's chilluns growed up en married off, dey all un 'em wanted dey daddy fer ter gin 'em Sandy fer a weddin' present. But Mars Marrabo knowed de res' wouldn' be satisfied ef he gin Sandy ter a'er one un 'em; so w'en dey wuz all done married, he fix it by 'lowin' one er his chilluns ter take Sandy fer a mont' er so, en den ernudder for a mont' er so, en so on dat erway tel dey had all had 'im de same lenk er time; en den dey would all take him roun' ag'in, 'cep'n' oncet in a w'ile w'en Mars Marrabo would len' 'im ter some er his yuther kinfolks 'roun' de country, w'en dey wuz short er han's; tel bimeby it got so Sandy didn' hardly knowed whar he wuz gwine ter stay fum one week's een' ter de yuther.

"One time w'en Sandy wuz lent out ez yushal, a spekilater come erlong wid a lot er niggers, en Mars Marrabo swap' Sandy's wife off fer a noo 'oman. W'en Sandy come back, Mars Marrabo gin 'im a dollar, en 'lowed he wuz monst'us sorry fer ter break up de fambly, but de spekilater had gin 'im big boot,[2] en times wuz hard en money skase, en so he wuz bleedst ter make de trade. Sandy tuk on some 'bout losin' his wife, but he soon seed dey want no use cryin' ober spilt merlasses; en bein' ez he lacked de looks er de noo 'oman, he tuk up wid her atter she'd be'n on de plantation a mont' er so.

"Sandy en his noo wife got on mighty well tergedder, en de niggers all 'mence' ter talk about how lovin' dey wuz. W'en Tenie wuz tuk sick oncet, Sandy useter set up all night wid 'er, en den go ter wuk in de mawnin' des lack he had his reg'lar sleep; en Tenie would 'a' done anythin' in de worl' for her Sandy.

"Sandy en Tenie hadn' be'n libbin' tergedder fer mo' d'n two mont's befo' Mars Marrabo's old uncle, w'at libbed down in Robeson County, sent up ter fin' out ef Mars Marrabo couldn' len' 'im er hire 'im a good han' fer a mont' er so. Sandy's marster wuz one er dese yer easy-gwine folks w'at wanter please eve'ybody, en he says yas, he could len' 'im Sandy. En Mars Marrabo tol' Sandy fer ter git ready ter go down ter Robeson nex' day, fer ter stay a mont' er so.

"It wuz monst'us hard on Sandy fer ter take 'im 'way fum Tenie. It wuz so fur down ter Robeson dat he didn' hab no chance er comin' back ter see her tel de time wuz up; he wouldn' 'a' mine comin' ten er fifteen mile at night ter see Tenie, but Mars Marrabo's uncle's plantation wuz mo' d'n forty mile off. Sandy wuz mighty sad en cas' down atter w'at Mars Marrabo tol' 'im, en he says ter Tenie, sezee:—

"'I'm gittin' monst'us ti'ed er dish yer gwine roun' so much. Here I is lent ter Mars Jeems dis mont', en I got ter do so-en-so; en ter Mars Archie de nex' mont', en I got ter do so-en-so; den I got ter go ter Miss Jinnie's: en hit's Sandy dis en Sandy dat, en Sandy yer en Sandy dere, tel it 'pears ter me I ain' got no home, ner no master, ner no mistiss, ner no nuffin. I can't eben keep a wife: my yuther ole 'oman wuz sol' away widout my gittin' a chance fer ter tell her good-by; en now I got ter go off en leab you, Tenie, en I dunno

[2] Gave him a good price.

whe'r I'm eber gwine ter see you ag'in er no. I wisht I wuz a tree, er a stump, er a rock, er sump'n w'at could stay on de plantation fer a w'ile.'

"Atter Sandy got thoo talkin', Tenie didn' say naer word, but des sot dere by de fier, studyin' en studyin'. Bimeby she up'n' says:—

" 'Sandy, is I eber tol' you I wuz a cunjuh 'oman?'

"Co'se Sandy hadn' nebber dremp' er nuffin lack dat, en he made a great 'miration w'en he hear w'at Tenie say. Bimeby Tenie went on:—

" 'I ain' goophered[3] nobody, ner done no cunjuh wuk, fer fifteen year er mo'; en w'en I got religion I made up my mine I wouldn' wuk no mo' goopher. But dey is some things I doan b'lieve it's no sin fer ter do; en ef you doan wanter be sent roun' fum pillar ter pos', en ef you doan wanter go down ter Robeson, I kin fix things so you won't haf ter. Ef you'll des say de word, I kin turn you ter w'ateber you wanter be, en you kin stay right where you wanter, ez long ez you mineter.'

"Sandy say he doan keer; he's willin' fer ter do anythin' fer ter stay close ter Tenie. Den Tenie ax 'im ef he doan wanter be turnt inter a rabbit.

"Sandy say, 'No, de dogs mought git atter me.'

" 'Shill I turn you ter a wolf?' sez Tenie.'

" 'No, eve'ybody 's skeered er a wolf, en I doan want nobody ter be skeered er me.'

" 'Shill I turn you ter a mawkin-bird?'

" 'No, a hawk mought ketch me. I wanter be turnt inter sump'n w'at'll stay in one place.'

" 'I kin turn you ter a tree,' sez Tenie. 'You won't hab no mouf ner years, but I kin turn you back oncet in a w'ile, so you kin git sump'n ter eat, en hear w'at's gwine on.'

"Well, Sandy say dat'll do. En so Tenie tuk 'im down by de aidge er de swamp, not fur fum de quarters, en turnt 'im inter a big pine-tree, en sot 'im out 'mongs' some yuther trees. En de nex' mawnin', ez some er de fiel' han's wuz gwine long dere, dey seed a tree w'at dey didn' 'member er habbin' seed befo'; it wuz monst'us quare, en dey wuz bleedst ter 'low dat dey hadn' 'membered right, er e'se one er de saplin's had be'n growin' monst'us fas.'

"W'en Mars Marrabo 'skiver' dat Sandy wuz gone, he 'lowed Sandy had runned away. He got de dogs out, but de las' place dey could track Sandy ter wuz de foot er dat pine-tree. En dere de dogs stood en barked, en bayed, en pawed at de tree, en tried ter climb up on it; en we'n dey wuz tuk roun' thoo de swamp ter look fer de scent, dey broke loose en made fer dat tree ag'in. It wuz de beatenis' thing de w'ite folks eber hearn of, en Mars Marrabo 'lowed dat Sandy must 'a' clim' up on de tree en jump' off on a mule er sump'n, en rid fur enuff fer ter spile de scent. Mars Marrabo wanted ter 'cuse some er de yuther niggers er heppin' Sandy off, but dey all 'nied it ter de las'; en eve'ybody knowed Tenie sot too much sto' by Sandy fer ter he'p 'im run away whar she couldn' nebber see 'im no mo'.

"W'en Sandy had be'n gone long ernuff fer folks ter think he done got clean away, Tenie useter go down ter de woods at night en turn 'im back, en den dey'd slip up ter

3 Placed a spell or curse on anyone.

de cabin en set by de fire en talk. But dey ha' ter be monst'us keerful, er e'se somebody would 'a' seed 'em, en dat would 'a' spile' de whole thing; so Tenie alluz turnt Sandy back in de mawnin' early, befo' anybody wuz a-stirrin'.

"But Sandy didn' git erlong widout his trials en tribberlations. One day a woodpecker come erlong en 'mence' ter peck at de tree; en de nex' time Sandy wuz turnt back he had a little roun' hole in his arm, des lack a sharp stick be'n stuck in it. Atter dat Tenie sot a sparrer-hawk fer ter watch de tree; en w'en de woodpecker come erlong nex' mawnin' fer ter finish his nes', he got gobble' up mos' 'fo' he stuck his bill in de bark.

"Nudder time, Mars Marrabo sent a nigger out in de woods fer ter chop tuppentime boxes. De man chop a box in dish yer tree, en hack' de bark up two er th'ee feet, fer ter let de tuppentime run. De nex' time Sandy wuz turnt back he had a big skyar on his lef' leg, des lack it be'n skunt; en it tuk Tenie nigh 'bout all night fer ter fix a mixtry ter kyo it up. Atter dat, Tenie sot a hawnet fer ter watch de tree; en w'en de nigger come back ag'in fer ter cut ernudder box on de yuther side'n de tree, de hawnet stung 'im so hard dat de ax slip en cut his foot nigh 'bout off.

"W'en Tenie see so many things happenin' ter de tree, she 'cluded she'd ha' ter turn Sandy ter sump'n e'se; en atter studyin' de matter ober, en talkin' wid Sandy one ebenin', she made up her mine fer ter fix up a goopher mixtry w'at would turn herse'f en Sandy ter foxes, er sump'n, so dey could run away en go some'rs whar dey could be free en lib lack w'ite folks.

"But dey ain' no tellin' w'at 's gwine ter happen in dis worl'. Tenie had got de night sot fer her en Sandy ter run away, w'en dat ve'y day one er Mars Marrabo's sons rid up ter de big house in his buggy, en say his wife wuz monst'us sick, en he want his mammy ter len' 'im a 'oman fer ter nuss his wife. Tenie's mistiss say sen' Tenie; she wuz a good nuss. Young mars wuz in a tarrible hurry fer ter git back home. Tenie wuz washin' at de big house dat day, en her mistiss say she should go right 'long wid her young marster. Tenie tried ter make some 'scuse fer ter git away en hide 'tel night, we'n she would have eve'ything fix' up fer her en Sandy; she say she wanter go ter her cabin fer ter git her bonnet. Her mistiss say it doan matter 'bout de bonnet; her head-hankcher wuz good ernuff. Den Tenie say she wanter git her bes' frock; her mistiss say no, she doan need no mo' frock, en w'en dat one got dirty she could git a clean one whar she wuz gwine. So Tenie had ter git in de buggy en go 'long wid young Mars Dunkin ter his plantation, which wuz mo' d'n twenty mile away; en dey wa'n't no chance er her seein' Sandy no mo' 'tel she come back home. De po' gal felt monst'us bad 'bout de way things wuz gwine on, en she knowed Sandy mus' be a wond'rin' why she didn' come en turn 'im back no mo'.

"W'iles Tenie wuz away nussin' young Mars Dunkin's wife, Mars Marrabo tuk a notion fer ter buil' 'im a noo kitchen; en bein' ez he had lots er timber on his place, he begun ter look 'roun' fer a tree ter hab de lumber sawed out'n. En I dunno how it come to be so, but he happen fer ter hit on de ve'y tree w'at Sandy wuz turnt inter. Tenie wuz gone, en dey wa'n't nobody ner nuffin fer ter watch de tree.

"De two men w'at cut de tree down say dey nebber had sech a time wid a tree befo': dey axes would glansh off, en didn' 'pear ter make no progress thoo de wood; en of all de creakin', en shakin', en wobblin' you eber see, dat tree done it w'en it commence' ter fall. It wuz de beatenis' thing!

"W'en dey got de tree all trim' up, dey chain it up ter a timber waggin, en start fer de sawmill. But dey had a hard time gittin' de log dere: fus' dey got stuck in de mud w'en dey wuz gwine crosst de swamp, en it wuz two er th'ee hours befo' dey could git out. W'en dey start' on ag'in, de chain kep' a-comin' loose, en dey had ter keep a-stoppin' en a-stoppin' fer ter hitch de log up ag'in. W'en dey commence' ter climb de hill ter de sawmill, de log broke loose, en roll down de hill en in 'mongs' de trees, en hit tuk nigh 'bout half a day mo' ter git it haul' up ter de sawmill.

"De nex' mawnin' atter de day de tree wuz haul' ter de sawmill, Tenie come home. W'en she got back ter her cabin, de fus' thing she done wuz ter run down ter de woods en see how Sandy wuz gittin' on. We'n she seed de stump standin' dere, wid de sap runnin' out'n it, en de limbs layin' scattered roun', she nigh 'bout went out'n her min'. She run ter her cabin, en got her goopher mixtry, en den follered de track er de timber waggin ter de sawmill. She knowed Sandy couldn' lib mo' d'n a minute er so ef she turnt him back, fer he wuz all chop' up so he'd 'a' be'n bleedst ter die. But she wanted ter turn 'im back long ernuff fer ter 'splain ter 'im dat she hadn' went off a-purpose, en lef' 'im ter be chop' down en sawed up. She didn' want Sandy ter die wid no hard feelin's to'ds her.

"De han's at de sawmill had des got de big log on de kerridge, en wuz startin' up de saw, w'en dey seed a 'oman runnin' up de hill, all out er bref, cryin' en gwine on des lack she wuz plumb 'stracted. It wuz Tenie; she come right inter de mill, en throwed herself on de log, right in front er de saw, a-hollerin' en cryin' ter her Sandy ter fergib her, en not ter think hard er her, fer it wa'n't no fault er hern. Den Tenie 'membered de tree didn' hab no years, en she wuz gittin' ready fer ter wuk her goopher mixtry so ez ter turn Sandy back, w'en de mill-hands kotch holt er her en tied her arms wid a rope, en fasten' her to one er de posts in de sawmill; en den dey started de saw up ag'in, en cut de log up inter bo'ds en scantlin's right befo' her eyes. But it wuz mighty hard wuk; fer of all de sweekin', en moanin', en groanin', dat log done it w'iles de saw wuz a-cuttin' thoo it. De saw wuz one er dese yer ole-timey, up-en-down saws, en hit tuk longer dem days ter saw a log 'en it do now. Dey greased de saw, but dat didn' stop de fuss; hit kep' right on, tel fin'ly dey got de log all sawed up.

"W'en de oberseah w'at run de sawmill come fum breakfas', de han's up en tell him 'bout de crazy 'oman—ez dey s'posed she wuz—w'at had come runnin' in de sawmill, a-hollerin' en gwine on, en tried ter th'ow herse'f befo' de saw. En de oberseah sent two er th'ee er de han's fer ter take Tenie back ter her marster's plantation.

"Tenie 'peered ter be out'n her min' fer a long time, en her marster ha' ter lock her up in de smoke-'ouse 'tel she got ober her spells. Mars Marrabo wuz monst'us mad, en hit would 'a' made yo' flesh crawl fer ter hear him cuss, 'caze he say de spekilater w'at he got Tenie fum had fooled 'im by wukkin' a crazy 'oman off on him. W'iles Tenie wuz lock up in de smoke-'ouse, Mars Marrabo tuk 'n' haul de lumber fum de sawnmill, en put up his noo kitchen.

"W'en Tenie got quiet' down, so she could be 'lowed ter go 'roun' der plantation, she up'n' tole her marster all erbout Sandy en de pine-tree; en w'en Mars Marrabo hearn it, he 'lowed she wuz de wuss 'stracted nigger he eber hearn of. He didn' know w'at ter do wid Tenie: fus' he thought he'd put her in de po'house; but fin'ly, seein' ez she didn' do no harm ter nobody ner nuffin, but des went 'roun' moanin', en groanin', en shakin' her head, he 'cluded ter let her stay on de plantation en nuss de little nigger chilluns w'en dey mammies wuz ter wuk in de cotton-fiel'.

"De noo kitchen Mars Marrabo buil' wuzn' much use, fer it hadn' be'n put up long befo' de niggers 'mence' ter notice quare things erbout it. Dey could hear sump'n moanin' en groanin' 'bout de kitchen in de night-time, en w'en de win' would blow dey could hear sump'n a-hollerin' en sweekin' lack it wuz in great pain en sufferin'. En it got so atter a w'ile dat it wuz all Mars Marrabo's wife could do ter git a 'oman ter stay in de kitchen in de daytime long ernuff ter do de cookin'; en dey wa'n't naer nigger on de plantation w'at wouldn' rudder take forty[4] dan ter go 'bout dat kitchen atter dark,—dat is, 'cep'n' Tenie; she didn' 'pear ter min' de ha'nts. She useter slip 'roun' at night, en set on de kitchen steps, en lean up agin de do'-jamb, en run on ter herse'f wid some kind er foolishness w'at nobody couldn' make out; fer Mars Marrabo had th'eaten' ter sen' her off'n de plantation ef she say anything ter any er de yuther niggers 'bout de pine-tree. But somehow er de 'nudder de niggers foun' out all erbout it, en dey all knowed de kitchen wuz ha'nted by Sandy's sperrit. En bimeby hit got so Mars Marrabo's wife herse'f wuz skeered ter go out in de yard atter dark.

"W'en it come ter dat, Mars Marrabo tuk en to' de kitchen down, en use' de lumber fer ter buil' dat ole school'ouse w'at you er talkin' 'bout pullin' down. De school'ouse wuzn' use' 'cep'n' in de daytime, en on dark nights folks gwine 'long de road would hear quare soun's en see quare things. Po' ole Tenie useter go down dere at night, en wander 'roun' de school'ouse; en de niggers all 'lowed she went fer ter talk wid Sandy's sperrit. En one winter mawnin', w'en one er de boys went ter school early fer ter start de fire, w'at should he fin' but po' ole Tenie, layin' on de flo', stiff, en col', en dead. Dere didn' 'pear ter be nuffin pertickler de matter wid her,—she had des grieve' herse'f ter def fer her Sandy. Mars Marrabo didn' shed no tears. He thought Tenie wuz crazy, en dey wa'n't no tellin' w'at she mought do nex'; en dey ain' much room in dis worl' fer crazy w'ite folks, let 'lone a crazy nigger.

"Hit wa'n't long atter dat befo' Mars Marrabo sol' a piece er his track er lan'; ter Mars Dugal' McAdoo,—*my* ole marster,—en dat's how de ole school'ouse happen to be on yo' place. W'en de wah broke out, de school stop', en de ole school'ouse be'n stannin' empty ever sence,—dat is, 'cep'n' fer de ha'nts. En folks sez dat de ole school'ouse, er any yuther house w'at got any er dat lumber in it w'at wuz sawed out'n de tree w'at Sandy wuz turnt inter, is gwine ter be ha'nted tel de las' piece er plank is rotted en crumble' inter dus'."

Annie had listened to this gruesome narrative with strained attention.

"What a system it was," she exclaimed, when Julius had finished, "under which such things were possible!"

"What things?" I asked, in amazement. "Are you seriously considering the possibility of a man's being turned into a tree?"

"Oh, no," she replied quickly, "not that"; and then she murmured absently, and with a dim look in her fine eyes, "Poor Tenie!"

---

[4] I.e., forty blows with a whip.

We ordered the lumber, and returned home. That night, after we had gone to bed, and my wife had to all appearances been sound asleep for half an hour, she startled me out of an incipient doze by exclaiming suddenly,—

"John, I don't believe I want my new kitchen built out of the lumber in that old schoolhouse."

"You wouldn't for a moment allow yourself," I replied, with some asperity, "to be influenced by that absurdly impossible yarn which Julius was spinning to-day?"

"I know the story is absurd," she replied dreamily, "and I am not so silly as to believe it. But I don't think I should ever be able to take any pleasure in that kitchen if it were built out of that lumber. Besides, I think the kitchen would look better and last longer if the lumber were all new."

Of course she had her way. I bought the new lumber, though not without grumbling. A week or two later I was called away from home on business. On my return, after an absence of several days, my wife remarked to me,—

"John, there has been a split in the Sandy Run Colored Baptist Church, on the temperance question. About half the members have come out from the main body, and set up for themselves. Uncle Julius is one of the seceders, and he came to me yesterday and asked if they might not hold their meetings in the old schoolhouse for the present."

"I hope you didn't let the old rascal have it," I returned, with some warmth. I had just received a bill for the new lumber I had bought.

"Well," she replied, "I couldn't refuse him the use of the house for so good a purpose."

"And I'll venture to say," I continued, "that you subscribed something toward the support of the new church?"

She did not attempt to deny it.

"What are they going to do about the ghost?" I asked, somewhat curious to know how Julius would get around this obstacle.

"Oh," replied Annie, "Uncle Julius says that ghosts never disturb religious worship, but that if Sandy's spirit *should* happen to stray into meeting by mistake, no doubt the preaching would do it good."

Chapter Nine

GRACE KING (1852–1935)

King began writing out of annoyance at what she considered the unfair treatment of her native New Orleans by George Washington Cable. Her *Balcony Stories* (1893), which included "The Little Convent Girl," are to be imagined as tales told among women sitting on a balcony on a hot New Orleans afternoon. King's work is in the tradition of women's regional realism, and her rejection of Cable's advanced views on civil rights places her also in the "plantation school" of conservative Southern fiction.

Nonetheless, "The Little Convent Girl" is an effective and nuanced story of a tragic mulatta. Much of the impact of her story comes from the girl's radical innocence, which the rough-hewn steamboat crew tries to protect. She has never seen the stars, because she has never been allowed outdoors at night. She is frightened and delighted by the world of experience opening to her, symbolized by the river beneath the river of the pilot's imagining. But this chaotic world includes the forces of sexuality and race in New Orleans, into which the little convent girl is about to be plunged.

Text: Grace King, *Balcony Stories* (New York: Century, 1893).

THE LITTLE CONVENT GIRL

She was coming down on the boat from Cincinnati, the little convent girl. Two sisters had brought her aboard. They gave her in charge of the captain, got her a state-room, saw that the new little trunk was put into it, hung the new little satchel up on the wall, showed her how to bolt the door at night, shook hands with her for good-by (good-bys have really no significance for sisters), and left her there. After a while the bells all rang, and the boat, in the awkward elephantine fashion of boats, got into midstream. The chambermaid found her sitting on the chair in the state-room where the sisters had left her, and showed her how to sit on a chair in the saloon. And there she sat until the captain came and hunted her up for supper. She could not do anything of herself; she had to be initiated into everything by some one else.

She was known on the boat only as "the little convent girl." Her name, of course, was registered in the clerk's office, but on a steamboat no one thinks of consulting the clerk's ledger. It is always the little widow, the fat madam, the tall colonel, the parson, etc. The captain, who pronounced by the letter, always called her the little convent girl. She was the beau-ideal of the little convent girl. She never raised her eyes except when spoken to. Of course she never spoke first, even to the chambermaid, and when she did speak it was in the wee, shy, furtive voice one might imagine a just-budding violet to have; and she walked with such soft, easy, carefully calculated steps that one naturally felt the penalties that must have secured them—penalties dictated by a black code of deportment.

She was dressed in deep mourning. Her black straw hat was trimmed with stiff new crape, and her stiff new bombazine dress had crape collar and cuffs. She wore her hair in two long plaits fastened around her head tight and fast. Her hair had a strong inclination to curl, but that had been taken out of it as austerely as the noise out of her footfalls. Her hair was as black as her dress; her eyes, when one saw them, seemed blacker than either, on account of the bluishness of the white surrounding the pupil. Her eyelashes were almost as thick as the black veil which the sisters had fastened around her hat with an extra pin the very last thing before leaving. She had a round little face, and a tiny pointed chin; her mouth was slightly protuberant from the teeth, over which she tried to keep her lips well shut, the effort giving them a pathetic little forced expression. Her complexion was sallow, a pale sallow, the complexion of a brunette bleached in darkened rooms. The only color about her was a blue taffeta ribbon from which a large silver medal of the Virgin hung over the place where a breast pin should have been. She was so little, so little, although she was eighteen, as the sisters told the captain; otherwise they would not have permitted her to travel all the way to New Orleans alone.

Unless the captain or the clerk remembered to fetch her out in front, she would sit all day in the cabin, in the same place, crocheting lace, her spool of thread and box of patterns in her lap, on the handkerchief spread to save her new dress. Never leaning back—oh, no! always straight and stiff, as if the conventual back board were there within call. She would eat only convent fare at first, notwithstanding the importunities of the waiters, and the jocularities of the captain, and particularly of the clerk. Every one knows the fund of humor possessed by a steamboat clerk, and what a field for display the table at meal-times affords. On Friday she fasted rigidly, and she never began to eat, or finished, without a little Latin movement of the lips and a sign of the cross. And always at six o'clock of the evening she remembered the angelus, although there was no church bell to remind her of it.

She was in mourning for her father, the sisters told the captain, and she was going to New Orleans to her mother. She had not seen her mother since she was an infant, on account of some disagreement between the parents, in consequence of which the father had brought her to Cincinnati, and placed her in the convent. There she had been for twelve years, only going to her father for vacations and holidays. So long as the father lived he would never let the child have any communication with her mother. Now that he was dead all that was changed, and the first thing that the girl herself wanted to do was to go to her mother.

The mother superior had arranged it all with the mother of the girl, who was to come personally to the boat in New Orleans, and receive her child from the captain, presenting a letter from the mother superior, a facsimile of which the sisters gave the captain.

It is a long voyage from Cincinnati to New Orleans, the rivers doing their best to make it interminable, embroidering themselves *ad libitum*[1] all over the country. Every

---

1 Latin: at will.

five miles, and sometimes oftener, the boat would stop to put off or take on freight, if not both. The little convent girl, sitting in the cabin, had her terrible frights at first from the hideous noises attendant on these landings—the whistles, the ringings of the bells, the running to and fro, the shouting. Every time she thought it was shipwreck, death, judgment, purgatory; and her sins! her sins! She would drop her crochet, and clutch her prayer-beads from her pocket, and relax the constraint over her lips, which would go to rattling off prayers with the velocity of a relaxed windlass. That was at first, before the captain took to fetching her out in front to see the boat make a landing. Then she got to liking it so much that she would stay all day just where the captain put her, going inside only for her meals. She forgot herself at times so much that she would draw her chair a little closer to the railing, and put up her veil, actually, to see better. No one ever usurped her place, quite in front, or intruded upon her either with word or look; for every one learned to know her shyness, and began to feel a personal interest in her, and all wanted the little convent girl to see everything that she possibly could.

And it was worth seeing—the balancing and *chasséeing*[2] and waltzing of the cumbersome old boat to make a landing. It seemed to be always attended with the difficulty and the improbability of a new enterprise; and the relief when it did sidle up anywhere within rope's-throw of the spot aimed at! And the roustabout throwing the rope from the perilous end of the dangling gang-plank! And the dangling roustabouts hanging like drops of water from it—dropping sometimes twenty feet to the land, and not infrequently into the river itself. And then what a rolling of barrels, and shouldering of sacks, and singing of Jim Crow songs, and pacing of Jim Crow steps; and black skins glistening through torn shirts, and white teeth gleaming through red lips, and laughing, and talking and—bewildering! entrancing! Surely the little convent girl in her convent walls never dreamed of so much unpunished noise and movement in the world!

The first time she heard the mate—it must have been like the first time woman ever heard man—curse and swear, she turned pale, and ran quickly, quickly into the saloon, and—came out again? No, indeed! not with all the soul she had to save, and all the other sins on her conscience. She shook her head resolutely, and was not seen in her chair on deck again until the captain not only reassured her, but guaranteed his reassurance. And after that, whenever the boat was about to make a landing, the mate would first glance up to the guards, and if the little convent girl was sitting there he would change his invective to sarcasm, and politely request the colored gentlemen not to hurry themselves—on no account whatever; to take their time about shoving out the plank; to send the rope ashore by post-office—write him when it got there; begging them not to strain their backs; calling them mister, colonel, major, general, prince, and your royal highness, which was vastly amusing. At night, however, or when the little convent girl was not there, language flowed in its natural curve, the mate swearing like a pagan to make up for lost time.

The captain forgot himself one day: it was when the boat ran aground in the most unexpected manner and place, and he went to work to express his opinion, as only steamboat captains can, of the pilot, mate, engineer, crew, boat, river, country, and the

---

[2] From French, here means maneuvering.

world in general, ringing the bell, first to back, then to head, shouting himself hoarser than his own whistle—when he chanced to see the little black figure hurrying through the chaos on the deck; and the captain stuck as fast aground in midstream as the boat had done.

In the evening the little convent girl would be taken on the upper deck, and going up the steep stairs there was such confusion, to keep the black skirts well over the stiff white petticoats; and, coming down, such blushing when suspicion would cross the unprepared face that a rim of white stocking might be visible; and the thin feet, laced so tightly in the glossy new leather boots, would cling to each successive step as if they could never, never make another venture; and then one boot would (there is but that word) hesitate out, and feel and feel around, and have such a pause of helpless agony as if indeed the next step must have been wilfully removed, or was nowhere to be found on the wide, wide earth.

It was a miracle that the pilot ever got her up into the pilot-house; but pilots have a lonely time, and do not hesitate even at miracles when there is a chance for company. He would place a box for her to climb to the tall bench behind the wheel, and he would arrange the cushions, and open a window here to let in air, and shut one there to cut off a draft, as if there could be no tenderer consideration in life for him than her comfort. And he would talk of the river to her, explain the chart, pointing out eddies, whirlpools, shoals, depths, new beds, old beds, cut-offs, caving banks, and making banks, as exquisitely and respectfully as if she had been the River Commission.

It was his opinion that there was as great a river as the Mississippi flowing directly under it—an underself of a river, as much a counterpart of the other as the second story of a house is of the first; in fact, he said they were navigating through the upper story. Whirlpools were holes in the floor of the upper river, so to speak; eddies were rifts and cracks. And deep under the earth, hurrying toward the subterranean stream, were other streams, small and great, but all deep, hurrying to and from that great mother-stream underneath, just as the small and great overground streams hurry to and from their mother Mississippi. It was almost more than the little convent girl could take in: at least such was the expression of her eyes; for they opened as all eyes have to open at pilot stories. And he knew as much of astronomy as he did of hydrology, could call the stars by name, and define the shapes of the constellations; and she, who had studied astronomy at the convent, was charmed to find that what she had learned was all true. It was in the pilot-house, one night, that she forgot herself for the first time in her life, and stayed up until after nine o'clock. Although she appeared almost intoxicated at the wild pleasure, she was immediately overwhelmed at the wickedness of it, and observed much more rigidity of conduct thereafter. The engineer, the boiler-men, the firemen, the stokers, they all knew when the little convent girl was up in the pilot-house: the speaking-tube became so mild and gentle.

With all the delays of river and boat, however, there is an end to the journey from Cincinnati to New Orleans. The latter city, which at one time to the impatient seemed at the terminus of the never, began, all of a sudden, one day to make its nearingness felt; and from that period every other interest paled before the interest in the immanence of arrival into port, and the whole boat was seized with a panic of preparation, the little convent girl with the others. Although so immaculate was she in person and effects that she might have been struck with a landing, as some good people might be struck with death, at any moment without fear of results, her trunk was packed and repacked, her satchel arranged and rearranged, and, the last day, her hair was brushed and plaited and smoothed over and over again until the very last glimmer of a curl disappeared. Her dress was whisked, as if for microscopic inspection; her face was washed; and her finger-nails were scrubbed with the hard convent nail-brush, until the disciplined little tips ached with a pristine soreness. And still there were hours to wait, and still the boat added up delays. But she arrived at last, after all, with not more than the usual and expected difference between the actual and the advertised time of arrival.

There was extra blowing and extra ringing, shouting, commanding, rushing up the gangway and rushing down the gangway. The clerks, sitting behind tables on the first deck, were plied, in the twinkling of an eye, with estimates, receipts, charges, countercharges, claims, reclaims, demands, questions, accusations, threats, all at topmost voices. None but steamboat clerks could have stood it. And there were throngs composed of individuals every one of whom wanted to see the captain first and at once: and those who could not get to him shouted over the heads of the others; and as usual he lost his temper and politeness, and began to do what he termed "hustle."

"Captain! Captain!" a voice called him to where a hand plucked his sleeve, and a letter was thrust toward him. "The cross, and the name of the convent." He recognized the envelop of the mother superior. He read the duplicate of the letter given by the sisters. He looked at the woman—the mother—casually, then again and again.

The little convent girl saw him coming, leading some one toward her. She rose. The captain took her hand first, before the other greeting, "Good-by, my dear," he said. He tried to add something else, but seemed undetermined what. "Be a good little girl—" It was evidently all he could think of. Nodding to the woman behind him, he turned on his heel, and left.

One of the deck-hands was sent to fetch her trunk. He walked out behind them, through the cabin, and the crowd on deck, down the stairs, and out over the gangway. The little convent girl and her mother went with hands tightly clasped. She did not turn her eyes to the right or left, or once (what all passengers do) look backward at the boat which, however slowly, had carried her surely over dangers that she wot[3] not of. All looked at her as she passed. All wanted to say good-by to the little convent girl, to see the mother who had been deprived of her so long. Some expressed surprise in a whistle; some in other ways. All exclaimed audibly, or to themselves, "Colored!"

It takes about a month to make the round trip from New Orleans to Cincinnati and back, counting five days' stoppage in New Orleans. It was a month to a day when the steamboat came puffing and blowing up to the wharf again, like a stout dowager after too long a walk; and the same scene of confusion was enacted, as it had been enacted twelve times a year, at almost the same wharf for twenty years; and the same calm, a death calmness by contrast, followed as usual the next morning.

---

3 Archaic English: knew.

The decks were quiet and clean; one cargo had just been delivered, part of another stood ready on the levee to be shipped. The captain was there waiting for his business to begin, the clerk was in his office getting his books ready, the voice of the mate could be heard below, mustering the old crew out and a new crew in; for if steamboat crews have a single principle,—and there are those who deny them any,—it is never to ship twice in succession on the same boat. It was too early yet for any but roustabouts, marketers, and church-goers; so early that even the river was still partly mist-covered; only in places could the swift, dark current be seen rolling swiftly along.

"Captain!" A hand plucked at his elbow, as if not confident that the mere calling would secure attention. The captain turned. The mother of the little convent girl stood there, and she held the little convent girl by the hand. "I have brought her to see you," the woman said. "You were so kind—and she is so quiet, so still, all the time, I thought it would do her a pleasure."

She spoke with an accent, and with embarrassment; otherwise one would have said that she was bold and assured enough.

"She don't go nowhere, she don't do nothing but make her crochet and her prayers, so I thought I would bring her for a little visit of 'How d' ye do' to you."

There was, perhaps, some inflection in the woman's voice that might have made known, or at least awakened, the suspicion of some latent hope or intention, had the captain's ear been fine enough to detect it. There might have been something in the little convent girl's face, had his eye been more sensitive—trifle paler, maybe, the lips a little tighter drawn, the blue ribbon a shade faded. He may have noticed that, but—And the visit of "How d' ye do" came to an end.

They walked down the stairway, the woman in front, the little convent girl—her hand released to shake hands with the captain—following, across the bared deck, out to the gangway, over to the middle of it. No one was looking, no one saw more than a flutter of white petticoats, a show of white stockings, as the little convent girl went under the water.

The roustabout dived, as the roustabouts always do, after the drowning, even at the risk of their good-for-nothing lives. The mate himself jumped overboard; but she had gone down in a whirlpool. Perhaps, as the pilot had told her whirlpools always did, it may have carried her through to the underground river, to that vast, hidden, dark Mississippi that flows beneath the one we see; for her body was never found.

Chapter Ten

E. LEVI BROWN (DATES OF BIRTH AND DEATH UNKNOWN)

E. Levi Brown's "At the Hermitage" was published in *Harper's Monthly* in 1893, and then included in William D. Howells and Henry Mills Alden's anthology, *Shapes That Haunt the Dusk* (1907). The story then sank into obscurity, and has not been collected again until now. No other published work by Brown has been discovered. Even the author's race and gender, concealed by the androgynous first initial, were unknown until recently, when the still unpublished research of Matthew Sivils revealed that Brown was an African American woman, the wife of a Southern minister.

The story takes us into a culture deeply steeped in conjure, of which the author must have had intimate knowledge. We see a curse thrown back on its perpetrator by a conjure doctor, as explained by Charles Chesnutt in his essay "Superstitions and Folk-Lore of the South." The intersecting families of the quarters and the big house also reveal the "degrading submissions," as Thomas Jefferson called them, of slavery and its aftermath. The rivals Mim and Tina are both daughters of the decadent white aristocrat John, and there is even a hint that Tina also may be his mistress.

Text: William Dean Howells and Henry Mills Alden, *Shapes That Haunt the Dusk: Harper's Novelettes* (New York: Harper and Brothers, 1907), 249–77.

AT THE HERMITAGE

The October sun was shining hot, but it was cool and pleasant inside the mill. The brown water in Sawny Creek lapped softly against the rocks in its bed, and the sycamore and cottonwood trees, which grew from the water's edge up the steep, muddy banks, stood straight and motionless in the warm sunny air, no touch of autumn upon them yet; only the sweet-gums were turning slightly yellow, and the black-gums were tinging red. It wanted two hours of sunset, but blackbirds were on their way home, and the thickets were noisy with their crying.

Inside the moss-grown old mill there was music and dancing going on, for, comfortably reclining on a pile of cotton seed in the rough ginning-room, with thick festoons of cobwebs everywhere, and bits of dusty lint clinging to every splinter in its walls, a young man was playing a banjo, and two others, with naked feet, were dancing as if for their lives. A slim dark girl in a blue and white homespun dress, her head turbaned with a square of the same, sat on a bag of seed cotton watching them.

"Now, boys, a break-down," called out the player, "and then I must gin out Religion's cotton; come, now, lively."

And they went lively enough.

"You bake the bread, and gimme the crus';
You sift the meal, and gimme the husk;
You bile the pot, and gimme the grease;
I have the crumbs, and you have the feast—
But mis' gwine gimme the ham-bone."

The loose boards shook and trembled under the heavy feet, the scattered cotton seed whirled away in little eddies, and baskets of cotton standing about tipped a little break-down of their own. Even the girl on the bag, whose sober, earnest face seemed out of keeping with the gayety, beat time with her bare feet. But by the time the miller threw his banjo aside, its strings still quivering, she was standing up, and the look of interest had given place to the old gravity. She had not a pretty feature, not even the usual pretty teeth. She was a homely black girl.

"See here, Religion," said the miller, "this here's Saturday evenin', and I keeps holiday like everybody else but you; can't you git along without that little tum of cotton? It ain't wuth ginnin'."

"I'm 'bliged to have it," she answered. "I didn't give nary day's work for rent this week; will pay the week's rent and git sumpin beside. We doesn't draw no ration."

"It's a mighty small heap o' ration you'll git out'n that tum of cotton after you pay fifty cents for your week's rent. Don't you find it cheaper to work out the week's rent than to pay it?"

"I git fifty cents a hundred for pickin'," she answered, simply, "and I kin pick two hundred and fifty a day, and scrap twenty-five more. We doesn't git but fifty cents fur a whole day's work on the plantation."

He looked at her admiringly, at the thin supple body and long light arms that could reach so far among the cotton bolls. He untied the bags and proceeded to fill the gin. A girl who could pick two hundred and seventy-five pounds of cotton a day was a person of some consequence.

The gin stopped its whir, and the clerk weighed the cotton. Religion watched him sharply, and counted the checks he handed her twice.

"If you pass 'em at the Hermitage," he said, "tell 'em to give you another five-cent check; I'm short to-night."

"I ain't goin' to the Hermitage store; I'm goin' to the ferry. They give me cash there for the checks."

"What do they take off?"

"They takes one cent out'n every five. But I'm 'bliged to have the hard money. We has to pay for a good many things we git for Min in hard money." She had taken up the empty bags, but still waited. "I wish you'd please, sir, see if you 'ain't got another check nowhere."

"You're a sight, Religion," he said, good-naturedly. "Here's a nickel."

With her bags on her arm she went out across the dry grass to where a little black mule, not much larger than a goat, was standing. Beck greeted her with a bray astonishing for one of her size, and a switch with her rope of a tail. Unheeding the cheerful greeting, Religion gave all her attention to untying the halter, and soon they were going along the sandy road straight through the woods.

The rickety box-wagon and the chain traces rattled noisily. Religion cracked her whip—it was a stick with a plaited leather string on the end. Beck was in a hurry to get home, and the wagon bumped along over roots and stumps until it was a wonder how Religion kept herself on the board which served for a seat. All the swamps and woods in Sawny were in bad repute. There was an old cemetery, rambling over many acres, lost in ivy and briers and immense trees, but abundant in ghost stories. There was the swamp through which Sherman's soldiers had cut a road, and near by was the hill-side where many sunken hollows marked their graves. A "spirit" could be raised there at a thought's notice. Beck flew past these unpleasant places, and her little hoofs were clattering over the loose bridge at the foot of the hill, where, the cemetery ending, the plantation road began, when she backed suddenly—so suddenly that the board tipped up and dropped Religion into the bottom of the wagon.

Beck had some tricks like all of her kind, and thinking this was one, Religion was scrambling up and readjusting her seat when she saw a face bending over her that she never forgot—a strange evil face, the lower part hidden by a short bushy beard, the upper by many thin braids of hair curling at the ends. Between the two crops of hair she saw a pair of small red eyes, dull and sleepy, but with a curious gleam in them like the eyes of the snakes in the swamp, and thick widespread nostrils. She only had time to note these features and the thick rings of gold in the great ears when the face disappeared, and, as if they floated in the air, she heard the words:

"I am the seventh son of the seventh daughter. I know all things. I can tell you what is killing your sister."

Religion pulled up her rope reins, and Beck flew up the road as if all Sherman's army were after her; nor did she slacken until she reached the great gateway which turned into the Hermitage. Only a flat-topped post remained of the gate, and a boy of twelve, with a face like Religion's, was perched on it.

"Hi, dar, 'Ligion! Ho, Beck!" he cried. "Take me in an' give me a piece of a ride anyway," and with a twinkle of his long ashy legs he landed safely in the wagon.

"What you doin' here, Bud?" questioned his sister. "Why ain't you to home with mammy and Min?"

"Min done had one o' she wussest spells, an' mammy sent me to Miss Tina fur calomel. I heerd youna comin', an' I waited; 'kase ridin' beats walkin' black and blue."

He looked up at her with a sly giggle, and crammed his mouth with persimmons. He expected a scolding for delaying with the calomel, but his sister only said:

"Quit eatin' them 'simmons. Pres'n'y we'll have to git calomel for youna."

They were passing through the quarter now, where every one was getting supper. The air was full of the appetizing odor of frying corn-bread and bacon and boiling coffee. Men sat on the door-steps or smoked in groups under the fine oaks which grew in the middle of the street, waiting for the call to supper. Up at the end of the row of houses, and separated a little from them by a wild-plum thicket, stood a house like a black stump just seen above the green around it. It had what none of the others possessed, a porch in front, but the rotten frame-work had dropped off piece by piece, until it was a mystery how the heavy scuppernong vine that grew upon it was supported. There were lilies and roses in the clean bit of front yard, and on a box was a number of geraniums flourishing in tin cans. There were boxes of violets, and a thick honeysuckle was hugging a post and sending out sweet yellow sprays. Beck drew up before the house with a jerk that had determination in it. Bud jumped out with a boyish shout, but his sister caught his arm.

"Hush, Bud! Don't you hear Min?"

"Min made up that piece to-day," responded Bud, in a roaring whisper. "Maw an' me's been scared pretty nigh to death. Miss Tina say it ain't Min singin', but that spell workin' on her."

The voice was sweet and rich, with an undercurrent of sadness running through that went to the heart. It seemed to wait and tremble, then float and float away, dying into softest melody. It was not the untaught music of the plantation singers; it was a voice exquisitely trained.

"Lord! Lord!" ejaculated Religion. The words held a heartful of trouble. She lowered the shafts gently and led Beck round the house.

"That you, Religion?" inquired a voice from somewhere in the yard.

She could hear milk straining into a pail, and the tramp of some animal over dry shucks.

"It's me, maw, an' I got enough to pay the rent, and there'll be some over."

"Youna mus' had good luck. Min'll be more'n middlin' glad of a few crackers. I thought sure the gal was gone to-day, Religion," and a tall form rose up from beside the cow and came towards the girl. "I sut'n'y thought she was gone to-day," continued the mother. "She just died off, and didn't 'pear to have no more life in her than a dead bird. I was mighty scared."

"Why youna didn't send fur me?"

"Chile, I didn't want to worry youna. Then the neighbors come in, 'kase I did a big piece o' hollerin', an' they worked on her and fotched her back; I 'ain't been no 'count since. See how my hand trembles now."

She placed her hand on her daughter's arm. It was large and hard, but all the ploughing, hoeing, and wood-cutting that she had done had not destroyed its fine shape. It was cold and trembling.

Religion took it between her own square thick ones. "Never mind, maw; she's better now, 'kase she's singin' a new piece. I'll go an' eat and do the errands, so as to git back. You won't feel so bad when I'm here."

The single thing which made the room she entered different from all the other rooms in the quarter was a white bed. The two other beds had the usual patchwork quilts and yellow slips. Religion touched a light-wood splinter to the fire, and holding the light above her head, went up to the white bed. The face on the pillow was of that pure lustrous whiteness which is sometimes seen in very young children; the features were perfect. She seemed a creature of an entirely different sphere—as different from Religion as a butterfly from a grub, and yet there was an indefinable likeness between the two.

"I was waiting for you, 'Ligion," she said, opening her eyes; "I want to tell you something; come close, so ma and Bud won't hear. A woman has been here, a little old woman, and she sat on the bed and told me some things. She told me that Tina had cut off a piece of my hair and hid it in a gum-tree in the swamp, and that I never would be well till my hair was found.

"I remember the night she combed my hair, and how Mauma Amy said it was bad luck to comb hair after dark; it was so thick and long then, and it has come out so since." She drew the long thin brown braid between her fingers. "Why should Tina want to hurt me? The only harm I ever did her was to love her."

She burst into tears, and Religion hugged her in mute sympathy; that was her only way to comfort. When Min was quiet, she stirred up the pillows and smoothed out the white spread. Then she took a tin cup full of clabber, poured a little syrup upon it, and ate it heartily. A plate of greens was hot on the hearth, and a corn-cake was browning beautifully in the bake-kettle. But there was no time to eat the dainties.

John Robinson, the owner of Hermitage, was a single man. He was old, feeble, and notoriously grasping, yet the dirty, ill-smelling room which Religion entered was strewn with choicest books, sheets of music lay on the table and chairs, and several rare violins lay on a piano, whose mother-of-pearl keys glowed in the red firelight.

"Who's that?" he called, in a cracked old voice, the instant he heard Religion's footsteps. He was wrapped in a cloak and sunk in an arm-chair before the fire.

"Me, Marse[1] John—Minnie's Religion.[2] I've come to pay the rent."

"Oh, come in, girl! Down, Bull!" he piped to a great hound that was slowly rising from a sheepskin. "It's fifty cents. Sure you've got it all, and no nickels with holes in them?"

She placed a little tobacco-bag in his hand, and he leaned forward to the light to count the money. He had a sharp, pinched old face surrounded by shaggy white hair. A portrait of him taken in a long-past day hung over the fireplace. In that he was a handsome man, with thick chestnut-brown hair. His hands shook so that the pieces of money dropped from them and rolled upon the brick hearth. A tall mulatto woman came from a near room and picked them up.

"Count it over again, Tina," he commanded, "and see if it's all there and no holes in it. You can't trust Religion herself with money. How's your sister?"

"Min ain't no better; she ain't never going to be no better in this world."

"Tut, tut!" he muttered. "There should be some strength of will in that girl. But, pshaw! she had a mother and a line of nonentities behind her. I forgot that. Is that money all right, Tina?"

"It's all right, Marse John."

Tina was a beautiful woman, with the smoothest brown skin, and black hair coiled many times around a perfectly shaped head.

The renters never waited long in Mr. Robinson's presence when their business was ended. But Religion only moved back a little and lingered. Tina, bringing a cup of cocoa, at last noticed her.

"Why, Religion, you're not gone."

"And why ain't you gone!" screamed the old man.

"I—I'm waiting for the receipt, sir."

---

1 Marse: Master.

2 Minnie's Religion: Minnie's daughter, Religion.

"Waiting for the receipt?" he shrieked. "God and fury! things have come to a pretty pass that a slave wench should wait in my house for a receipt. Get out of this, or—Bull!"

"Stand still, Religion," cried Tina, as the dog leaped up. "Down, Bull! Marse John"—and her voice sank to a sweet, soothing tone—"you'd better not upset yourself so; you'll be sick."

She stroked his face and hair tenderly, and when he lay back quiet in his chair, worn out with his passion, she beckoned to Religion to follow her. They went into one of the rooms. The candle burning in it showed a bed, with posts reaching to the ceiling, and an ancient mahogany chest. A handful of fire burned in the deep fireplace, and before it crouched Mack, an old slave of Mr. Robinson's—a miserable idiot, with just mind enough to perform a very few menial services.

"Trick yer! trick yer!"[3] he piped, in a high thin voice, like an old woman's. "Done got de blacksnake's head an' de dead baby's hand right hyar. Trick yer! trick yer! Git out quick!" He kept up the cry while Tina wrote the receipt, and when she led the way to the door he pattered after them. "Git out quick, 'fore Tina trick yer. I done hope Tina trick Min."

Religion turned fiercely. "Has you tricked my sister and brung her to what she is?"

Tina laughed contemptuously. "Who says I put a spell on Min?"

"Min says it, an' Mack says it, an' I b'lieves it. You always was jealous of her, 'kase Marse John taught her, and made more of her than he did of you."

"Then it's likely this *spell* will put her out of my way," said Tina, all the sweetness gone out of her voice and face, and nothing but venom left. She turned to go in, but Religion dropped on her knees and clasped her feet.

"Oh, Tina! if you did put a spell on Min, take it off, for Christ's sake. Nobody kin do it but you. Our pooty, pooty Min! she be dyin' there before our eyes, and we-uns can't do nothin'. Take the ban off, an' I'll work for you the longest day I live."

Tina dragged herself away and shut the door heavily.

Religion was in the field scattering pine straw, and Beck was there too, harnessed in company with a very lean Texas pony. Her mother and Bud were in the same occupation, but Mollie, the old brown cow, drew their wagon.

Religion was crooning a solemn old ditty, as she always did when alone and thinking.

"I just made up my mind this mornin' that I'd got to do sumpin when Mr. Frye come for we-uns to scatter this straw. An' I wish I knowed what to do. Oh, Lord, don't I wish I knowed what to do. There's Min been down on that air bed one whole year come Christmas, and nobody can't say what is the matter with her. Sich a heap o' calomel, and quinine, and turpentine, and doctor's stuff as she has took, and 'tain't done no good. I can't count the times I been to the tavern. I know I brung off more'n two gallons of the best whiskey, an' it's been mixed up with pine-top, an' snakeroot, an' mullein, an' I dun'no' what all, an' none of it 'ain't done no good. An' Min is dyin' just as fast as she can die. Oh, Lord!"

[3] As Tina glosses below, to "trick" means to place a spell or curse on someone.

A fine mule, drawing a light road-cart, trotted past. The driver was a short, squat man, his face almost hidden in hair. It was Dr. Buzzard. He was known for miles as a successful "conjurer" and giver of "hands." Most of the people around had perfect faith in his cures and revelations, and had advised Religion to try him, but the girl objected, vaguely questioning reason and conscience, and Min was getting worse. It was despair, not belief, which made her whisper to herself, "I'm goin' to see him this very night."

"Great day! 'ain't we-uns had trouble! Lord, Lord! I b'lieve one-half this wurl' has all the trouble fur all the rest, anyhow!"

Religion was on her way, and thinking over the family record as she walked. The sun had set, the cotton-pickers were in, and odors of supper were afloat. Religion was eating hers as she walked and thought—it was a finely browned ash-cake, richly flavored with the cabbage leaves in which it was baked.

The Beckets had always been very poor, hard-working people, without any especial grace or finer touch of nature about them. The two brothers had married two sisters, and such marriages were considered unlucky.

When Religion was a little girl her father broke his contract with his employer, and to escape imprisonment he ran away. Religion remembered his stolen visits at night, and his silent caresses of her. After a while the visits stopped. They heard of him in a distant city, but he never came back. His brother had died long before.

The widowed sisters stayed on the plantation, and both were favorites of Mr. Robinson. Min and Tina were half-sisters. They were as opposite in character as they were in appearance; everybody loved Min; she sang like a bird, and her voice had been carefully trained, and some especial provision had been made for its further cultivation when this strange sickness overtook her.

Good nursing was unknown on the plantations, or perhaps the slight cold, which was the beginning of the end with Min, might have been cured. Since no member of the family had died with consumption, it was not believed that she could have it.

When all the home remedies and doctors' prescriptions failed, there was but one verdict, Min was "hurt." It was known that her half-sister was not very friendly nor over-scrupulous, and it was believed that Tina, out of jealousy, had thrown an evil spell.

The light was still lingering when Religion, turning out of the road, ran down a narrow lane bordered with turpentine woods on one side, and on the other by a field of dead pines. Away back among the latter was a substantial log house, with good brick chimneys at either end. There were several smaller buildings in the yard, and in one a woman was stooping over the fire frying cakes, a young man was thrumming a banjo, and a little boy in scantiest jeans was careening around to the inspiring strains of "Old Joe kicking up behind and before."

Inside, the large low-ceiled room was in a blaze of light. There was a tumbled bed in one corner, a table covered with dusty dishes and glass-ware in another, and a large case filled with bottles, jugs, and bundles occupied a third. Walls and ceiling were hidden by packages of herbs and strings of roots, while over the fireplace were three shelves piled high with cigar-boxes, carefully labelled.

Half buried in a great chair, his breast bare, his sleeves rolled up above his elbows, the veins in his arms standing out like cords, his legs wrapped in a blanket and resting upon a stool, sat Dr. Buzzard, to all appearances in a deep sleep. On the floor, close to the hearth, was a most evil-looking old crone, continually stirring a pot bubbling on the coals. She threw one glance at Religion, and went on stirring. The doctor never moved. A splendid-looking mulatto noiselessly brought a box, and the girl subsided upon it.

There were other visitors. A young man wanted help to get money that was due him; another sought assistance in settling a difficulty. A woman with a child in her arms wanted to charm her recreant husband back to her; a sick one desired relief from the spell which was making her cough her life out.

But the great man slumbered on with a gentle snore, and the old woman stirred the pot. There was not a sound in the room save his snore, the swish of the spoon, and the occasional dropping of a coal. Every one sat in silent, intense expectation, waiting for—they knew not what.

The oaken logs had died down to a bed of glowing coals when suddenly a red glare flashed from it. Religion closed her eyes, blinded by the light. When she opened them the doctor was sitting upright, his head hanging back, his eyes wide open and staring upward, and his breast heaving as if in pain. His wife was in the room holding whispered consultations with each person. The men stated their complaints briefly, but the women detained her longer. When she had been the round she glided back to the side of the doctor.

Then in a low chant, sweet and sorrowful, she repeated the story which each had told her, running them into a continuous recitative. The old woman rose from the floor, and joining in the chant in a quavering croon, sprinkled salt at the thresholds of the doors and at the feet of every person, ending by throwing a large handful up the chimney. It fell back and sputtered and cracked in the fire. Seizing one of the cigar-boxes, she sprinkled a pinch of its contents over the fire. A dense gray vapor rose. The doctor raised his arms, and let them fall slowly, three times.

"The fire holds many secrets," he uttered, in a hollow, unnatural voice, like one talking in his sleep; "he who would see his enemy about his work of destruction, let him look in the fire."

With eyes ready to start from her head, Religion with the rest bent forward to look. She saw, or thought she saw, in the curling gray cloud a woman's face. It seemed to take shape and expression, as she gazed, until it grew familiar. The forsaken woman, who had seen the face of a successful rival, sank heavily upon the floor. Some of the others screamed, some moaned and prayed. The cloud over the fire was repeated many times, and dissolving into fantastic shapes, pictured to the excited fancy of the others their enemies and distresses. At last the exhibition ended, and the visitors were sent from the room, and called in again, separately, to receive directions, medicines, and charms against further evil.

Religion found the doctor sitting at the table, surrounded by jugs, bottles, and boxes, his wife and the old woman standing on either side. He still slept, breathing heavily. His hands were on the table.

"A girl named Religion Becket inquiring for her sister," spoke the doctor in the same strange voice. "The sister seems to be dying."

"Say yes close to his right ear," instructed the wife, and Religion did so.

"The doctors know nothing about the case," responded the conjurer. "A red scorpion is inside her body feeding on her vitals. I see a woman hiding something in a black-gum tree that hangs over running water. It is at the hour when spirits walk. The first creature that runs over the cleft where the hand is hidden is the one to torment your sister. That first creature is a red scorpion. Its young one lives in your sister's side. I, even I, can withdraw it."

Like one moved by some power outside of himself, his hands moved in the array before him, lightly touching this or that bottle and bundle until he found what he sought. And like a careful druggist he deliberately measured each ingredient, giving clear directions at the same time. When Religion came out she had a large bottle of medicine, several huge plasters, and orders for a bewildering list of root teas, with a promise of an early visit from the great man himself.

Religion was feeding the cane-mill. Bud was on the other side drawing out the crushed cane; the mother was under the shed stirring the boiling syrup. Beck was travelling round and round doing the grinding. The sun was set. It would soon be time to stop work. Religion seemed to be expecting some one; she never stooped to pick up an armful of stalks without glancing up the road.

"What you keep lookin' up the road for, 'Ligion?" inquired her mother, her body swaying back and forth as she drew or pushed the long wooden ladle.

"Nuthin'. I ain't lookin' fur nuthin'."

"I b'lieve there's a spell on youna too," said her mother, surveying her anxiously. "I wish youna'd be more keerful and not put your fingers so close to the teeth."

"It's time to quit, anyhow," put in Bud; "the sun's 'way down, an' I'm more'n middlin' hungry."

"You kin take the mule out an' go home an' make the fire. Will you go an' git supper, Religion, or stay an' stir?"

"I reckon I'll stay and stir. You kin bring me some supper when you come. We'll be here half the night."

With another look up the road, where the sunlight was fast fading, she took up the wet bags which protected her dress, and passed under the shed, glad to sit down and rest her aching limbs. The shed was a primitive affair, but everything was convenient for syrup-boiling, and the two long boilers were full of the golden-brown liquid. There was nothing to do but to stir continually and keep a steady fire.

The short autumn twilight had died out, and the fields and woods were slipping into gloom. The cane-mill was in the overseer's yard, and back of it the quarter began. A multitude of sounds came up to Religion's ear—the crying of babies, the laughing of children, the barking of dogs, the whistle of the boys rubbing off the mules, the scolding and calling of women for wood and water. Night was closing in. Religion stirred and thought.

All Dr. Buzzard's instructions had been carefully followed. He had come many times, performed a variety of strange operations, frightened and gladdened them all one day by declaring that the red scorpion had passed out of her body through her foot and run into the fire, that now all danger was passed, pocketed thirty dollars which Minnie and

Religion had obtained by giving a lien on Beck, the old cow, all the corn in the crib, and every article of furniture their cabin held; and still Min was no better—was worse, indeed, with the worry of it all.

Some one was coming. "Is that you, Bud?" she called.

The unnatural laugh that answered her could belong to no one but Mack. Lifting a blazing stick above her head, she peered out into the darkness.

"Come fur youna," he mumbled. "Miss Tina goin' on drefful; come fur youna quick."

"You go, Religion," said a woman who had come unperceived. "The Lord's gwine to cl'ar up some t'ings what's took place in this quarter. You go, an' I'll stay an' stir."

Religion hurried away. She found Tina tossing about in a pretty white bed, her hands and feet bound in onions, her whole body swathed in red flannel saturated with turpentine, and her head bandaged with dock leaves wet with vinegar. There was a hot fire, and the room was crowded with men and women.

Dr. Buzzard was there, with a black calico bag, from which he frequently drew a black bottle, examined it sharply at the lamp, then gravely replaced it, after which he always looked at and pinched Tina's fingers.

"Mother," he said at last, addressing himself to Tina's mother, "the time has come for me to show you the cause of your daughter's illness. She has been hurt. She was too beautiful and well loved to suit all I could name. An evil hand was laid on her."

He took out his watch, looked at it gravely, and laid it upon the table. Removing his coat, he turned back the cuffs of his brown shirt, then took off the bandages from Tina's hands and feet.

He rubbed each arm from the shoulder to the end of the fingers with one sweep, first lightly, then harder, snapping his fingers violently after every stroke. Tina writhed under the treatment, then screamed loudly, and tried to leap from the bed. He called two men to hold her, and the rubbing went on.

With each stroke he grew more and more excited. He lifted his arms high above his head, and bore down upon Tina painfully. His eyes were burning, and the perspiration pouring down his face. He broke into a low humming, and the women took it up, moaning in concert, and rocking their bodies in sympathy.

Suddenly he yelled out, "Ah! there it is; see there, see there; there he goes into the fire, the miserable lizard, which was purposely put into Tina's drink, and has grown in her, and poisoned her blood until I came to drive it out!"

Every one jumped to see the lizard, and saw nothing but the glowing logs. There was a faint smell of burning flesh. The women fell back into their seats, staring fearfully into each other's faces. Tina sprang upright in bed.

"Min is down by the Black Run calling me, an' I'm goin' to her. He told me to put her hair and some stuff he give me into a hole in the black-gum that hangs over the stone, and I did it. Before God! I never meant to hurt her. I hated her because Marse thought more of her than he did me. He taught her, but he never taught me, and we was both his children. But I never meant to hurt her. Tell Religion so. I'm comin', Min; yes, I'm comin'; wait for me!"

She leaped upon the floor, but the unnatural strength supplied by the delirium of fever had fled. She dropped at Religion's feet with a cry like a wounded dog.

Daylight found Religion in the lonely swamp: only great pools of thick black water and leaning trees shrouded in long gray moss. The water lay still in those levels until the sun dried it up. In just one place was there the slightest movement. A short descent sent a stream slowly curling away under masses of green briers.

The only stone known to be in the whole swamp was at the head of the stream, on a tiny hillock formed of logs and the débris of many freshets. It was known as Cuffee's Stone, and the story was that a slave escaping from his master, and hiding in the swamp, had carried the stone there to build his fire upon. Close by, its sprawling roots washed by the running water, was an immense black-gum, in the branches of which the same Cuffee had built himself a covert of branches, from which he watched his pursuers in their vain hunt for him. Had Cuffee's shade, which was said still to haunt the tree, been abroad at that hour, it would have seen a girl narrowly scanning the rough stem, to find some crack or cleft in which anything might be hidden.

And she found a small crevice which would have escaped any but her searching eyes. They lit up as if she had found a rare treasure. Inserting the point of a knife, she drew out a little bag wet and mouldy. She never stopped to examine it, but leaped from log to log through the briers and water out of the swamp.

"Here's your hair, Min. Curl it round your finger three times and throw it in the fire. Oh, Min, now youna'll get well!"

A light shone in the sick girl's eyes. "Yes, I shall get well. Come out and listen to the music, Religion."

"There isn't any music, Min. See the hair."

"Yes, I see the hair; but, oh, the beautiful music! If I could only learn it!"

Religion clasped her close in her arms. The water-oaks were in a golden-brown haze, and the room was full of rich light. But it swam in darkness before the exhausted girl.

A moment after she recovered herself, but Min was well.

Chapter Eleven

KATE CHOPIN (1851–1904)

Kate O'Flaherty Chopin was born in St. Louis into a bilingual family (her mother's family spoke French) and lived in francophone rural Louisiana for several years after her husband's early death. Her two published collections of stories, *Bayou Folk* (1894) and *A Night in Arcady* (1897), are in the tradition of women's regional realism (or, less precisely, local color), filtered through a distinctly non-Anglo-Saxon sensibility. She was a translator of Guy de Maupassant, and her stories often have his characteristic twist or reversal, as does "Désirée's Baby." Like her contemporary Charles Chesnutt, her reputation did not survive her transition from short stories to the novel form, and *The Awakening* (1899) was excoriated and banned. But again, like Chesnutt, her reputation soared after rediscovery in the more tolerant 1960s.

Chopin uses Gothic tropes to great effect: a foundling, a gloomy mansion, a hidden manuscript and a heroine fleeing the villain in her flimsy nightgown. As in so many Southern Gothic stories, a hidden genealogy is at its core.

Readers should consider not only the interaction of Désirée and Armand, but also the role of secondary characters. La Blanche, for instance, never actually appears in the story, but is a presence lurking off stage, and becomes a kind of double for Désirée. Note that Désirée's epiphany occurs when she compares her son with La Blanche's son.

Text: Kate Chopin, *Bayou Folk* (Boston, MA: Hougton, Mifflin, 1894).

DÉSIRÉE'S BABY

As the day was pleasant, Madame Valmondé drove over to L'Abri to see Désirée and the baby.

It made her laugh to think of Désirée with a baby. Why, it seemed but yesterday that Désirée was little more than a baby herself; when Monsieur in riding through the gateway of Valmondé had found her lying asleep in the shadow of the big stone pillar.

The little one awoke in his arms and began to cry for "Dada." That was as much as she could do or say. Some people thought she might have strayed there of her own accord, for she was of the toddling age. The prevailing belief was that she had been purposely left by a party of Texans, whose canvas-covered wagon, late in the day, had crossed the ferry that Coton Maïs kept, just below the plantation. In time Madame Valmondé abandoned every speculation but the one that Désirée had been sent to her by a beneficent Providence to be the child of her affection, seeing that she was without child of the flesh. For the girl grew to be beautiful and gentle, affectionate and sincere,—the idol of Valmondé.

It was no wonder, when she stood one day against the stone pillar in whose shadow she had lain asleep, eighteen years before, that Armand Aubigny riding by and seeing her there, had fallen in love with her. That was the way all the Aubignys fell in love, as if struck by a pistol shot. The wonder was that he had not loved her before; for he had known her since his father brought him home from Paris, a boy of eight, after his mother died there. The passion that awoke in him that day, when he saw her at the gate, swept along like an avalanche, or like a prairie fire, or like anything that drives headlong over all obstacles.

Monsieur Valmondé grew practical and wanted things well considered: that is, the girl's obscure origin. Armand looked into her eyes and did not care. He was reminded that she was nameless. What did it matter about a name when he could give her one of the oldest and proudest in Louisiana? He ordered the *corbeille*[1] from Paris, and contained himself with what patience he could until it arrived; then they were married.

Madame Valmondé had not seen Désirée and the baby for four weeks. When she reached L'Abri she shuddered at the first sight of it, as she always did. It was a sad looking place, which for many years had not known the gentle presence of a mistress, old Monsieur Aubigny having married and buried his wife in France, and she having loved her own land too well ever to leave it. The roof came down steep and black like a cowl, reaching out beyond the wide galleries that encircled the yellow stuccoed house. Big, solemn oaks grew close to it, and their thick-leaved, far-reaching branches shadowed it like a pall. Young Aubigny's rule was a strict one, too, and under it his negroes had forgotten how to be gay, as they had been during the old master's easy-going and indulgent lifetime.

The young mother was recovering slowly, and lay full length, in her soft white muslins and laces, upon a couch. The baby was beside her, upon her arm, where he had fallen asleep, at her breast. The yellow nurse woman sat beside a window fanning herself.

Madame Valmondé bent her portly figure over Désirée and kissed her, holding her an instant tenderly in her arms. Then she turned to the child.

"This is not the baby!" she exclaimed, in startled tones. French was the language spoken at Valmondé in those days.

"I knew you would be astonished," laughed Désirée, "at the way he has grown. The little *cochon de lait!*[2] Look at his legs, mamma, and his hands and finger-nails,—real finger-nails. Zandrine had to cut them this morning. Isn't it true, Zandrine?"

The woman bowed her turbaned head majestically, "*Mais si*,[3] Madame."

"And the way he cries," went on Désirée, "is deafening. Armand heard him the other day as far away as La Blanche's cabin."

Madame Valmondé had never removed her eyes from the child. She lifted it and walked with it over to the window that was lightest. She scanned the baby narrowly, then looked as searchingly at Zandrine whose face was turned to gaze across the fields.

---

1 Wedding gifts.
2 Suckling piglet.
3 Yes, indeed!

"Yes, the child has grown, has changed," said Madame Valmondé, slowly, as she replaced it beside its mother. "What does Armand say?"

Désirée's face became suffused with a glow that was happiness itself.

"Oh, Armand is the proudest father in the parish, I believe, chiefly because it is a boy, to bear his name; though he says not,—that he would have loved a girl as well. But I know it isn't true. I know he says that to please me. And mamma," she added, drawing Madame Valmondé's head down to her, and speaking in a whisper, "he hasn't punished one of them—not one of them—since baby is born. Even Négrillon, who pretended to have burnt his leg that he might rest from work—he only laughed, and said Négrillon was a great scamp. Oh, mamma, I'm so happy; it frightens me."

What Désirée said was true. Marriage, and later the birth of his son had softened Armand Aubigny's imperious and exacting nature greatly. This was what made the gentle Désirée so happy, for she loved him desperately. When he frowned she trembled, but loved him. When he smiled she asked no greater blessing of God. But Armand's dark, handsome face had not often been disfigured by frowns since the day he fell in love with her.

When the baby was about three months old, Désirée awoke one day to the conviction that there was something in the air menacing her peace. It was at first too subtle to grasp. It had only been a disquieting suggestion; an air of mystery among the blacks; unexpected visits from far-off neighbors who could hardly account for their coming. Then a strange, an awful change in her husband's manner, which she dared not ask him to explain. When he spoke to her, it was with averted eyes, from which the old love-light seemed to have gone out. He absented himself from home; and when there, avoided her presence and that of her child, without excuse. And the very spirit of Satan seemed suddenly to take hold of him in his dealings with the slaves. Désirée was miserable enough to die.

She sat in her room, one hot afternoon, in her *peignoir*,[4] listlessly drawing through her fingers the strands of her long, silky brown hair that hung about her shoulders. The baby, half naked, lay asleep upon her own great mahogany bed, that was like a sumptuous throne, with its satin-lined hall canopy. One of La Blanche's little quadroon boys—half naked too—stood fanning the child slowly with a fan of peacock feathers. Désirée's eyes had been fixed absently and sadly upon the baby, while she was striving to penetrate the threatening mist that she felt closing about her. She looked from her child to the boy who stood beside him, and back again; over and over. "Ah!" It was a cry that she could not help; which she was not conscious of having uttered. The blood turned like ice in her veins, and a clammy moisture gathered upon her face.

She tried to speak to the little quadroon[5] boy; but no sound would come, at first. When he heard his name uttered, he looked up, and his mistress was pointing to the door. He laid aside the great, soft fan, and obediently stole away, over the polished floor, on his bare tiptoes.

---

[4] Dressing gown.

[5] An archaic term for someone with one grandparent of African origin.

She stayed motionless, with gaze riveted upon her child, and her face the picture of fright.

Presently her husband entered the room, and without noticing her, went to a table and began to search among some papers which covered it.

"Armand," she called to him, in a voice which must have stabbed him, if he was human. But he did not notice. "Armand," she said again. Then she rose and tottered towards him. "Armand," she panted once more, clutching his arm, "look at our child. What does it mean? tell me."

He coldly but gently loosened her fingers from about his arm and thrust the hand away from him. "Tell me what it means!" she cried despairingly.

"It means," he answered lightly, "that the child is not white; it means that you are not white."

A quick conception of all that this accusation meant for her nerved her with unwonted courage to deny it. "It is a lie; it is not true, I am white! Look at my hair, it is brown; and my eyes are gray, Armand, you know they are gray. And my skin is fair," seizing his wrist. "Look at my hand; whiter than yours, Armand," she laughed hysterically.

"As white as La Blanche's," he returned cruelly; and went away leaving her alone with their child.

When she could hold a pen in her hand, she sent a despairing letter to Madame Valmondé.

"My mother, they tell me I am not white. Armand has told me I am not white. For God's sake tell them it is not true. You must know it is not true. I shall die. I must die. I cannot be so unhappy, and live."

The answer that came was as brief:

"My own Désirée: Come home to Valmondé; back to your mother who loves you. Come with your child."

When the letter reached Désirée she went with it to her husband's study, and laid it open upon the desk before which he sat. She was like a stone image; silent, white, motionless after she placed it there.

In silence he ran his cold eyes over the written words. He said nothing. "Shall I go, Armand?" she asked in tones sharp with agonized suspense.

"Yes, go."

"Do you want me to go?"

"Yes, I want you to go."

He thought Almighty God had dealt cruelly and unjustly with him; and felt, somehow, that he was paying Him back in kind when he stabbed thus into his wife's soul. Moreover he no longer loved her, because of the unconscious injury she had brought upon his home and his name.

She turned away like one stunned by a blow, and walked slowly towards the door, hoping he would call her back.

"Good-by, Armand," she moaned.

He did not answer her. That was his last blow at fate.

Désirée went in search of her child. Zandrine was pacing the sombre gallery with it. She took the little one from the nurse's arms with no word of explanation, and descending the steps, walked away, under the live-oak branches.

It was an October afternoon; the sun was just sinking. Out in the still fields the negroes were picking cotton.

Désirée had not changed the thin white garment nor the slippers which she wore. Her hair was uncovered and the sun's rays brought a golden gleam from its brown meshes. She did not take the broad, beaten road which led to the far-off plantation of Valmondé. She walked across a deserted field, where the stubble bruised her tender feet, so delicately shod, and tore her thin gown to shreds.

She disappeared among the reeds and willows that grew thick along the banks of the deep, sluggish bayou; and she did not come back again.

Some weeks later there was a curious scene enacted at L'Abri. In the centre of the smoothly swept back yard was a great bonfire. Armand Aubigny sat in the wide hallway that commanded a view of the spectacle; and it was he who dealt out to a half dozen negroes the material which kept this fire ablaze.

A graceful cradle of willow, with all its dainty furbishings, was laid upon the pyre, which had already been fed with the richness of a priceless *layette*.[6] Then there were silk gowns, and velvet and satin ones added to these; laces, too, and embroideries; bonnets and gloves; for the corbeille had been of rare quality.

The last thing to go was a tiny bundle of letters; innocent little scribblings that Désirée had sent to him during the days of their espousal. There was the remnant of one back in the drawer from which he took them. But it was not Désirée's; it was part of an old letter from his mother to his father. He read it. She was thanking God for the blessing of her husband's love:—

"But, above all," she wrote, "night and day, I thank the good God for having so arranged our lives that our dear Armand will never know that his mother, who adores him, belongs to the race that is cursed with the brand of slavery."

---

6 Baby linens.

Chapter Twelve

M. E. M. DAVIS (1852–1909)

Although largely forgotten today, Mollie Evelyn Moore Davis had a long and commercially successful career as an editor, poet and writer of fiction and nonfiction. She wrote a popular history of Texas, *Under Six Flags* (1897), for young readers. She spent much of her youth on a cotton plantation in Texas and, after her marriage, settled in New Orleans and maintained a fashionable home on Royal Street.

"At La Glorieuse," published in *Harper's Monthly*, was selected by William Dean Howells and Henry Mills Alden for inclusion in *Shapes That Haunt the Dusk* (1907), their collection of tales that occupy "the borderland between experience and illusion" (p. v.). As we have seen, E. Levi Brown's "At the Hermitage" also found its way into this useful and long-neglected anthology.

Davis's story creates its uncanny effect through a blend of glamor, nastiness and broken taboos. The ghost of a "soulless" woman haunts a shuttered ballroom and returns for seduction and revenge.

Text: William Dean Howells and Henry Mills Alden, eds, *Shapes That Haunt the Dusk: Harper's Novelettes* (New York: Harper and Brothers, 1907), 177–222.

AT LA GLORIEUSE

Madame Raymonde-Arnault leaned her head against the back of her garden chair, and watched the young people furtively from beneath her half-closed eyelids. "He is about to speak,"[1] she murmured under her breath; "she, at least, will be happy!" and her heart fluttered violently, as if it had been her own thin bloodless hand which Richard Keith was holding in his; her dark sunken eyes, instead of Félice's brown ones, which drooped beneath his tender gaze.

Marcelite, the old bonne,[2] who stood erect and stately behind her mistress, permitted herself also to regard them for a moment with something like a smile relaxing her sombre yellow face; then she too turned her turbaned head discreetly in another direction.

The plantation house at La Glorieuse is built in a shining loop of Bayou L'Eperon. A level grassy lawn, shaded by enormous live-oaks, stretches across from the broad stone steps to the sodded levee, where a flotilla of small boats, drawn up among the flags and lily-pads, rise and fall with the lapping waves. On the left of the house the white cabins of the quarter show their low roofs above the shrubbery; to the right the plantations of

[1] Speak: here means to propose marriage.

[2] Maid.

cane, following the inward curve of the bayou, sweep southward field after field, their billowy blue-green reaches blending far in the rear with the indistinct purple haze of the swamp. The great square house, raised high on massive stone pillars, dates back to the first quarter of the century; its sloping roof is set with rows of dormer-windows, the big red double chimneys rising oddly from their midst; wide galleries with fluted columns enclose it on three sides; from the fourth is projected a long narrow wing, two stories in height, which stands somewhat apart from the main building, but is connected with it by a roofed and latticed passageway. The lower rooms of this wing open upon small porticos, with balustrades of wrought ironwork rarely fanciful and delicate. From these you may step into the rose garden—a tangled pleasaunce[3] which rambles away through alleys of wild-peach and magnolia to an orange grove, whose trees are gnarled and knotted with the growth of half a century.

The early shadows were cool and dewy there that morning; the breath of damask-roses was sweet on the air; brown, gold-dusted butterflies were hovering over the sweet-pease abloom in sunny corners; birds shot up now and then from the leafy aisles, singing, into the clear blue sky above; the chorus of the negroes at work among the young cane floated in, mellow and resonant, from the fields. The old mistress of La Glorieuse saw it all behind her drooped eyelids. Was it not April too, that long-gone unforgotten morning? And were not the bees busy in the hearts of the roses, and the birds singing, when Richard Keith, the first of the name who came to La Glorieuse, held her hand in his, and whispered his love-story yonder, by the ragged thicket of crêpe-myrtle? Ah, Félice, my child, thou art young, but I too have had my sixteen years; and yellow as are the curls on the head bent over thine, those of the first Richard were more golden still. And the second Richard, he who—

Marcelite's hand fell heavily on her mistress's shoulder. Madame Arnault opened her eyes and sat up, grasping the arms of her chair. A harsh grating sound had fallen suddenly into the stillness, and the shutters of one of the upper windows of the wing which overlooked the garden were swinging slowly outward. A ripple of laughter, musical and mocking, rang clearly on the air; at the same moment a woman appeared, framed like a portrait in the narrow casement. She crossed her arms on the iron window-bar, and gazed silently down on the startled group below. She was strangely beautiful and young, though an air of soft and subtle maturity pervaded her graceful figure. A glory of yellow hair encircled her pale oval face, and waved away in fluffy masses to her waist; her full lips were scarlet; her eyes, beneath their straight dark brows, were gray, with emerald shadows in their luminous depths. Her low-cut gown, of some thin, yellowish-white material, exposed her exquisitely rounded throat and perfect neck; long, flowing sleeves of spidery lace fell away from her shapely arms, leaving them bare to the shoulder; loose strings of pearls were wound around her small wrists, and about her throat was clasped a strand of blood-red coral, from which hung to the hollow of her bosom a single translucent drop of amber. A smile at once daring and derisive parted her lips; an elusive light came and went in her eyes.

3 A garden or pleasure ground attached to a mansion.

Keith had started impatiently from his seat at the unwelcome interruption. He stood regarding the intruder with mute, half-frowning inquiry.

Félice turned a bewildered face to her grandmother. "Who is it, mère?" she whispered. "Did—did you give her leave?"

Madame Arnault had sunk back in her chair. Her hands trembled convulsively still, and the lace on her bosom rose and fell with the hurried beating of her heart. But she spoke in her ordinary measured, almost formal tones, as she put out a hand and drew the girl to her side. "I do not know, my child. Perhaps Suzette Beauvais has come over with her guests from Grandchamp. I thought I heard but now the sound of boats on the bayou. Suzette is ever ready with her pranks. Or perhaps—"

She stopped abruptly. The stranger was drawing the batten blinds together. Her ivory-white arms gleamed in the sun. For a moment they could see her face shining like a star against the dusky glooms within; then the bolt was shot sharply to its place.

Old Marcelite drew a long breath of relief as she disappeared. A smothered ejaculation had escaped her lips, under the girl's intent gaze; an ashen gray had overspread her dark face. "Mam'selle Suzette, she been an' dress up one o' her young ladies jes fer er trick," she said, slowly, wiping the great drops of perspiration from her wrinkled forehead.

"Suzette?" echoed Félice, incredulously. "She would never dare! Who can it be?"

"It is easy enough to find out," laughed Keith. "Let us go and see for ourselves who is masquerading in my quarters."

He drew her with him as he spoke along the winding violet-bordered walks which led to the house. She looked anxiously back over her shoulder at her grandmother. Madame Arnault half arose, and made an imperious gesture of dissent; but Marcelite forced her gently into her seat, and leaning forward, whispered a few words rapidly in her ear.

"Thou art right, Marcelite," she acquiesced, with a heavy sigh. 'Tis better so."

They spoke in nègre, that mysterious patois which is so uncouth in itself, so soft and caressing on the lips of women. Madame Arnault signed to the girl to go on. She shivered a little, watching their retreating figures. The old bonne threw a light shawl about her shoulders, and crouched affectionately at her feet. The murmur of their voices as they talked long and earnestly together hardly reached beyond the shadows of the wild-peach-tree beneath which they sat.

"How beautiful she was!" Félice said, musingly, as they approached the latticed passageway.

"Well, yes," her companion returned, carelessly. "I confess I do not greatly fancy that style of beauty myself." And he glanced significantly down at her own flower-like face.

She flushed, and her brown eyes drooped, but a bright little smile played about her sensitive mouth. "I cannot see," she declared, "how Suzette could have dared to take her friends into the ballroom!"

"Why?" he asked, smiling at her vehemence.

She stopped short in her surprise. "Do you not know, then?" She sank her voice to a whisper. "The ballroom has never been opened since the night my mother died. I was but a baby then, though sometimes I imagine that I remember it all. There was a grand ball there that night. La Glorieuse was full of guests, and everybody from all the plantations around was here. Mère has never told me how it was, nor Marcelite; but the other servants used to talk to me about my beautiful young mother, and tell me how she died suddenly in her ball dress, while the ball was going on. My father had the whole wing closed at once, and no one was ever allowed to enter it. I used to be afraid to play in its shadow, and if I did stray anywhere near it, my father would always call me away. Her death must have broken his heart. He rarely spoke; I never saw him smile; and his eyes were so sad that I could weep now at remembering them. Then he too died while I was still a little girl, and now I have no one in the world but dear old mère." Her voice trembled a little, but she flushed, and smiled again beneath his meaning look. "It was many years before even the lower floor was reopened, and I am almost sure that yours is the only room there which has ever been used."

They stepped, as she concluded, into the hall.

"I have never been in here before," she said, looking about her with shy curiosity. A flood of sunlight poured through the wide arched window at the foot of the stair. The door of the room nearest the entrance stood open; the others, ranging along the narrow hall, were all closed.

"This is my room," he said, nodding towards the open door.

She turned her head quickly away, with an impulse of girlish modesty, and ran lightly up the stair. He glanced downward as he followed, and paused, surprised to see the flutter of white garments in a shaded corner of his room. Looking more closely, he saw that it was a glimmer of light from an open window on the dark polished floor.

The upper hall was filled with sombre shadows; the motionless air was heavy with a musty, choking odor. In the dimness a few tattered hangings were visible on the walls; a rope, with bits of crumbling evergreen clinging to it, trailed from above one of the low windows. The panelled double door of the ballroom was shut; no sound came from behind it.

"The girls have seen us coming," said Félice, picking her way daintily across the dust-covered floor, "and they have hidden themselves inside."

Keith pushed open the heavy valves, which creaked noisily on their rusty hinges. The gloom within was murkier still; the chill dampness, with its smell of mildew and mould, was like that of a funeral vault.

The large, low-ceilinged room ran the entire length of the house. A raised dais, whose faded carpet had half rotted away, occupied an alcove at one end; upon it four or five wooden stools were placed; one of these was overturned; on another a violin in its baggy green baize cover was lying. Straight high-backed chairs were pushed against the walls on either side; in front of an open fireplace with a low wooden mantel two small cushioned divans were drawn up, with a claw-footed table between them. A silver salver filled with tall glasses was set carelessly on one edge of the table; a half-open fan of sandal-wood lay beside it; a man's glove had fallen on the hearth just within the tarnished brass fender. Cobwebs depended from the ceiling, and hung in loose threads from the mantel; dust was upon everything, thick and motionless; a single ghostly ray of light that filtered in through a crevice in one of the shutters was weighted with gray lustreless motes. The room was empty and silent. The visitors, who had come so stealthily, had as stealthily departed, leaving no trace behind them.

"They have played us a pretty trick," said Keith, gayly. "They must have fled as soon as they saw us start towards the house." He went over to the window from which the girl had looked down into the rose garden, and gave it a shake. The dust flew up in a suffocating cloud, and the spiked nails which secured the upper sash rattled in their places.

"That is like Suzette Beauvais," Félice replied, absently. She was not thinking of Suzette. She had forgotten even the stranger, whose disdainful eyes, fixed upon herself, had moved her sweet nature to something like a rebellious anger. Her thoughts were on the beautiful young mother of alien race, whose name, for some reason, she was forbidden to speak. She saw her glide, gracious and smiling, along the smooth floor; she heard her voice above the call and response of the violins; she breathed the perfume of her laces, backward-blown by the swift motion of the dance!

She strayed dreamily about, touching with an almost reverent finger first one worm-eaten object and then another, as if by so doing she could make the imagined scene more real. Her eyes were downcast; the blood beneath her rich dark skin came and went in brilliant flushes on her cheeks; the bronze hair, piled in heavy coils on her small, well-poised head, fell in loose rings on her low forehead and against her white neck; her soft gray gown, following the harmonious lines of her slender figure, seemed to envelop her like a twilight cloud.

"She is adorable," said Richard Keith to himself.

It was the first time that he had been really alone with her, though this was the third week of his stay in the hospitable old mansion where his father and his grandfather before him had been welcome guests. Now that he came to think of it, in that bundle of yellow, time-worn letters from Félix Arnault to Richard Keith, which he had found among his father's papers, was one which described at length a ball in this very ballroom. Was it in celebration of his marriage, or of his home-coming after a tour abroad? Richard could not remember. But he idly recalled portions of other letters, as he stood with his elbow on the mantel watching Félix Arnault's daughter.

"Your son and my daughter," the phrase which had made him smile when he read it yonder in his Maryland home, brought now a warm glow to his heart. The half-spoken avowal, the question that had trembled on his lips a few moments ago in the rose garden, stirred impetuously within him.

Félice stepped down from the dais where she had been standing, and came swiftly across the room, as if his unspoken thought had called her to him. A tender rapture possessed him to see her thus drawing towards him; he longed to stretch out his arms and fold her to his breast. He moved, and his hand came in contact with a small object on the mantel. He picked it up. It was a ring, a band of dull worn gold, with a confused tracery graven upon it. He merely glanced at it, slipping it mechanically on his finger. His eyes were full upon hers, which were suffused and shining.

"Did you speak?" she asked, timidly. She had stopped abruptly, and was looking at him with a hesitating, half-bewildered expression.

"No," he replied. His mood had changed. He walked again to the window and examined the clumsy bolt. "Strange!" he muttered. "I have never seen a face like hers," he sighed, dreamily.

"She was very beautiful," Félice returned, quietly. "I think we must be going," she added. "Mère will be growing impatient." The flush had died out of her cheek, her arms hung listlessly at her side. She shuddered as she gave a last look around the desolate room. "They were dancing here when my mother died," she said to herself.

He preceded her slowly down the stair. The remembrance of the woman began vaguely to stir his senses. He had hardly remarked her then, absorbed as he had been in another idea. Now she seemed to swim voluptuously before his vision; her tantalizing laugh rang in his ears; her pale perfumed hair was blown across his face; he felt its filmy strands upon his lips and eyelids. "Do you think," he asked, turning eagerly on the bottom step, "that they could have gone into any of these rooms?"

She shrank unaccountably from him. "Oh no," she cried. "They are in the rose garden with mère, or they have gone around to the lawn. Come"; and she hurried out before him.

Madame Arnault looked at them sharply as they came up to where she was sitting. "No one!" she echoed, in response to Keith's report. "Then they really have gone back?"

"Madame knows dat we is hear de boats pass up de bayou whilse m'sieu an' mam'selle was inside," interposed Marcelite, stooping to pick up her mistress's cane.

"I would not have thought Suzette so—so indiscreet," said Félice. There was a note of weariness in her voice.

Madame Arnault looked anxiously at her and then at Keith. The young man was staring abstractedly at the window, striving to recall the vision that had appeared there, and he felt, rather than saw, his hostess start and change color when her eyes fell upon the ring he was wearing. He lifted his hand covertly, and turned the trinket around in the light, but he tried in vain to decipher the irregular characters traced upon it.

"Let us go in," said the old madame. "Félice, my child, thou art fatigued."

Now when in all her life before was Félice ever fatigued? Félice, whose strong young arms could send a pirogue[4] flying up the bayou for miles; Félice, who was ever ready for a tramp along the rose-hedged lanes to the swamp lakes when the water-lilies were in bloom; to the sugar-house in grinding-time, down the levee road to St. Joseph's, the little brown ivy-grown church, whose solitary spire arose slim and straight above the encircling trees.

Marcelite gave an arm to her mistress, though, in truth, she seemed to walk a little unsteadily herself. Félice followed with Keith, who was silent and self-absorbed.

The day passed slowly, a constraint had somehow fallen upon the little household. Madame Arnault's fine high-bred old face wore its customary look of calm repose, but her eyes now and then sought her guest with an expression which he could not have fathomed if he had observed it. But he saw nothing. A mocking red mouth; a throat made for the kisses of love; white arms strung with pearls—these were ever before him, shutting away even the pure sweet face of Félice Arnault.

"Why did I not look at her more closely when I had the opportunity, fool that I was?" he asked himself, savagely, again and again, revolving in his mind a dozen pretexts for going at once to the Beauvais plantation, a mile or so up the bayou. But he felt an inexplicable shyness at the thought of putting any of these plans into action, and so

[4] A Cajun style of flat-bottomed boat.

allowed the day to drift by. He arose gladly when the hour for retiring came—that hour which he had hitherto postponed by every means in his power. He kissed, as usual, the hand of his hostess, and held that of Félice in his for a moment; but he did not feel its trembling, or see the timid trouble in her soft eyes.

His room in the silent and deserted wing was full of fantastic shadows. He threw himself on a chair beside a window without lighting his lamp. The rose garden outside was steeped in moonlight; the magnolia bells gleamed waxen-white against their glossy green leaves; the vines on the tall trellises threw a soft network of dancing shadows on the white-shelled walks below; the night air stealing about was loaded with the perfume of roses and sweet-olive; a mocking-bird sang in an orange-tree, his mate responding sleepily from her nest in the old summer-house.

"To-morrow," he murmured, half aloud, "I will go to Grandchamp and give her the ring she left in the old ballroom."

He looked at it glowing dully in the moonlight; suddenly he lifted his head, listening. Did a door grind somewhere near on its hinges? He got up cautiously and looked out. It was not fancy. She was standing full in view on the small balcony of the room next his own. Her white robes waved to and fro in the breeze; the pearls on her arms glistened. Her face, framed in the pale gold of her hair, was turned towards him; a smile curved her lips; her mysterious eyes seemed to be searching his through the shadow. He drew back, confused and trembling, and when, a second later, he looked again, she was gone.

He sat far into the night, his brain whirling, his blood on fire. Who was she, and what was the mystery hidden in this isolated old plantation house? His thoughts reverted to the scene in the rose garden, and he went over and over all its details. He remembered Madame Arnault's agitation when the window opened and the girl appeared; her evident discomfiture—of which at the time he had taken no heed, but which came back to him vividly enough now—at his proposal to visit the ballroom; her startled recognition of the ring on his finger; her slurring suggestion of visitors from Grandchamp; the look of terror on Marcelite's face. What did it all mean? Félice, he was sure, knew nothing. But here, in an unused portion of the house, which even the members of the family had never visited, a young and beautiful girl was shut up a prisoner, condemned perhaps to a life-long captivity.

"Good God!" He leaped to his feet at the thought. He would go and thunder at Madame Arnault's door, and demand an explanation. But no; not yet. He calmed himself with an effort. By too great haste he might injure her. "Insane?" He laughed aloud at the idea of madness in connection with that exquisite creature.

It dawned upon him, as he paced restlessly back and forth, that although his father had been here more than once in his youth and manhood, he had never heard him speak of La Glorieuse nor of Félix Arnault, whose letters he had read after his father's death a few months ago—those old letters whose affectionate warmth indeed had determined him, in the first desolation of his loss, to seek the family which seemed to have been so bound to his own. Morose and taciturn as his father had been, surely he would sometimes have spoken of his old friend if—Worn out at last with conjecture; beaten back, bruised and breathless, from an enigma which he could not solve; exhausted by listening with strained attention for some movement in the next room, he threw himself on his bed, dressed as he was, and fell into a heavy sleep, which lasted far into the forenoon of the next day.

When he came out (walking like one in a dream), he found a gay party assembled on the lawn in front of the house. Suzette Beauvais and her guests, a bevy of girls, had come from Grandchamp. They had been joined, as they rowed down the bayou, by the young people from the plantation houses on the way. Half a dozen boats, their long paddles laid across the seats, were added to the home fleet at the landing. Their stalwart black rowers were basking in the sun on the levee, or lounging about the quarter. At the moment of his appearance, Suzette herself was indignantly disclaiming any complicity in the jest of the day before.

"Myself, I was making o'ange-flower conserve," she declared; "an' anyhow I wouldn't go in that ballroom unless madame send me."

"But who was it, then?" insisted Félice.

Mademoiselle Beauvais spread out her fat little hands and lifted her shoulders. "Mo pas connais,"[5] she laughed, dropping into patois.

Madame Arnault here interposed. It was but the foolish conceit of some teasing neighbor, she said, and not worth further discussion. Keith's blood boiled in his veins at this calm dismissal of the subject, but he gave no sign. He saw her glance warily at himself from time to time.

"I will sift the matter to the bottom," he thought, "and I will force her to confess the truth, whatever it may be, before the world."

The noisy chatter and meaningless laughter around him jarred upon his nerves; he longed to be alone with his thoughts; and presently, pleading a headache—indeed his temples throbbed almost to bursting, and his eyes were hot and dry—he quitted the lawn, seeing but not noting until long afterwards, when they smote his memory like a two-edged knife, the pain in Félice's uplifted eyes, and the little sorrowful quiver of her mouth. He strolled around the corner of the house to his apartment. The blinds of the arched window were drawn, and a hazy twilight was diffused about the hall, though it was mid-afternoon outside. As he entered, closing the door behind him, the woman at that moment uppermost in his thoughts came down the dusky silence from the further end of the hall. She turned her inscrutable eyes upon him in passing, and flitted noiselessly and with languid grace up the stairway, the faint swish of her gown vanishing with her. He hesitated a moment, overpowered by conflicting emotion; then he sprang recklessly after her.

He pushed open the ballroom door, reaching his arms out blindly before him. Once more the great dust-covered room was empty. He strained his eyes helplessly into the obscurity. A chill reaction passed over him; he felt himself on the verge of a swoon. He did not this time even try to discover the secret door or exit by which she had disappeared; he looked, with a hopeless sense of discouragement, at the barred windows, and turned to leave the room. As he did so, he saw a handkerchief lying on the threshold of the door. He picked it up eagerly, and pressed it to his lips. A peculiar delicate perfume which

[5] French patois: "I don't know."

thrilled his senses lurked in its gossamer folds. As he was about thrusting it into his breast-pocket, he noticed in one corner a small blood-stain fresh and wet. He had then bitten his lip in his excitement.

"I need no further proof," he said aloud, and his own voice startled him, echoing down the long hall. "She is beyond all question a prisoner in this detached building, which has mysterious exits and entrances. She has been forced to promise that she will not go outside of its walls, or she is afraid to do so. I will bring home this monstrous crime. I will release this lovely young woman who dares not speak, yet so plainly appeals to me." Already he saw in fancy her starlike eyes raised to his in mute gratitude, her white hand laid confidingly on his arm.

The party of visitors remained at La Glorieuse overnight. The negro fiddlers came in, and there was dancing in the old-fashioned double parlors and on the moonlit galleries. Félice was unnaturally gay. Keith looked on gloomily, taking no part in the amusement.

"Il est bien bête,[6] your yellow-haired Marylander," whispered Suzette Beauvais to her friend.

He went early to his room, but he watched in vain for some sign from his beautiful neighbor. He grew sick with apprehension. Had Madame Arnault—But no; she would not dare. "I will wait one more day," he finally decided; "and then—"

The next morning, after a late breakfast, some one proposed impromptu charades and tableaux. Madame Arnault good-naturedly sent for the keys to the tall presses built into the walls, which contained the accumulated trash and treasure of several generations. Mounted on a stepladder, Robert Beauvais explored the recesses, and threw down to the laughing crowd embroidered shawls and scarfs yellow with age, soft muslins of antique pattern, stiff big-flowered brocades, scraps of gauze ribbon, gossamer laces. On one topmost shelf he came upon a small wooden box inlaid with mother-of-pearl. Félice reached up for it, and, moved by some undefined impulse, Richard came and stood by her side while she opened it. A perfume which he recognized arose from it as she lifted a fold of tissue-paper. Some strings of Oriental pearls of extraordinary size, and perfect in shape and color, were coiled underneath, with a coral necklace, whose pendant of amber had broken off and rolled into a corner. With them—he hardly restrained an exclamation, and his hand involuntarily sought his breast-pocket at sight of the handkerchief with a drop of fresh blood in one corner! Félice trembled without knowing why. Madame Arnault, who had just entered the room, took the box from her quietly, and closed the lid with a snap. The girl, accustomed to implicit obedience, asked no questions; the others, engaged in turning over the old-time finery, had paid no attention.

"Does she think to disarm me by such puerile tricks?" he thought, turning a look of angry warning on the old madame; and in the steady gaze which she fixed on him he read a haughty defiance.

He forced himself to enter into the sports of the day, and he walked down to the boat-landing a little before sunset to see the guests depart. As the line of boats swept away, the black rowers dipping their oars lightly in the placid waves, he turned with a

6 French: "He is a complete fool."

sense of release, leaving Madame Arnault and Félice still at the landing, and went down the levee road towards St. Joseph's. The field gang, whose red, blue, and brown blouses splotched the squares of cane with color, was preparing to quit work; loud laughter and noisy jests rang out on the air; high-wheeled plantation wagons creaked along the lanes; negro children, with dip-nets and fishing-poles over their shoulders, ran homeward along the levee, the dogs at their heels barking joyously; a schooner, with white sail outspread, was stealing like a fairy bark around a distant bend of the bayou; the silvery waters were turning to gold under a sunset sky.

It was twilight when he struck across the plantation, and came around by the edge of the swamp to the clump of trees in a corner of the home field which he had often remarked from his window. As he approached, he saw a woman come out of the dense shadow, as if intending to meet him, and then draw back again. His heart throbbed painfully, but he walked steadily forward. It was only Félice. Only Félice! She was sitting on a flat tombstone. The little spot was the Raymonde-Arnault family burying-ground. There were many marble headstones and shafts, and two broad low tombs side by side and a little apart from the others. A tangle of rose-briers covered the sunken graves, a rank growth of grass choked the narrow paths, the little gate interlaced and overhung with honeysuckle sagged away from its posts, the fence itself had lost a picket here and there, and weeds flaunted boldly in the gaps. The girl looked wan and ghostly in the lonely dusk.

"This is my father's grave, and my mother is here," she said, abruptly, as he came up and stood beside her. Her head was drooped upon her breast, and he saw that she had been weeping. "See," she went on, drawing her finger along the mildewed lettering: " 'Félix Marie-Joseph Arnault ... âgé de trente-quatre ans' ... 'Hélène Pallacier, épouse de Félix Arnault ... décédée à l'âge de dix-neuf ans.' Nineteen years old," she repeated, slowly. "My mother was one year younger than I am when she died—my beautiful mother!"

Her voice sounded like a far-away murmur in his ears. He looked at her, vaguely conscious that she was suffering. But he did not speak, and after a little she got up and went away. Her dress, which brushed him in passing, was wet with dew. He watched her slight figure, moving like a spirit along the lane, until a turn in the hedge hid her from sight. Then he turned again towards the swamp, and resumed his restless walk.

Some hours later he crossed the rose garden. The moon was under a cloud; the trunks of the crêpe-myrtles were like pale spectres in the uncertain light. The night wind blew in chill and moist from the swamp. The house was dark and quiet, but he heard the blind of an upper window turned stealthily as he stepped into the latticed arcade.

"The old madame is watching me—and her," he said to himself.

His agitation had now become supreme. The faint familiar perfume that stole about his room filled him with a kind of frenzy. Was this the chivalric devotion of which he had so boasted? this the desire to protect a young and defenceless woman? He no longer dared question himself. He seemed to feel her warm breath against his cheeks. He threw up his arms with a gesture of despair. A sigh stirred the deathlike stillness. At last! She was there, just within his doorway; the pale glimmer of the veiled moon fell upon her. Her trailing laces wrapped her about like a silver mist; her arms were folded across her bosom; her eyes—he dared not interpret the meaning which he read in those wonderful eyes. She turned slowly and went down the hall. He followed her, reeling like a drunkard. His feet seemed clogged, the blood ran thick in his veins, a strange roaring was in his ears. His hot eyes strained after her as she vanished, just beyond his touch, into the room next his own. He threw himself against the closed door in a transport of rage. It yielded suddenly, as if opened from within. A full blaze of light struck his eyes, blinding him for an instant; then he saw her. A huge four-posted bed with silken hangings occupied a recess in the room. Across its foot a low couch was drawn. She had thrown herself there. Her head was pillowed on crimson gold-embroidered cushions; her diaphanous draperies, billowing foamlike over her, half concealed, half revealed her lovely form; her hair waved away from her brows, and spread like a shower of gold over the cushions. One bare arm hung to the floor; something jewel-like gleamed in the half-closed hand; the other lay across her forehead, and from beneath it her eyes were fixed upon him. He sprang forward with a cry …

At first he could remember nothing. The windows were open; the heavy curtains which shaded them moved lazily in the breeze; a shaft of sunlight that came in between them fell upon the polished surface of the marble mantel. He examined with languid curiosity some trifles that stood there—a pair of Dresden figures, a blue Sèvres vase of graceful shape, a bronze clock with gilded rose-wreathed Cupids; and then raised his eyes to the two portraits which hung above. One of these was familiar enough—the dark melancholy face of Félix Arnault, whose portrait by different hands and at different periods of his life hung in nearly every room of La Glorieuse. The blood surged into his face and receded again at sight of the other. Oh, so strangely like! The yellow hair, the slumberous eyes, the full throat clasped about with a single strand of coral. Yes, it was she! He lifted himself on his elbow. He was in bed. Surely this was the room into which she had drawn him with her eyes. Did he sink on the threshold, all his senses swooning into delicious faith? Or had he, indeed, in that last moment thrown himself on his knees by her couch? He could not remember, and he sank back with a sigh.

Instantly Madame Arnault was bending over him. Her cool hands were on his forehead. "Dieu merci!" she exclaimed, "thou art thyself once more, mon fils."

He seized her hand imperiously. "Tell me, madame," he demanded—"tell me, for the love of God! What is she? Who is she? Why have you shut her away in this deserted place? Why—"

She was looking down at him with an expression half of pity, half of pain.

"Forgive me," he faltered, involuntarily, all his darker suspicions somehow vanishing; "but—oh, tell me!"

"Calm thyself, Richard," she said, soothingly, seating herself on the side of the bed, and stroking his hand gently. Too agitated to speak, he continued to gaze at her with imploring eyes. "Yes, yes, I will relate the whole story," she added, hastily, for he was panting and struggling for speech. "I heard you fall last night," she continued, relapsing for greater ease into French; "for I was full of anxiety about you, and I lingered long at my window watching for you. I came at once with Marcelite, and found you lying insensible across the threshold of this room. We lifted you to the bed, and bled you after the old fashion, and then I gave you a tisane[7] of my own making, which threw you into a quiet sleep. I have watched beside you until your waking. Now you are but a little weak from fasting and excitement, and when you have rested and eaten—"

"No," he pleaded; "now, at once!"

"Very well," she said, simply. She was silent a moment, as if arranging her thoughts. "Your grandfather, a Richard Keith like yourself," she began, "was a college-mate and friend of my brother, Henri Raymonde, and accompanied him to La Glorieuse during one of their vacations. I was already betrothed to Monsieur Arnault, but I—No matter! I never saw Richard Keith afterwards. But years later he sent your father, who also bore his name, to visit me here. My son, Félix, was but a year or so younger than his boy, and the two lads became at once warm friends. They went abroad, and pursued their studies side by side, like brothers. They came home together, and when Richard's father died, Félix spent nearly a year with him on his Maryland plantation. They exchanged, when apart, almost daily letters. Richard's marriage, which occurred soon after they left college, strengthened rather than weakened this extraordinary bond between them. Then came on the war. They were in the same command, and hardly lost sight of each other during their four years of service.

"When the war was ended, your father went back to his estates. Félix turned his face homeward, but drifted by some strange chance down to Florida, where he met her"—she glanced at the portrait over the mantel. "Hélène Pallacier was Greek by descent, her family having been among those brought over some time during the last century as colonists to Florida from the Greek islands. He married her, barely delaying his marriage long enough to write me that he was bringing home a bride. She was young, hardly more than a child, indeed, and marvellously beautiful"—Keith moved impatiently; he found these family details tedious and uninteresting—"a radiant soulless creature, whose only law was her own selfish enjoyment, and whose coming brought pain and bitterness to La Glorieuse. These were her rooms. She chose them because of the rose garden, for she had a sensuous and passionate love of nature. She used to lie for hours on the grass there, with her arms flung over her head, gazing dreamily on the fluttering leaves above her. The pearls—which she always wore—some coral ornaments, and a handful of amber beads were her only dower, but her caprices were the insolent and extravagant caprices of a queen. Félix, who adored her, gratified them at whatever expense; and I think at first she had a careless sort of regard for him. But she hated the little Félice, whose coming gave her the first pang of physical pain she had ever known. She never offered the child a caress. She sometimes looked at her with a suppressed rage which filled me with terror and anxiety.

"When Félice was a little more than a year old, your father came to La Glorieuse to pay us a long-promised visit. His wife had died some months before, and you, a child of six or seven years, were left in charge of relatives in Maryland. Richard was in the full vigor of manhood, broad-shouldered, tall, blue-eyed, and blond-haired, like his father and like you. From the moment of their first meeting Hélène exerted all the power of her fascination to draw him to her. Never had she been so whimsical, so imperious, so

[7] French: Medicinal tea.

bewitching! Loyal to his friend, faithful to his own high sense of honor, he struggled against a growing weakness, and finally fled. I will never forget the night he went away. A ball had been planned by Félix in honor of his friend. The ballroom was decorated under his own supervision. The house was filled with guests from adjoining parishes; everybody, young and old, came from the plantations around. Hélène was dazzling that night. The light of triumph in her cheeks; her eyes shone with a softness which I had never seen in them before. I watched her walking up and down the room with Richard, or floating with him in the dance. They were like a pair of radiant godlike visitants from another world. My heart ached for them in spite of my indignation and apprehension; for light whispers were beginning to circulate, and I saw more than one meaning smile directed at them. Félix, who was truth itself, was gayly unconscious.

"Towards midnight I heard far up the bayou the shrill whistle of the little packet which passed up and down then, as now, twice a week; and presently she swung up to our landing. Richard was standing with Hélène by the fireplace. They had been talking for some time in low earnest tones. A sudden look of determination came into his eyes. I saw him draw from his finger a ring which she had one day playfully bade him wear, and offer it to her. His face was white and strained; hers wore a look which I could not fathom. He quitted her side abruptly, and walked rapidly across the room, threading his way among the dancers, and disappeared in the press about the door. A few moments later a note was handed me. I heard the boat steam away from the landing as I read it. It was a hurried line from Richard. He said that he had been called away on urgent business, and he begged me to make his adieux to Madame Arnault and Félix. Félix was worried and perplexed by the sudden departure of his guest. Hélène said not a word, but very soon I saw her slipping down the stair, and I knew that she had gone to her room. Her absence was not remarked, for the ball was at its height. It was almost daylight when the last dance was concluded, and the guests who were staying in the house had retired to their rooms.

"Félix, having seen to the comfort of all, went at last to join his wife. He burst into my room a second later almost crazed with horror and grief. I followed him to this room. She was lying on a couch at the foot of the bed. One arm was thrown across her forehead, the other hung to the floor, and in her hand she held a tiny silver bottle with a jewelled stopper. A handkerchief, with a single drop of blood upon it, was lying on her bosom. A faint curious odor exhaled from her lips and hung about the room, but the poison had left no other trace.

"No one save ourselves and Marcelite ever knew the truth. She had danced too much at the ball that night, and she had died suddenly of heart-disease. We buried her out yonder in the old Raymonde-Arnault burying-ground. I do not know what the letter contained which Félix wrote to Richard. He never uttered his name afterwards. The ballroom, the whole wing, in truth, was at once closed. Everything was left exactly as it was on that fatal night. A few years ago, the house being unexpectedly full, I opened the room in which you have been staying, and it has been used from time to time as a guest-room since. My son lived some years, prematurely old, heart-broken, and desolate. He died with her name on his lips."

Madame Arnault stopped.

A suffocating sensation was creeping over her listener. Only in the past few moments had the signification of the story begun to dawn upon him. "Do you mean," he gasped, "that the girl whom I—that she is—was—"

"Hélène, the dead wife of Félix Arnault," she replied, gravely. "Her restless spirit has walked here before. I have sometimes heard her tantalizing laugh echo through the house, but no one had ever seen her until you came—so like the Richard Keith she loved!"

"When I read your letter," she went on, after a short silence, "which told me that you wished to come to those friends to whom your father had been so dear, all the past arose before me, and I felt that I ought to forbid your coming. But I remembered how Félix and Richard had loved each other before she came between them. I thought of the other Richard Keith whom I—I loved once; and I dreamed of a union at last between the families. I hoped, Richard, that you and Félice—"

But Richard was no longer listening. He wished to believe the whole fantastic story an invention of the keen-eyed old madame herself. Yet something within him confessed to its truth. A tumultuous storm of baffled desire, of impotent anger, swept over him. The ring he wore burned into his flesh. But he had no thought of removing it—the ring which had once belonged to the beautiful golden-haired woman who had come back from the grave to woo him to her!

He turned his face away and groaned.

Her eyes hardened. She rose stiffly. "I will send a servant with your breakfast," she said, with her hand on the door. "The down boat will pass La Glorieuse this afternoon. You will perhaps wish to take advantage of it."

He started. He had not thought of going—of leaving her—her! He looked at the portrait on the wall and laughed bitterly.

Madame Arnault accompanied him with ceremonious politeness to the front steps that afternoon.

"Mademoiselle Félice?" he murmured, inquiringly, glancing back at the windows of the sitting-room.

"Mademoiselle Arnault is occupied," she coldly returned. "I will convey to her your farewell."

He looked back as the boat chugged away. Peaceful shadows enwrapped the house and overspread the lawn. A single window in the wing gleamed like a balefire[8] in the rays of the setting sun.

The years that followed were years of restless wandering for Richard Keith. He visited his estate but rarely. He went abroad and returned, hardly having set foot to land; he buried himself in the fastnesses of the Rockies; he made a long, aimless sea-voyage. Her image accompanied him everywhere. Between him and all he saw hovered her faultless face; her red mouth smiled at him; her white arms enticed him. His own face became worn and his step listless. He grew silent and gloomy. "He is madder than the old colonel, his father, was," his friends said, shrugging their shoulders.

---

8 A bonfire or signal fire; but also, a funeral pyre.

One day, more than three years after his visit to La Glorieuse, he found himself on a deserted part of the Florida seacoast. It was late in November, but the sky was soft and the air warm and balmy. He bared his head as he paced moodily to and fro on the silent beach. The waves rolled languidly to his feet and receded, leaving scattered half-wreaths of opalescent foam on the snowy sands. The wind that fanned his face was filled with the spicy odors of the sea. Seized by a capricious impulse, he threw off his clothes and dashed into the surf. The undulating billows closed around him; a singular lassitude passed into his limbs as he swam; he felt himself slowly sinking, as if drawn downward by an invisible hand. He opened his eyes. The waves lapped musically above his head; a tawny glory was all about him, a luminous expanse in which he saw strangely formed creatures moving, darting, rising, falling, coiling, uncoiling.

"You was jes on de eedge er drowndin', Mars Dick," said Wiley, his black body-servant, spreading his own clothes on the porch of the little fishing-hut to dry. "In de name o' Gawd whar mek you wanter go in swimmin' dis time o' de yea', anyhow? Ef I hadn' er splunge in an' fotch you out, dey'd er been mo'nin' yander at de plantation, sho!"

His master laughed lazily. "You are right, Wiley," he said; "and you are going to smoke the best tobacco in Maryland as long as you live." He felt buoyant. Youth and elasticity seemed to have come back to him at a bound. He stretched himself on the rough bench, and watched the blue rings of smoke curl lightly away from his cigar. Gradually he was aware of a pair of wistful eyes shining down on him. His heart leaped. They were the eyes of Félice Arnault! "My God, have I been mad!" he muttered. His eyes sought his hand. The ring, from which he had never been parted, was gone. It had been torn from his finger in his wrestle with the sea. "Get my traps together at once, Wiley," he said. "We are going to La Glorieuse."

"Now you talkin', Mars Dick," assented Wiley, cheerfully.

It was night when he reached the city. First of all, he made inquiries concerning the little packet. He was right; the Assumption would leave the next afternoon at five o'clock for Bayou L'Eperon. He went to the same hotel at which he had stopped before when on his way to La Glorieuse. The next morning, too joyous to sleep, he rose early, and went out into the street. A gray uncertain dawn was just struggling into the sky. A few people on their way to market or to early mass were passing along the narrow banquettes; sleepy-eyed women were unbarring the shutters of their tiny shops; high-wheeled milk-carts were rattling over the granite pavements; in the vine-hung court-yards, visible here and there through iron grilles, parrots were scolding on their perches; children pattered up and down the long, arched corridors; the prolonged cry of an early clothes-pole man echoed, like the note of a winding horn, through the close alleys. Keith sauntered carelessly along.

"In so many hours," he kept repeating to himself, "I shall be on my way to La Glorieuse. The boat will swing into the home landing; the negroes will swarm across the gang-plank, laughing and shouting; Madame Arnault and Félice will come out on the gallery and look, shading their eyes with their hands. Oh, I know quite well that the old madame will greet me coldly at first. Her eyes are like steel when she is angry. But when she knows that I am once more a sane man—And Félice, what if she—But no! Félice is not the kind of woman who loves more than once; and she did love me, God bless her! unworthy as I was."

A carriage, driven rapidly, passed him; his eyes followed it idly, until it turned far away into a side street. He strayed on to the market, where he seated himself on a high stool in L'Appel du Matin coffee stall. But a vague, teasing remembrance was beginning to stir in his brain. The turbaned woman on the front seat of the carriage that had rolled past him yonder, where had he seen that dark, grave, wrinkled face, with the great hoops of gold against either cheek? Marcelite! He left the stall and retraced his steps, quickening his pace almost to a run as he went. Félice herself, then, might be in the city. He hurried to the street into which the carriage had turned, and glanced down between the rows of white-eaved cottages with green doors and batten shutters. It had stopped several squares away; there seemed to be a number of people gathered about it. "I will at least satisfy myself," he thought.

As he came up, a bell in a little cross-crowned tower began to ring slowly. The carriage stood in front of a low red brick house, set directly on the street; a silent crowd pressed about the entrance. There was a hush within. He pushed his way along the banquette to the steps. A young nun, in a brown serge robe, kept guard at the door. She wore a wreath of white artificial roses above her long coarse veil. Something in his face appealed to her, and she found a place for him in the little convent chapel.

Madame Arnault, supported by Marcelite, was kneeling in front of the altar, which blazed with candles. She had grown frightfully old and frail. Her face was set, and her eyes were fixed with a rigid stare on the priest who was saying mass. Marcelite's dark cheeks were streaming with tears. The chapel, which wore a gala air with its lights and flowers, was filled with people. On the left of the altar, a bishop, in gorgeous robes, was sitting, attended by priests and acolytes; on the right, the wooden panel behind an iron grating had been removed, and beyond, in the nun's choir, the black-robed sisters of the order were gathered. Heavy veils shrouded their faces and fell to their feet. They held in their hands tall wax-candles, whose yellow flames burned steadily in the semi-darkness. Five or six young girls knelt, motionless as statues, in their midst. They also carried tapers, and their rapt faces were turned towards the unseen altar within, of which the outer one is but the visible token. Their eyelids were downcast. Their white veils were thrown back from their calm foreheads, and floated like wings from their shoulders.

He felt no surprise when he saw Félice among them. He seemed to have foreknown always that he should find her thus on the edge of another and mysterious world into which he could not follow her.

Her skin had lost a little of its warm rich tint; the soft rings of hair were drawn away under her veil; her hands were thin, and as waxen as the taper she held. An unearthly beauty glorified her pale face.

"Is it forever too late?" he asked himself in agony, covering his face with his hands. When he looked again the white veil on her head had been replaced by the sombre one of the order. "If I could but speak to her!" he thought; "if she would but once lift her eyes to mine, she would come to me even now!"

Félice! Did the name break from his lips in a hoarse cry that echoed through the hushed chapel, and silenced the voice of the priest? He never knew. But a faint color

swept into her cheeks. Her eyelids trembled. In a flash the rose-garden at La Glorieuse was before him; he saw the turquoise sky, and heard the mellow chorus of the field gang; the smell of damask-roses was in the air; her little hand was in his … he saw her coming swiftly towards him across the dusk of the old ballroom; her limpid innocent eyes were smiling into his own … she was standing on the grassy lawn; the shadows of the leaves flickered over her white gown …

At last the quivering eyelids were lifted. She turned her head slowly, and looked steadily at him. He held his breath. A cart rumbled along the cobble-stones outside; the puny wail of a child sounded across the stillness; a handful of rose leaves from a vase at the foot of the altar dropped on the hem of Madame Arnault's dress. It might have been the gaze of an angel in a world where there is no marrying nor giving in marriage, so pure was it, so passionless, so free of anything like earthly desire.

As she turned her face again towards the altar the bell in the tower above ceased tolling; a triumphant chorus leaped into the air borne aloft by joyous organ tones. The first rays of the morning sun streamed in through the small windows. Then light penetrated into the nuns' choir, and enveloped like a mantle of gold Sister Mary of the Cross, who in the world had been Félicité Arnault

II

BACKGROUND

Chapter Thirteen

J. HECTOR ST. JOHN DE CRÈVECOEUR (1735–1813)

Crèvecoeur (born Michel-Guillaume de Crèvecoeur) was a French soldier who became a naturalized citizen of New York. The early chapters of his *Letters from an American Farmer* (1782) describe an idealized life in rural New York in the years before the Revolution. He celebrates an early vision of the American Dream, in which European peoples are blended to create a new and perfect democracy.

But on a visit to South Carolina, Crèvecoeur takes a walk on a pleasant sunny day, enters a wood and encounters something that shatters his vision of simple republican virtue. What he finds in the woods forces him to acknowledge that "we certainly are not that class of beings which we vainly think ourselves to be." This is a true moment of the Gothic uncanny.

Text: J. Hector St. John de Crèvecoeur, *Letters from an American Farmer*, reprinted from the original edition (New York: Duffield, 1904). A small number of obvious misprints have been silently corrected and present-day conventions for quotation marks applied.

LETTER IX

Description of Charles-Town; Thoughts on Slavery; on Physical Evil; a Melancholy Scene

CHARLES-TOWN is, in the north, what Lima is in the south; both are Capitals of the richest provinces of their respective hemispheres: you may therefore conjecture, that both cities must exhibit the appearances necessarily resulting from riches. Peru abounding in gold, Lima is filled with inhabitants who enjoy all those gradations of pleasure, refinement, and luxury, which proceed from wealth. Carolina produces commodities, more valuable perhaps than gold, because they are gained by greater industry; it exhibits also on our northern stage, a display of riches and luxury, inferior indeed to the former, but far superior to what are to be seen in our northern towns. Its situation is admirable, being built at the confluence of two large rivers, which receive in their course a great number of inferior streams; all navigable in the spring, for flat boats. Here the produce of this extensive territory concentres;[1] here therefore is the seat of the most valuable exportation; their wharfs, their docks, their magazines, are extremely convenient to facilitate this great commercial business. The inhabitants are the gayest in America; it

[1] Comes together.

is called the centre of our beau monde,[2] and is always filled with the richest planters of the province, who resort hither in quest of health and pleasure. Here are always to be seen a great number of valetudinarians from the West-Indies, seeking for the renovation of health, exhausted by the debilitating nature of their sun, air, and modes of living. Many of these West-Indians have I seen, at thirty, loaded with the infirmities of old age; for nothing is more common in those countries of wealth, than for persons to lose the abilities of enjoying the comforts of life, at a time when we northern men just begin to taste the fruits of our labour and prudence. The round of pleasure, and the expenses of those citizens' tables, are much superior to what you would imagine: indeed the growth of this town and province has been astonishingly rapid. It is pity that the narrowness of the neck on which it stands prevents it from increasing; and which is the reason why houses are so dear. The heat of the climate, which is sometimes very great in the interior parts of the country, is always temperate in Charles-Town; though sometimes when they have no sea breezes the sun is too powerful. The climate renders excesses of all kinds very dangerous, particularly those of the table; and yet, insensible or fearless of danger, they live on, and enjoy a short and a merry life: the rays of their sun seem to urge them irresistibly to dissipation and pleasure: on the contrary, the women, from being abstemious, reach to a longer period of life, and seldom die without having had several husbands. An European at his first arrival must be greatly surprised when he sees the elegance of their houses, their sumptuous furniture, as well as the magnificence of their tables. Can he imagine himself in a country, the establishment of which is so recent?

The three principal classes of inhabitants are, lawyers, planters, and merchants; this is the province which has afforded to the first the richest spoils, for nothing can exceed their wealth, their power, and their influence. They have reached the *ne plus ultra*[3] of worldly felicity; no plantation is secured, no title is good, no will is valid, but what they dictate, regulate, and approve. The whole mass of provincial property is become tributary to this society; which, far above priests and bishops, disdain to be satisfied with the poor Mosaical portion of the tenth.[4] I appeal to the many inhabitants, who, while contending perhaps for their right to a few hundred acres, have lost by the mazes of the law their whole patrimony. These men are more properly law givers than interpreters of the law; and have united here, as well as in most other provinces, the skill and dexterity of the scribe with the power and ambition of the prince: who can tell where this may lead in a future day? The nature of our laws, and the spirit of freedom, which often tends to make us litigious, must necessarily throw the greatest part of the property of the colonies into the hands of these gentlemen. In another century, the law will possess in the north, what now the church possesses in Peru and Mexico.

While all is joy, festivity, and happiness in Charles-Town, would you imagine that scenes of misery overspread in the country? Their ears by habit are become deaf, their hearts are hardened; they neither see, hear, nor feel for the woes of their poor slaves, from

---

2 French: "beautiful world," here meaning fashionable society.

3 Latin: Literally, "No more beyond," here meaning the farthest or utmost point.

4 That is, the tithe, a tenth of one's income given to charity or the church.

whose painful labours all their wealth proceeds. Here the horrors of slavery, the hardship of incessant toils, are unseen; and no one thinks with compassion of those showers of sweat and of tears which from the bodies of Africans daily drop, and moisten the ground they till. The cracks of the whip urging these miserable beings to excessive labour, are far too distant from the gay Capital to be heard. The chosen race eat, drink, and live happy, while the unfortunate one grubs up the ground, raises indigo, or husks the rice; exposed to a sun full as scorching as their native one; without the support of good food, without the cordials of any cheering liquor. This great contrast has often afforded me subjects of the most conflicting meditation. On the one side, behold a people enjoying all that life affords most bewitching and pleasurable, without labour, without fatigue, hardly subjected to the trouble of wishing. With gold, dug from Peruvian mountains, they order vessels to the coasts of Guinea; by virtue of that gold, wars, murders, and devastations are committed in some harmless, peaceable African neighbourhood, where dwelt innocent people, who even knew not but that all men were black. The daughter torn from her weeping mother, the child from the wretched parents, the wife from the loving husband; whole families swept away and brought through storms and tempests to this rich metropolis! There, arranged like horses at a fair, they are branded like cattle, and then driven to toil, to starve, and to languish for a few years on the different plantations of these citizens. And for whom must they work? For persons they know not, and who have no other power over them than that of violence, no other right than what this accursed metal has given them! Strange order of things! Oh, Nature, where art thou?—Are not these blacks thy children as well as we? On the other side, nothing is to be seen but the most diffusive misery and wretchedness, unrelieved even in thought or wish! Day after day they drudge on without any prospect of ever reaping for themselves; they are obliged to devote their lives, their limbs, their will, and every vital exertion to swell the wealth of masters; who look not upon them with half the kindness and affection with which they consider their dogs and horses. Kindness and affection are not the portion of those who till the earth, who carry the burdens, who convert the logs into useful boards. This reward, simple and natural as one would conceive it, would border on humanity; and planters must have none of it!

If negroes are permitted to become fathers, this fatal indulgence only tends to increase their misery: the poor companions of their scanty pleasures are likewise the companions of their labours; and when at some critical seasons they could wish to see them relieved, with tears in their eyes they behold them perhaps doubly oppressed, obliged to bear the burden of nature—a fatal present—as well as that of unabated tasks. How many have I seen cursing the irresistible propensity, and regretting, that by having tasted of those harmless joys, they had become the authors of double misery to their wives. Like their masters, they are not permitted to partake of those ineffable sensations with which nature inspires the hearts of fathers and mothers; they must repel them all, and become callous and passive. This unnatural state often occasions the most acute, the most pungent of their afflictions; they have no time, like us, tenderly to rear their helpless offspring, to nurse them on their knees, to enjoy the delight of being parents. Their paternal fondness is embittered by considering, that if their children live, they must live to be slaves like themselves; no time is allowed them to exercise their pious office, the mothers must fasten them on their backs, and, with this double load, follow their husbands in the fields, where they too often hear no other sound than that of the voice or whip of the task-master, and the cries of their infants, broiling in the sun. These unfortunate creatures cry and weep like their parents, without a possibility of relief; the very instinct of the brute, so laudable, so irresistible, runs counter here to their master's interest; and to that god, all the laws of nature must give way. Thus planters get rich; so raw, so unexperienced am I in this mode of life, that were I to be possessed of a plantation, and my slaves treated as in general they are here, never could I rest in peace; my sleep would be perpetually disturbed by a retrospect of the frauds committed in Africa, in order to entrap them; frauds surpassing in enormity everything which a common mind can possibly conceive. I should be thinking of the barbarous treatment they meet with on ship-board; of their anguish, of the despair necessarily inspired by their situation, when torn from their friends and relations; when delivered into the hands of a people differently coloured, whom they cannot understand; carried in a strange machine over an ever agitated element, which they had never seen before; and finally delivered over to the severities of the whippers, and the excessive labours of the field. Can it be possible that the force of custom should ever make me deaf to all these reflections, and as insensible to the injustice of that trade, and to their miseries, as the rich inhabitants of this town seem to be? What then is man; this being who boasts so much of the excellence and dignity of his nature, among that variety of unscrutable mysteries, of unsolvable problems, with which he is surrounded? The reason why man has been thus created, is not the least astonishing! It is said, I know that they are much happier here than in the West-Indies; because land being cheaper upon this continent than in those islands, the fields allowed them to raise their subsistence from, are in general more extensive. The only possible chance of any alleviation depends on the humour of the planters, who, bred in the midst of slaves, learn from the example of their parents to despise them; and seldom conceive either from religion or philosophy, any ideas that tend to make their fate less calamitous; except some strong native tenderness of heart, some rays of philanthropy, overcome the obduracy contracted by habit.

I have not resided here long enough to become insensible of pain for the objects which I every day behold. In the choice of my friends and acquaintance, I always endeavour to find out those whose dispositions are somewhat congenial with my own. We have slaves likewise in our northern provinces; I hope the time draws near when they will be all emancipated: but how different their lot, how different their situation, in every possible respect! They enjoy as much liberty as their masters, they are as well clad, and as well fed; in health and sickness they are tenderly taken care of; they live under the same roof, and are, truly speaking, a part of our families. Many of them are taught to read and write, and are well instructed in the principles of religion; they are the companions of our labours, and treated as such; they enjoy many perquisites, many established holidays, and are not obliged to work more than white people. They marry where inclination leads them; visit their wives every week; are as decently clad as the common people; they are indulged in educating, cherishing, and chastising their children, who are taught subordination to them as to their lawful parents: in short, they participate in many of the benefits of our society, without being obliged to bear any of its burdens. They are fat, healthy, and hearty, and far from repining at their fate; they think themselves happier than many of the lower class whites: they share with their masters the wheat and meat provision they help to raise; many of those whom the good Quakers have emancipated have received that great benefit with tears of regret, and have never quitted, though free, their former masters and benefactors.

But is it really true, as I have heard it asserted here, that those blacks are incapable of feeling the spurs of emulation, and the cheerful sound of encouragement? By no means; there are a thousand proofs existing of their gratitude and fidelity: those hearts in which such noble dispositions can grow, are then like ours, they are susceptible of every generous sentiment, of every useful motive of action; they are capable of receiving lights, of imbibing ideas that would greatly alleviate the weight of their miseries. But what methods have in general been made use of to obtain so desirable an end? None; the day in which they arrive and are sold, is the first of their labours; labours, which from that hour admit of no respite; for though indulged by law with relaxation on Sundays, they are obliged to employ that time which is intended for rest, to till their little plantations. What can be expected from wretches in such circumstances? Forced from their native country, cruelly treated when on board, and not less so on the plantations to which they are driven; is there anything in this treatment but what must kindle all the passions, sow the seeds of inveterate resentment, and nourish a wish of perpetual revenge? They are left to the irresistible effects of those strong and natural propensities; the blows they receive, are they conducive to extinguish them, or to win their affections? They are neither soothed by the hopes that their slavery will ever terminate but with their lives; or yet encouraged by the goodness of their food, or the mildness of their treatment. The very hopes held out to mankind by religion, that consolatory system, so useful to the miserable, are never presented to them; neither moral nor physical means are made use of to soften their chains; they are left in their original and untutored state; that very state wherein the natural propensities of revenge and warm passions are so soon kindled. Cheered by no one single motive that can impel the will, or excite their efforts; nothing but terrors and punishments are presented to them; death is denounced if they run away; horrid delaceration[5] if they speak with their native freedom; perpetually awed by the terrible cracks of whips, or by the fear of capital punishments, while even those punishments often fail of their purpose.

A clergyman settled a few years ago at George-Town, and feeling as I do now, warmly recommended to the planters, from the pulpit, a relaxation of severity; he introduced the benignity of Christianity, and pathetically made use of the admirable precepts of that system to melt the hearts of his congregation into a greater degree of compassion toward their slaves than had been hitherto customary; "Sir," said one of his hearers, "we pay you a genteel salary to read to us the prayers of the liturgy, and to explain to us such parts of the Gospel as the rule of the church directs; but we do not want you to teach us what we are to do with our blacks." The clergyman found it prudent to with-hold any farther admonition. Whence this astonishing right, or rather this barbarous custom, for most certainly we have no kind of right beyond that of force? We are told, it is true,

5 Tearing to pieces.

that slavery cannot be so repugnant to human nature as we at first imagine, because it has been practised in all ages, and in all nations: the Lacedemonians[6] themselves, those great assertors of liberty, conquered the Helotes with the design of making them their slaves; the Romans, whom we consider as our masters in civil and military policy, lived in the exercise of the most horrid oppression; they conquered to plunder and to enslave. What a hideous aspect the face of the earth must then have exhibited! Provinces, towns, districts, often depopulated! their inhabitants driven to Rome, the greatest market in the world, and there sold by thousands! The Roman dominions were tilled by the hands of unfortunate people, who had once been, like their victors, free, rich, and possessed of every benefit society can confer; until they became subject to the cruel right of war, and to lawless force. Is there then no superintending power who conducts the moral operations of the world, as well as the physical? The same sublime hand which guides the planets round the sun with so much exactness, which preserves the arrangement of the whole with such exalted wisdom and paternal care, and prevents the vast system from falling into confusion; doth it abandon mankind to all the errors, the follies, and the miseries, which their most frantic rage, and their most dangerous vices and passions can produce?

The history of the earth! doth it present anything but crimes of the most heinous nature, committed from one end of the world to the other? We observe avarice, rapine, and murder, equally prevailing in all parts. History perpetually tells us of millions of people abandoned to the caprice of the maddest princes, and of whole nations devoted to the blind fury of tyrants. Countries destroyed; nations alternately buried in ruins by other nations; some parts of the world beautifully cultivated, returned again to the pristine state; the fruits of ages of industry, the toil of thousands in a short time destroyed by a few! If one corner breathes in peace for a few years, it is, in turn subjected, torn, and levelled; one would almost believe the principles of action in man, considered as the first agent of this planet, to be poisoned in their most essential parts. We certainly are not that class of beings which we vainly think ourselves to be; man an animal of prey, seems to have rapine and the love of bloodshed implanted in his heart; nay, to hold it the most honourable occupation in society: we never speak of a hero of mathematics, a hero of knowledge of humanity; no, this illustrious appellation is reserved for the most successful butchers of the world. If Nature has given us a fruitful soil to inhabit, she has refused us such inclinations and propensities as would afford us the full enjoyment of it. Extensive as the surface of this planet is, not one half of it is yet cultivated, not half replenished; she created man, and placed him either in the woods or plains, and provided him with passions which must for ever oppose his happiness; everything is submitted to the power of the strongest; men, like the elements, are always at war; the weakest yield to the most potent; force, subtlety, and malice, always triumph over unguarded honesty and simplicity. Benignity, moderation, and justice, are virtues adapted only to the humble paths of life: we love to talk of virtue and to admire its beauty, while in the

6 Spartans. The Helots (usual present spelling) were a large class of slaves, controlled by harsh laws, who performed most of the farming and other heavy labor of Sparta.

shade of solitude and retirement; but when we step forth into active life, if it happen to be in competition with any passion or desire, do we observe it to prevail? Hence so many religious impostors have triumphed over the credulity of mankind, and have rendered their frauds the creeds of succeeding generations, during the course of many ages; until worn away by time, they have been replaced by new ones. Hence the most unjust war, if supported by the greatest force, always succeeds; hence the most just ones, when supported only by their justice, as often fail. Such is the ascendancy of power; the supreme arbiter of all the revolutions which we observe in this planet: so irresistible is power, that it often thwarts the tendency of the most forcible causes, and prevents their subsequent salutary effects, though ordained for the good of man by the Governor of the universe. Such is the perverseness of human nature; who can describe it in all its latitude?

In the moments of our philanthropy we often talk of an indulgent nature, a kind parent, who for the benefit of mankind has taken singular pains to vary the genera of plants, fruits, grain, and the different productions of the earth; and has spread peculiar blessings in each climate. This is undoubtedly an object of contemplation which calls forth our warmest gratitude; for so singularly benevolent have those parental intentions been, that where barrenness of soil or severity of climate prevail, there she has implanted in the heart of man, sentiments which overbalance every misery, and supply the place of every want. She has given to the inhabitants of these regions, an attachment to their savage rocks and wild shores, unknown to those who inhabit the fertile fields of the temperate zone. Yet if we attentively view this globe, will it not appear rather a place of punishment, than of delight? And what misfortune! that those punishments should fall on the innocent, and its few delights be enjoyed by the most unworthy. Famine, diseases, elementary convulsions, human feuds, dissensions, etc., are the produce of every climate; each climate produces besides, vices, and miseries peculiar to its latitude. View the frigid sterility of the north, whose famished inhabitants hardly acquainted with the sun, live and fare worse than the bears they hunt: and to which they are superior only in the faculty of speaking. View the arctic and antarctic regions, those huge voids, where nothing lives; regions of eternal snow: where winter in all his horrors has established his throne, and arrested every creative power of nature. Will you call the miserable stragglers in these countries by the name of men? Now contrast this frigid power of the north and south with that of the sun; examine the parched lands of the torrid zone, replete with sulphureous exhalations; view those countries of Asia subject to pestilential infections which lay nature waste; view this globe often convulsed both from within and without; pouring forth from several mouths, rivers of boiling matter, which are imperceptibly leaving immense subterranean graves, wherein millions will one day perish! Look at the poisonous soil of the equator, at those putrid slimy tracks, teeming with horrid monsters, the enemies of the human race; look next at the sandy continent, scorched perhaps by the fatal approach of some ancient comet, now the abode of desolation. Examine the rains, the convulsive storms of those climates, where masses of sulphur, bitumen, and electrical fire, combining their dreadful powers, are incessantly hovering and bursting over a globe threatened with dissolution. On this little shell, how very few are the spots where man can live and flourish? even under those mild climates which seem to breathe peace and happiness, the poison of slavery, the fury of despotism, and the rage of superstition, are all combined against man! There only the few live and rule, whilst the many starve and utter ineffectual complaints: there, human nature appears more debased, perhaps than in the less favoured climates. The fertile plains of Asia, the rich low lands of Egypt and of Diarbeck, the fruitful fields bordering on the Tigris and the Euphrates, the extensive country of the East Indies in all its separate districts; all these must to the geographical eye, seem as if intended for terrestrial paradises: but though surrounded with the spontaneous riches of nature, though her kindest favours seem to be shed on those beautiful regions with the most profuse hand; yet there in general we find the most wretched people in the world. Almost everywhere, liberty so natural to mankind is refused, or rather enjoyed but by their tyrants; the word slave, is the appellation of every rank, who adore as a divinity, a being worse than themselves; subject to every caprice, and to every lawless rage which unrestrained power can give. Tears are shed, perpetual groans are heard, where only the accents of peace, alacrity, and gratitude should resound. There the very delirium of tyranny tramples on the best gifts of nature, and sports with the fate, the happiness, the lives of millions: there the extreme fertility of the ground always indicates the extreme misery of the inhabitants!

Every where one part of the human species are taught the art of shedding the blood of the other; of setting fire to their dwellings; of levelling the works of their industry: half of the existence of nations regularly employed in destroying other nations. What little political felicity is to be met with here and there, has cost oceans of blood to purchase; as if good was never to be the portion of unhappy man. Republics, kingdoms, monarchies, founded either on fraud or successful violence, increase by pursuing the steps of the same policy, until they are destroyed in their turn, either by the influence of their own crimes, or by more successful but equally criminal enemies.

If from this general review of human nature, we descend to the examination of what is called civilised society; there the combination of every natural and artificial want, makes us pay very dear for what little share of political felicity we enjoy. It is a strange heterogeneous assemblage of vices and virtues, and of a variety of other principles, for ever at war, for ever jarring, for ever producing some dangerous, some distressing extreme. Where do you conceive then that nature intended we should be happy? Would you prefer the state of men in the woods, to that of men in a more improved situation? Evil preponderates in both; in the first they often eat each other for want of food, and in the other they often starve each other for want of room. For my part, I think the vices and miseries to be found in the latter, exceed those of the former; in which real evil is more scarce, more supportable, and less enormous. Yet we wish to see the earth peopled; to accomplish the happiness of kingdoms, which is said to consist in numbers. Gracious God! to what end is the introduction of so many beings into a mode of existence in which they must grope amidst as many errors, commit as many crimes, and meet with as many diseases, wants, and sufferings!

The following scene will I hope account for these melancholy reflections, and apologize for the gloomy thoughts with which I have filled this letter: my mind is, and always has been, oppressed since I became a witness to it. I was not long since invited to dine with a planter who lived three miles from ——, where he then resided. In order to avoid the heat of the sun, I resolved to go on foot, sheltered in a small path, leading through a pleasant wood. I was leisurely travelling along, attentively examining some peculiar plants which I had collected, when all at once I felt the air strongly agitated, though the day was perfectly calm and sultry. I immediately cast my eyes toward the cleared ground, from which I was but at a small distance, in order to see whether it was not occasioned by a sudden shower; when at that instant a sound resembling a deep rough voice, uttered, as I thought, a few inarticulate monosyllables. Alarmed and surprised, I precipitately looked all round, when I perceived at about six rods distance[7] something resembling a cage, suspended to the limbs of a tree; all the branches of which appeared covered with large birds of prey, fluttering about, and anxiously endeavouring to perch on the cage. Actuated by an involuntary motion of my hands, more than by any design of my mind, I fired at them; they all flew to a short distance, with a most hideous noise: when, horrid to think and painful to repeat, I perceived a negro, suspended in the cage, and left there to expire! I shudder when I recollect that the birds had already picked out his eyes, his cheek bones were bare; his arms had been attacked in several places, and his body seemed covered with a multitude of wounds. From the edges of the hollow sockets and from the lacerations with which he was disfigured, the blood slowly dropped, and tinged the ground beneath. No sooner were the birds flown, than swarms of insects covered the whole body of this unfortunate wretch, eager to feed on his mangled flesh and to drink his blood. I found myself suddenly arrested by the power of affright and terror; my nerves were convulsed; I trembled, I stood motionless, involuntarily contemplating the fate of this negro, in all its dismal latitude. The living spectre, though deprived of his eyes, could still distinctly hear, and in his uncouth dialect begged me to give him some water to allay his thirst. Humanity herself would have recoiled back with horror; she would have balanced whether to lessen such reliefless distress, or mercifully with one blow to end this dreadful scene of agonising torture! Had I had a ball in my gun, I certainly should have despatched him; but finding myself unable to perform so kind an office, I sought, though trembling, to relieve him as well as I could. A shell ready fixed to a pole, which had been used by some negroes, presented itself to me; filled it with water, and with trembling hands I guided it to the quivering lips of the wretched sufferer. Urged by the irresistible power of thirst, he endeavoured to meet it, as he instinctively guessed its approach by the noise it made in passing through the bars of the cage. "Tankè, you whitè man, tankè you, putè somè poison and givè me." "How long have you been hanging there?" I asked him. "Two days, and me no die; the birds, the birds; aaah me!" Oppressed with the reflections which this shocking spectacle afforded me, I mustered strength enough to walk away, and soon reached the house at which I intended to dine. There I heard that the reason for this slave being thus punished, was on account of his having killed the overseer of the plantation. They told me that the laws of self-preservation rendered such executions necessary; and supported the doctrine of slavery with the arguments generally made use of to justify the practice; with the repetition of which I shall not trouble you at present.

Adieu.

[7] Ninety-nine feet or a bit over 30 meters.

Chapter Fourteen

THOMAS JEFFERSON (1743–1826)

The third president of the United States shared with Crèvecoeur both a vision of the American dream and its gothic inversion. In Query XIX of *Notes on the State of Virginia* (1784) he describes the simple life of the yeoman farmer as the core of republican virtue. But in the chapter before, Query XVIII, he had lamented the corrosive effect of slavery on the morals of the state: "The whole commerce between master and slave is a perpetual exercise of the most boisterous passions, the most unremitting despotism on the one part, and degrading submissions on the other."

We read this passage today knowing that Jefferson was speaking of his own boisterous passions, since DNA testing has confirmed what was long rumored, his fathering of children with his slave Sally Hemmings. Query XVIII takes us to the core of Southern racial Gothic, where we glimpse the sexual exploitation of enslaved women, their racially mixed offspring, the guilt of their masters and their fear of slave rebellion.

Text: Thomas Jefferson, *Notes on the State of Virginia* (London: John Stockdale, 1787).

QUERY XVIII

The particular *customs and manners that may happen to be received in that state?*

Manners

It is difficult to determine on the standard by which the manners of a nation may be tried, whether *catholic*,[1] or *particular*. It is more difficult for a native to bring to that standard the manners of his own nation, familiarized to him by habit. There must doubtless be an unhappy influence on the manners of our people produced by the existence of slavery among us. The whole commerce between master and slave is a perpetual exercise of the most boisterous passions, the most unremitting despotism on the one part, and degrading submissions on the other. Our children see this, and learn to imitate it; for man is an imitative animal. This quality is the germ of all education in him. From his cradle to his grave he is learning to do what he sees others do. If a parent could find no motive either in his philanthropy or his self-love, for restraining the intemperance of passion towards his slave, it should always be a sufficient one that his child is present. But generally it is not sufficient. The parent storms, the child looks on, catches the lineaments of wrath, puts on the same airs in the circle of smaller slaves, gives a loose to his worst of passions, and thus nursed, educated, and daily exercised in tyranny, cannot but be stamped by it with

1 Catholic: universal.

odious peculiarities. The man must be a prodigy who can retain his manners and morals undepraved by such circumstances. And with what execration should the statesman be loaded, who permitting one half the citizens thus to trample on the rights of the other, transforms those into despots, and these into enemies, destroys the morals of the one part, and the amor patriæ[2] of the other. For if a slave can have a country in this world, it must be any other in preference to that in which he is born to live and labour for another: in which he must lock up the faculties of his nature, contribute as far as depends on his individual endeavours to the evanishment of the human race, or entail his own miserable condition on the endless generations proceeding from him. With the morals of the people, their industry also is destroyed. For in a warm climate, no man will labour for himself who can make another labour for him. This is so true, that of the proprietors of slaves a very small proportion indeed are even seen to labour. And can the liberties of a nation be thought secure when we have removed their only firm basis, a conviction in the minds of the people that these liberties are of the gift of God? That they are not to be violated but with his wrath? Indeed I tremble for my country when I reflect that God is just: that his justice cannot sleep for ever: that considering numbers, nature and natural means only, a revolution of the wheel of fortune, an exchange of situation, is among possible events: that it may become probable by supernatural interference! The Almighty has no attribute which can take side with us in such a contest.—But it is impossible to be temperate and to pursue this subject through the various considerations of policy, of morals, of history natural and civil. We must be contented to hope they will force their way into every one's mind. I think a change already perceptible, since the origin of the present revolution. The spirit of the master is abating, that of the slave rising from the dust, his condition mollifying, the way I hope preparing, under the auspices of heaven, for a total emancipation, and that this is disposed, in the order of events, to be with the consent of the masters, rather than by their extirpation.

---

2 Latin: love of country.

Chapter Fifteen

JEAN-JACQUES DESSALINES (1758–1806)

Dessalines was the first leader of an independent Haiti. As a young man, he became embittered by the extreme brutality with which enslaved people in Haiti, then a French colony, were treated. In the Haiti Revolution, he rose to power after the betrayal and capture of Toussaint L'Ouverture by the French. After declaring Haiti an independent nation in 1804, Dessalines ordered the mass execution of French settlers, resulting in the deaths of 3,000–5,000 people of all ages and genders. In September 1804 Dessalines was declared Emperor Jacques I of Haiti by a group of Revolutionary generals. He was assassinated in 1806.

Text: Jean-Jacques Dessalines, "Liberty or Death Proclamation, 1 January 1804," https://mjp.univ-perp.fr/constit/ht1804.htm, downloaded on July 18, 2019. Translated by Susan Castillo Street.

LIBERTY OR DEATH PROCLAMATION

Jean-Jacques Dessalines, Governor-General, to the Inhabitants of Haiti
The most extraordinary crimes heard of, that would cause Nature itself to shudder, have been committed. The vessel has overflowed … At last the moment of revenge has arrived, and the implacable enemies of the Rights of Man have suffered just punishment for their crimes.

My arm, raised over their guilty heads, had refrained too long from striking. At that signal from a just God, your righteously armed hands have brought down the axe on the ancient tree of slavery and prejudice. Time, and the infernal politics of Europeans, had surrounded it with a triple shield of brass. You have torn away its armour and have placed it on your own hearts so that you can become as cruel and pitiless as your natural enemies. Like a mighty torrent that overflows its banks, your vengeful rage has swept all before it. Thus may all perish all those who tyrannise innocence, all those who oppress humankind.

And now? Burdened for centuries under an iron yoke, the sport of human passions, of their injustices and the whims of fate; mutilated victims of the greed of white Frenchmen, insatiable bloodsuckers who have fattened themselves on our toil; we suffered with unprecedented patience and resignation: should we watch these heathen hordes attempt our destruction, without regard to sex or age? Should we, men stripped of energy and virtue and delicate sensibility, not plunge the dagger of despair into their breasts? Where is the vile Haitian, unworthy of his own regeneration, who believes that he has not carried out the decrees of the Eternal by exterminating these bloodthirsty tigers? If there is one, may he flee far; outraged Nature repels him from our bosom. May he hide himself far from here; the air we breathe is not fit for his crude organs. It is the pure air of freedom, august and triumphant.

Yes, we have repaid these true cannibals war for war, crime for crime, outrage for outrage. Yes, I have saved my country; I have avenged America.[1] The confession I make of this is my pride and glory. What matters to me the opinion that contemporary and future generations may have of my conduct? I have carried out my duty; I am at ease with my own conscience. For me that is enough. What can I say? The deliverance of my unfortunate brothers and the testimony of my own conscience are not my only reward. I have seen two classes of men born to love, assist, and succour one another, mixed and blended together, crying out for vengeance and disputing the honour of striking the first blow.

Blacks and Yellows,[2] whom the refined duplicity of Europeans has for so long attempted to divide; you who are now allied and make up one family; without a doubt it was necessary that your perfect reconciliation be sealed with the blood of your butchers.

[…] sooner or later Divine Justice will unleash mighty winds on this earth, superior to the weakness of everyday things, for the loss and the terror of the wicked. Tremble, tyrants, usurpers, scourges of the New World! Our daggers are sharpened, your punishment awaits. Sixty thousand men duly equipped, hardened fighters, obedient to my orders, are burning with the desire to offer a new holocaust to the severed locks of their brothers whose throats have been cut. Is there any power mad enough to dare to attack me? Already, as it approaches, the enraged spirit of Haiti is rising from the depths of the ocean; its menacing aspect confounds the waves, creates storms, drives off their ships or dashes them to bits; the laws of Nature obey its terrible voice; diseases, plague, famine and flames are its minions. But why count on the assistance of the climate and the elements? Should I forget that I command exceptional souls, nourished by adversity, whose audacity shakes off obstacles and is increased by danger? Let these murderous cohorts come! I shall await them with firmness and a steady eye. I freely concede to them the seashore and the places where once there were cities, but woe to those who approach the mountains! Better for them that the sea receive them into its depths, than to be devoured by the rage of the children of Haiti.

War to the death against tyrants! is my motto.

Freedom and independence! is our rallying cry.

Generals, officers, soldiers: unlike my predecessor the ex-general Toussaint L'Ouverture,[3] I have been faithful to the promise I made to you to take up arms against tyranny; as long as there is breath in my body I shall keep my promise. *Never again shall a*

---

1 "America" here refers to the Americas or the Western Hemisphere.

2 People of mixed race.

3 Toussaint L'Ouverture led the 1791 slave revolt in St. Domingue and gained control over the whole island. In 1802 he was forced to resign by Napoleon Bonaparte in order to restore slavery and reinstitute French control of the island. He was betrayed and condemned to prison in France, where he died in 1803.

colonist or European set foot upon this land with the title of master or proprietor. This resolution shall henceforth be the fundamental basis of our constitution.

[…] As it goes against my character and my own dignity to punish innocents for the faults of their neighbours, a few whites, who motivated by the religion they profess have chosen to live with us in the woods, have experienced mercy from me. I have ordered that they not be put to the sword and that they be left unmolested.

I recommend anew and order all the generals of the region to grant succour, encouragement, and protection to neutral nations and to friends who wish to establish commercial relations with this island.

From the Quartel-General in Le Cap, 28 April 1804, the first year of independence.

The Governor-General

(Signed) DESSALINES

A true copy. The Sec'y-General Juste Chanlatte[4]

[4] Juste Chanlatte (1766–1828), Haitian editor, journalist and poet.

Chapter Sixteen

CHARLES BROCKDEN BROWN (1771–1810)

Charles Brockden Brown is considered the first American professional novelist, and in four Gothic novels written in a burst of creative energy (*Wieland* (1798), *Arthur Mervyn* (1799), *Ormond* (1799) and *Edgar Huntly* (1799)) he anticipated the themes and techniques of later Gothic authors such as Poe and Hawthorne.

Brown was a progressive and feminist who was influenced by the radical thought of William Godwin and Mary Wollstonecraft. In his dialogue *Alcuin* (published in parts in 1798, but not in its entirety until 1971), he imagines a utopia in which women are completely free.

In the essay below, Brown turns his attention to Caribbean slavery. Written and published in 1805, while the revolution in Haiti was still unfolding, Brown's essay shows an intelligent and thoughtful white American grappling with historic changes that challenged received ideas. His conclusions will strike readers of our own time as sometimes enlightened, sometimes disappointing. While he understood the need for the emancipation of women, he could not make that leap for enslaved Africans, instead calling for a gradual improvement of their condition.

Text: Charles Brockden Brown, "On the Consequences of Abolishing the Slave Trade in the West Indian Colonies," *Literary Magazine, and the American Register* 4 (November 1805), 375–81.

ON THE CONSEQUENCES OF ABOLISHING THE SLAVE TRADE TO THE WEST INDIAN COLONIES

The probable fate of the negro race in the American colonies, is an interesting subject at all times, in a merely speculative view. It comprehends various questions of high importance in the philosophy of man; it touches on the destines of a large portion of the species, on the event to be expected from the grandest and most cruel experiment that ever was tried upon human nature; the sudden and violent transportation of immense multitudes of savages to distant regions and new climates, and their forcible and instantaneous exposure to a state of comparative civilization. The fate of a large empire, with all its wealth and power, depends on this experiment. The colonial establishments of Europe in the new world, form a mass of dominion scarcely inferior in magnitude to the proudest dynasties of ancient or modern times; and though their ruin would not necessarily involve that of the mother countries, it would completely subvert all the established relations between the different members of the European commonwealth, besides absolutely diminishing their prosperity.

What form will the colonial society assume during the continuance of the slave trade? In all human probability, one of two events will speedily happen; either the fate of St. Domingo will suddenly become the fate of all the negro settlements, or the West Indian system will remain a little longer on the present footing. The impending blow may possibly be warded off for a season: negroes will continue to be driven, tortured, and wasted, in proportion as new recruits can always be obtained from Africa. A scanty portion of the dregs of Europe will still reside in the islands, and compose the whole of that colonial body on whom the preservation of the system depends. Each attempt of the enemy in St. Domingo, or each effort of the slaves themselves to imitate the example of that settlement, will shake to its base the whole western wing of the European community, till, in the course of a few years, the frail tenure will give way, on which are held those fine possessions; and all the monuments of Europe, in the insular part of the new world, will vanish before the tempest which a short-sighted and wicked policy has for ages been raising.

With emancipated Africans there can be no faith, no treaties, no fixed connexions of neutrality, not even the honourable and settled relations of modern warfare. The suppression of such a monster of policy is a duty incumbent on every civilized state connected with the West Indian system. The efforts of France and Spain may possibly be successful in St. Domingo, but what will be the effects of a contrary event on the colonies that remain tranquil? The negroes in St. Domingo are already acquiring something like a navy; they have proposed to Great Britain conditions of alliance, which no civilized government can listen to. These two facts speak loudly of the dangers necessarily inherent in such a neighbourhood. What has England to expect? or what can she do to brighten her prospects? Till the slave trade is at once boldly and totally abolished (for in the present circumstances delay is not prudence; it is rashness, in fact, though it may result, like many other kinds of temerity, from real cowardice); till the root of all the evil is hardily struck at, and the main, universal cause of all danger is destroyed, an hour's quiet cannot be expected in the slave colonies, nor any sensible alleviation of the manifold evils which crowd the picture of West Indian society. Whether all the mischiefs of negro liberty come at once, or only undermine the system gradually, and then cover it with ruin in the end, the alternative is almost equal. The abolition of the slave trade alone can rectify those abuses, and counteract those frightful dangers. But what are the steps by which the abolition is likely to lead to so desirable a consequence?

Every one is aware of the dangers of the slave trade in its natural effects upon the *security* of the West Indian establishments. Nothing can tend more obviously to prevent proprietors from residing on their plantations, than the constant, and, at present, just fear of insurrection. When a native of Europe is about to leave a home, in which the value of perfect security is only overlooked because it knows no interruption, he is forced to reflect on the blessings he has hitherto enjoyed, and to consider that they are not the gift of every government. In his choice of a new place of residence, the change on climate enters perhaps far less into his comparative views, than the change from a state of safety and protection to one of perpetual alarm; of real dangers, which no length of time can disarm of their terrors; and sufferings, which no seasoning can palliate. Even in the regular communities of the old worlds, the difference of the rights enjoyed under various governments, has no small influence on emigrants in fixing on new abodes. And what are all the fears of banishment to Siberia, or of French conscription, compared with the risks to which every white inhabitant of Jamaica is exposed, so long as Dessalines is emperor of Hayti, and has a troop of allies in the slaves of every British plantation? In proportion as the number and attachments of those allies is diminished; that is, in proportion as the British plantations are peopled by homebred negroes, whom their masters are forced to treat well by the impossibility of filling their places; the danger of the planter is diminished, and the just obstacles to choosing the colonies for a place of residence is removed.

The tendency of men is always to follow their stock. When it is vested in foreign trade, they *may* remain at home; but they generally reside where they see it oftenest. When vested in the carrying trade, it generally draws them to one of the spots between which it circulates. When vested in foreign agriculture, it seldom fails to draw them after it. In these employments, no doubt, impolitic restrictions may prevent the capitalist from following his stock; climate is seldom any obstacle: the general tendency is strong, and as soon as artificial impediments are removed, this tendency is manifest. And this would cause the great colonial proprietors to reside on their plantations, were not two principal causes now to prevent them; the dangerous nature of their colonial residence, and the superior attractions of European society. The latter is of much less consequence than the former, because it operates chiefly on the more wealthy and less valuable, as well as less numerous class of inhabitants, and because it must daily lessen as the improvements of the colonies advances. We have proofs, in all the accounts of St. Domingo during the last year of its greatness that the whites were rapidly increasing, in numbers, elegance, and even splendour, merely from the strength of those inducements which connect men with their property; and such inducements operate with accelerated force; for every family that removes to the island, is a new tie to those which remain. Nothing but the dangers of insurrection could permanently counteract this propensity, and the measure which removes or lessens that danger, will remove or lessen the non-residence, hitherto so hurtful, both to the interests of the proprietors themselves, and to the general character of colonial society.

The excellent management of the negroes in the colonies where no supply can be procured, and where the great proportion of the whites reside, is sufficient proof of these propositions. Various circumstances have placed the settlements of Spain and Portugal nearly in this predicament. Scarcely any of the blacks, in these colonies, are of African birth; the trade being extremely insignificant, and the natural increase of the blacks very rapid. The whites, too, reside upon their properties, and in the large towns scattered over South America, in a proportion elsewhere unknown. The privileges of slaves have gradually been extended, first by custom, and then by law, till the period has actually arrived, when a Spanish or Portuguese slave hardly conceives himself less comfortable, or even less important, than the lower order of free inhabitants. The good treatment of those negroes is partly owing to the residence of their masters, who are guided by their own eyes and interests, not their overseer's, and in its turn tends to encourage that custom of residing; and to the difficulty of procuring recruits from Africa, the necessity of which is lessened by the consequences of this treatment. The condition of the slaves in those states of North America, where importation has long been discontinued, is another striking proof of the truth of this representation.

That the bad qualities ascribed to the negroes, often with great justice, belong rather to their habits rather than their nature, and are derived either from the low state of civilization in which the whole race at present is placed, or from the manifold hardships of their situation in the colonies, is not only consistent with analogy, but is deducible from facts. The travelers who have visited interior Africa, where the influence of the slave-trade is much less felt than on the west coast, assure us, that the natural dispositions of the negro race are mild, gentle, and amiable in a high degree: that, far from wanting ingenuity, they have made no contemptible progress in the arts; and have even united into political societies of great extent and complicated structure, notwithstanding the obstacles arising from their remote situation, and their want of water-carriage: that their disposition to voluntary and continued exertions of body and mind, their capacity of industry, the great promoter of all human improvement, is not inferior to the same principle in other tribes, in similar situations: in fine, that they have the same propensity to improve both their condition, their faculties, and their virtues, conspicuous in the human character over all the rest of the world. Let us compare the general circumstances of any European nation; the character, both for talents and virtues of its inhabitants, at two distant periods. How remarkable is the contrast between them! Little more than a century ago, Russia was covered with hordes of barbarians; cheating, drinking, brutal lust, and ferocious rage, were as well known, and as little blamed, among the nobles of the czar's court, as the more polished and mitigated forms of the same vices are at this day in Petersburgh; literature never appeared among its inhabitants; and you might travel several days journey, without meeting a man, even among the higher classes, qualified for one moment's rational conversation. ...[1] Though the various circumstances of *external* improvement will not totally conceal, even at this day, and among the first classes, the "*vestigia rurus*,"[2] yet no one can deny that the stuff of which Russians are made has been greatly and fundamentally improved; that their capacities and virtues rapidly unfolding, as their habits have been changed, and their communication with the rest of mankind extended. A century ago, it would have been just as miraculous to read a tolerable Russian poem, or find a society of Boyars where a rational person could spend his time with satisfaction, as it would be at this day, to find the same prodigies at Houssa or Tombuctoo:[3] and those who argue about races, and despise the effect of circumstances, would have had the same right to decide upon the fate of all the Russias, from an inspection of the Calmuc[4] skull, as they now have to condemn all Africa to everlasting barbarism, from the craniums, colour, and wool of its inhabitants. If we allow that there will always be a sensible difference between the negro and the European, yet why should we suppose that this disparity will be greater

1 Ellipsis in original.

2 Latin: Traces of rural life.

3 Houssa: a possibly mythical city on the Niger; Tombuctoo (now usually Timbuktu): an ancient city in Mali.

4 The Calmucs or Kalmyks are an ethnic group in Russia.

than between the Sclavonian and the Gothic nations?[5] No one denies that all the families of mankind are capable of great improvement. And though, after all, some tribes should remain inferior to others, it would be ridiculous of that account to deny the possibility of greatly civilizing even the most untoward tribe, or the importance of the least considerable advances which it may be capable of making. That the progress of any race of men, or of the whole species, in the various branches of virtue and power, must be infinite, was never maintained by sound reasoners. But that this progress is indefinite; that no limit can be assigned to its extent or acceleration, is beyond all reasonable controversy.

The superiority of a negro in the interior of Africa to one of the Slave Coast is notorious. The enemies of the slave-trade reasonably impute the degeneracy of the maritime tribes to that baneful commerce. Its friends have, on the other hand, deduced from thence an argument against the negro character, which, say they, is not improved by intercourse with civilized nations. But that *fact* is admitted. Mr. Park observed it in the north, and Mr. Barrow[6] in the tribes south of the line, who increase in civilization as you leave the Slave Coast. Compare the accounts given by these travellers, of the skill, the industry, the excellent moral qualities of the Africans in Houssa and Tombuctoo, &c., with the pictures that have been drawn of the same race, living in all the barbarity with which the supply of slave ships requires; you will be convinced that the negro is as much improved by a change of circumstances as the white. The state of slavery is in no case favourable to improvement; yet, compare the Creole[7] negro with the imported slave, and you will find that even the most debasing form of servitude, though it necessarily eradicates most of the moral qualities of the African, has not prevented him from profiting intellectually by the intercourse of more civilized men. The war of St. Domingo reads us a memorable lesson; negroes organizing immense armies; laying plans of campaigns and sieges, which, if not scientific, have at least been successful against the finest European troops; arranging forms of government, and even proceeding some length in executing the most difficult of human enterprizes; entering into commercial relations with foreigners, and conceiving the idea of alliances; acquiring something like a maritime force, and, at any rate, navigating vessels in the tropical seas, with as much skill and foresight as that complicated operation requires.

This spectacle ought to teach us the effects of circumstances upon the human faculties, and prescribe bounds to that arrogance, which would confine to one race, the characteristics of the species. We have torn those men from their country, on the vain pretence, that their nature is radially inferior to our own. We have treated them so as to stunt the natural growth of their virtues and their reason. Our efforts have partly succeeded; for the West Indian, like all other slaves, has copied some of the tyrant's vices. But their ingenuity has advanced apace, under all disadvantages; and the negroes are already so much improved, that while we madly continue to despise them, and to justify

5 I.e., between Eastern and Western Europeans.

6 Mungo Park (1711–1806) was a Scottish adventurer who explored West Africa; Sir John Barrow (1764–1848) explored and mapped Southern Africa.

7 Creole here means born in the Americas.

the crimes which have transplanted them, it has really become doubtful how long they will suffer us to exist in the islands.

We may be told, that brute force and adaptation to the climate, are the only faculties which the negroes of the West Indies possess. But something more than this must concur to form and maintain armies, and to distribute civil powers in a state. And the negroes, who in Africa cannot count ten, and bequeath the same portion of arithmetic to their children, must somewhat improve before they can use the mariner's compass; rig square-sailed vessels; and cultivate whole districts of cotton and coffee for their own profit in the Antilles.

The improvement visible in the negroes brought over to Europe as domestics, and their superiority to their countrymen in Africa or the West Indies, is a new evidence of these truths. There is surely a wider difference between one of those blacks and a native of the Slave Coast, than between a London chairman and the Irish shepherd who lived a few centuries ago. The fidelity, courage, and other good qualities, remarkable in freed negroes, distinguish them as much from the slaves, of whose cowardice and treachery such pictures have been drawn, as the feats of valour recorded in the annals of the Welsh, place them above those wretched Britons who resisted their invaders only with groans.

There is nothing in the physical or moral constitution of the negro, which renders him an exception to the general character of the species, and prevents him from improving in all estimable qualities, when placed in favourable circumstances. Nay, under all possible disadvantages, we see the progress he is capable of making, whether insulated by the deserts of Africa, or surrounded by the slave factories of Europeans, or groaning under the cruelties of the West Indian system. This progress will be accelerated in proportion as those impediments are removed; while Africa is civilized by legitimate commerce with the more polished nations of the world, the negroes already in the West Indies will rapidly improve, as soon as the abolition shall begin to ameliorate their treatment.

It will not be long before milder treatment will increase the productive powers of negro labour. The first two or three seasons may possibly be less prosperous, in consequence of the change. Indeed, changes of every kind have a tendency at the beginning to produce disorder in all political systems; for, it is true, though lamentable, that the correction of the greatest evils in society generally increases, for a time, the bad effects of the original error. But the connexion is so constant between freedom and industry, that we may reasonable expect these evils to be of short duration. The history of all Europe demonstrates the effects which the mild treatment of the labouring orders naturally produces on the value of their industry.

The proprietors of Hungary, almost immediately after the reform of Maria Theresa,[8] began to feel the salutary consequences of the limitations of the corvées[9] due from their peasants. When, instead of full power over the whole of the serf's labour, the lord

---

8 Maria Theresa (1717–1780) was the ruler of the Austrian-Hungarian Empire and the only female Hapsburg monarch.

9 Labor owed by a vassal to his lord, usually used in construction or maintenance of roads or other public works.

could only take two days in each week, he found those two worth much more than all the seven had been before; though at the same time, he lost the right of retaining the peasant on his ground against his will. If such mitigations are favourable to the master, still more advantageous must they be to the slave. And can any improvement be made in the condition of the lower orders, more effectually, than by augmenting their wealth, and their importance to the upper classes? It is not unlikely that the number of holidays will next be increased, or the hours of work in the day diminished; that the negro will, by degrees, be left more and more to his own care, and will begin to feel himself more dependent on the produce of his industry. The less interference from the laws, the better for the master, and still more for the slave. The mutual interest of the parties will be the best law, and, indeed, the only one capable of being accurately executed. When something like industry has taken root, it may be time to introduce, in the same silent, gradual, and voluntary manner, the grand improvement of task-work. This has already been attempted, with the happiest effects, in several of the colonies; in Brazil; on some parts of the Spanish main; in the Bahamas, and elsewhere. It has been introduced also into Surinam; though, from peculiar circumstances, it has not there produced such salutary changes as in other settlements. Indeed, while the bad effects of the old system flourish in full vigour, preventing the general improvement of the slaves in their habits of voluntary exertion, it is only in certain kinds of work that tasks can be distributed. The new mode of treatment would render *universal* task-work, not only an easy, but a necessary improvement. And when these changes shall have been effected slowly, and with the consent of all proprietors, not taken by vote, but freely given by each individual; will not the lower orders in the islands be exactly in the state of the *ascripti glebae*[10] under the milder feudal governments of the old world? It is but one step to make them *coloni partiarii*, or serf tenants paying a proportion of their crops to their lord. Such they are already in some parts of Spanish and Portuguese America, where the richest ores and pearls are obtained, by means of this very contract between the master and his slave. Nor does it much signify in what form the last change of all shall then be effected by the total emancipation of the negro. He will, by this natural gradation, have become civilized to a certain degree, and fully capable of enjoying the station of a free man, for which all are fitted by nature. In the course of time, we may hope to see the same relaxation of prejudice against him among the whites, which has made the European baron cease to look down upon his serf as an inferior animal. The mixture even of the races, is a thing by no means impossible, and will remove the only pretext that can remain for supposing the West Indian society, as new-modelled by the abolition, to be in the smallest degree different from the society of Europe, after the successors of the Romans ceased to procure slaves in commerce.

---

[10] Latin. A slave or serf who was attached to a particular piece of land, and thus would be part of the property transferred with the land from one owner to another.

Chapter Seventeen

LEONORA SANSAY (1773–1821)

Leonora Sansay was born in Philadelphia in 1773. Her father died at sea shortly thereafter, and her mother's second husband owned the Half Moon Tavern, which was a gathering place for local politicians. It is possible that she may have met her patron Aaron Burr there. The nature of their relationship has been the subject of debate; most critics agree that she was his mistress, though others maintain that they were simply friends. Whatever the case, she married Louis Sansay, a New York merchant who had fled from St. Domingue following the turbulence in the wake of the slave revolt in the 1790s. In 1802, Louis Sansay traveled to St. Domingue to reclaim his plantation, taking Leonora with him. Burr had given assurances to Leonora that the French forces would subdue the rebellion in less than a month, but in 1803, the black army was victorious against the French, and Leonora and her husband fled to Cuba. Aaron Burr's fortunes also took a downturn. After killing Alexander Hamilton in a duel, he was acquitted on charges of treason, after which he fled to Europe for four years.

Leonora Sansay was aware that her relationship with Burr had become a liability. She managed, however, to transform her eyewitness experiences in St. Domingue and her love affair with Burr into very considerable assets, exploiting the reading public's fascination with accounts of racialized violence and news of Burr's controversial career. Her *Secret History* caused a sensation when it was published in 1808, offering readers a vivid eyewitness account of the people, places and events in Haiti at the time of the Haitian Revolution.

Text: Leonora Sansay, *Secret History* caused sensation on its publication in 1802, offering to readers an extraordinarily eyewitness account of events in Haiti, with its vivid evocation of the historical moment it describes. (Philadelphia, PA: Bradford & Inskeep, 1808).

LETTER II

Cape Francois.[1]

What a change has taken place here since my last letter was written! I mentioned that there was to be a grand review, and I also mentioned that the confidence General Le Clerc[2] placed in the negroes was highly blamed, and justly, as he has found to his cost.

---

1 A port city on the north coast of Haiti.

2 General Charles Le Clerc was sent by his brother-in-law Napoleon Bonaparte to subdue the slave rebellion in Haiti, accompanied by 23,000 French troops. He landed in Haiti in 1802 and soon took possession of most of the island, made peace with the rebel leaders Toussaint

On the day of the review, when the troops of the line and the guarde nationale[3] were assembled on the field, a plot was discovered, which had been formed by the negroes in the town, to seize the arsenal and to point the cannon of a fort, which overlooked the place of review, on the troops; whilst Clairvaux,[4] the mulatto general, who commanded the advanced posts, was to join the negroes of the plain, overpower the guards, and entering the town, complete the destruction of the white inhabitants. The first part of the plot was discovered and defeated. But Clairvaux made good his escape, and in the evening attacked the post General Le Clerc had so imprudently confided to him. The consternation was terrible. The guarde nationale, composed chiefly of Creoles, did wonders. The American captains and sailors volunteered their services; they fought bravely, and many of them perished. The negroes were repulsed; but if they gained no ground they lost none, and they occupy at present the same posts as before. The pusillanimous General Le Clerc, shrinking from danger of which his own imprudence had been the cause, thought only of saving himself. He sent his plate and valuable effects on board the admiral's vessel, and was preparing to embark secretly with his suite, but the brave admiral La Touche de Treville[5] sent him word that he would fire with more pleasure on those who abandoned the town, than on those who attacked it.

The ensuing morning presented a dreadful spectacle. Nothing was heard but the groans of the wounded, who were carried through the streets to their homes, and the cries of the women for their friends who were slain.

The general, shut up in his house, would see nobody; ashamed of the weakness which had led to this disastrous event, and of the want of courage he had betrayed: a fever seized him and he died in three days.

Madame Le Clerc, who had not loved him whilst living, mourned his death like the Ephesian matron,[6] cut off her hair, which was very beautiful, to put it in his coffin; refused all sustenance and all public consolation.

General Rochambeau,[7] who is at Port au Prince, has been sent for by the inhabitants of the Cape to take the command. Much good is expected from the change, he is said to be a brave officer and an excellent man.

L'Ouverture and Dessalines. By treachery, he betrayed L'Ouverture and sent him to prison in France.

3 National Guard.

4 Augustin Clairveaux was a mixed-race general who fought alongside L'Ouverture. He is one of the signatories of the Haitian Declaration of Independence, along with Dessalines. He died of yellow fever in 1804.

5 Admiral Louis Rene Levassor de la Touche Treville was the commandant of a French naval expedition sent to Haiti. After the restoration of slavery by the French in 1802, he defended the harbours in the south of the island.

6 A reference to T*he Widow of Ephesus,* by Petronius, a Roman writer of the first century AD. In it, he describes the extravagant displays of grief by a widow, who then consoles herself with one of the men guarding her late husband's grave.

7 General Rochambeau led French expeditionary forces in an attempt to gain control of Cap Francois after General Le Clerc's death.

Monsieur D'Or is in the interim Captain General, and unites in himself the three principal places in the government: Prefect Colonial, Ordonnateur,[8] and General in Chief.

All this bustle would be delightful if it was not attended with such melancholy consequences. It keeps us from petrifying, of which I was in danger.

I have become acquainted with some Creole ladies who, having staid in the Island during the revolution, relate their sufferings in a manner which harrows up the soul; and dwell on the recollection of their long lost happiness with melancholy delight. St. Domingo was formerly a garden. Every inhabitant lived on his estate like a Sovereign ruling his slaves with despotic sway, enjoying all that luxury could invent, or fortune procure.

The pleasures of the table were carried to the last degree of refinement. Gaming knew no bounds, and libertinism, called love, was without restraint. The Creole is generous hospitable, magnificent, but vain, inconstant, and incapable of serious application; and in this abode of pleasure and luxurious ease vices have reigned at which humanity must shudder. The jealousy of the women was often terrible in its consequences. One lady, who had a beautiful negro girl continually about her person, thought she saw some symptoms of tendresse in the eyes of her husband, and all the furies of jealousy seized her soul.

She ordered one of her slaves to cut off the head of the unfortunate victim, which was instantly done. At dinner her husband said he felt no disposition to eat, to which his wife, with the air of a demon, replied, perhaps I can give you something that will excite your appetite; it has at least had that effect before. She rose and drew from a closet the head of Coomba. The husband, shocked beyond expression, left the house and sailed immediately for France, in order never again to behold such a monster.

Many similar anecdotes have been related by my Creole friends; but one of them, after having excited my warmest sympathy, made me laugh heartily in the midst of my tears. She told me that her husband was stabbed in her arms by a slave whom he had always treated as his brother; that she had seen her children killed, and her house burned, but had been herself preserved by a faithful slave, and conducted, after incredible sufferings, and through innumerable dangers to the Cape. The same slave, she added, and the idea seemed to console her for every other loss, saved all my madrass[9] handkerchiefs.

The Creole ladies have an air of voluptuous languor which renders them extremely interesting. Their eyes, their teeth, and their hair are remarkably beautiful, and they have acquired from the habit of commanding their slaves, an air of dignity which adds to their charms. Almost too indolent to pronounce their words they speak with a drawling accent that is very agreeable: but since they have been roused by the pressure of misfortune many of them have displayed talents and found resources in the energy of their own minds which it would have been supposed impossible for them to possess.

They have naturally a taste for music; dance with a lightness, a grace, an elegance peculiar to themselves, and those who, having been educated in France, unite the French

8 Organizer or administrator.

9 A lightweight cotton fabric of plaid design.

vivacity to the Creole sweetness, are the most irresistible creatures that the imagination can conceive. In the ordinary intercourse of life they are delightful; but if I wanted a friend on any extraordinary occasion I would not venture to rely on their stability.

LETTER XXI

St. Jago de Cuba
General Rochambeau, after having made a shameful capitulation with the negroes, has evacuated the Cape. He presented his superb horses to Dessalines,[10] and then embarked with his suite, and all the inhabitants who chose to follow him, intending to fight his way through the British ships. They were, however, soon overpowered and taken. The English admiral would not admit the general in chief into his presence. He has been sent to Jamaica, from whence he will be transported to England.

Many of the inhabitants of the Cape have arrived here, after having lost every thing they possessed. Numbers have remained. After the articles of capitulation were signed three days were allowed for the evacuation, during which the negroes entered the town, and were so civil and treated the inhabitants with so much kindness and respect, that many who had embarked their effects, allured by the prospect of making a fortune rapidly, paid great sums to have them relanded, supposing they would be protected as they had been in the time of Toussaint. But in less than a week they found that they had flattered themselves with false hopes. A proclamation was issued by Dessalines, in which every white man was declared an enemy of the indigenes, as they call themselves, and their colour alone deemed sufficient to make them hated and to devote them to destruction. The author of this eloquent production, a white man, became himself the first sacrifice.

The destined victims were assembled in a public square, where they were slaughtered by the negroes with the most unexampled cruelty. One brave man, who had often distinguished himself in the defence of the Cape, and who had been weak enough to stay in it, seized with desperate fury the sword of one of the negroes, and killing several, at length fell, overpowered by numbers. A few were preserved from this day's massacre by their slaves. Some were concealed by the American merchants, though it was very dangerous to venture on such benevolent actions. One vessel was searched, and several inhabitants being found on board, they were taken and hanged. The mate of the vessel, though an American, shared their fate. The captain saved himself by declaring that he was ignorant of their being on board. Major B——, whom I have so often mentioned, had also the folly to stay. One of his slaves concealed him on the day of the massacre, and, shut up in a hogshead, he was put on board an American vessel. After many perilous

[10] Jean-Jacques Dessalines (1758–1806) defeated a French army at the Battle of Vertières in 1803 and declared Haiti an independent nation in 1804, after which he was chosen by a council of generals to assume the office of governor-general. In 1804, he ordered the massacre of French settlers in Haiti, resulting in the deaths of between 3,000 and 5,000 people.

adventures he has arrived here, and relates scenes which cannot be thought of without horror.

The women have not yet been killed; but they are exposed to every kind of insult, are driven from their houses, imprisoned, sent to work on the public roads; in fine, nothing can be imagined more dreadful than their situation.

Two amiable girls, whom I knew, hung to the neck of their father when the negroes seized him. They wept and entreated these monsters to spare him; but he was torn rudely from their arms. The youngest, attempting to follow him, received a blow on the head with a musquet which laid her lifeless on the ground. The eldest, frantic with terror, clung to her father, when a ruthless negro pierced her with his bayonet, and she fell dead at his feet. The hapless father gave thanks to God that his unfortunate children had perished before him, and had not been exposed to lingering suffering's and a more dreadful fate.

Some ladies have found protectors in the American merchants, who conceal them in their stores. Some have been saved by the British officers; but the greatest number have been driven into the streets, and many are forced to carry on their heads baskets of cannon balls from the arsenal to the fosset, a distance of at least three miles.

I enquired after a most accomplished and exemplary woman, who with three beautiful daughters remained at the Cape after the evacuation, and I have wept at the story of their sufferings till I am unable to relate them.

What could have induced these infatuated people to confide in the promises of the negroes? Yet to what will not people submit to avoid the horrors of poverty, or allured by the hope of making a rapid fortune.

During the reign of Toussaint[11] the white inhabitants had been generally respected, and many of them, engaging in commerce, had accumulated money which they sent to the United States, where they are now living at their ease. Even at the arrival of the French fleet, the lives of the people, except in a few solitary instances, had been spared. These considerations had without doubt great weight, but alas! how soon were their hopes blasted, and how dearly have they paid for their credulity. Yet even these monsters, thirsting after blood, and unsated with carnage, preserved from among the devoted victims those whose talents could be useful to themselves. A printer and several artists have been suffered to live, but are closely guarded, and warned that their lives will be the forfeit of the first attempt to escape. With the sword suspended over their heads they still cherish perhaps a secret hope of eluding the vigilance of their savage masters.

[11] Toussaint L'Ouverture led the 1791 slave revolt in St. Domingue, gaining control over the whole island. In 1802, he was forced to resign by Napoleon Bonaparte in order to restore slavery and reinstitute French domination. He was betrayed and condemned to prison in France, where he died in 1803.

Chapter Eighteen

THOMAS RUFFIN GRAY (1800–?) AND NAT TURNER (1800–1831)

Nat Turner led a slave uprising in 1831 in which some sixty white Virginians were killed. Gray was a young lawyer who interviewed Turner, his exact contemporary, while Turner was awaiting trial. It is impossible to determine the accuracy of the resulting pamphlet, "The Confessions of Nat Turner" (1832). There has been much critical discussion over the degree to which Turner's authentic voice can be heard in Gray's retelling.

Gray's pamphlet is the basis for William Styron's controversial novel by the same name, which won the Pulitzer Prize for 1967.

Text: Thomas Ruffin Gray, *The Confessions of Nat Turner, the Leader of the Late Insurrection in Southhampton, Va. as Fully and Voluntarily Made to Thomas R. Gray* (Baltimore, MD: Thomas Ruffin Gray, 1831). Downloaded from DigitalCommons@University of Nebraska-Lincoln. A small number of obvious spelling errors have been silently corrected.

"THE CONFESSIONS OF NAT TURNER"

CONFESSION. Agreeable to his own appointment, on the evening he was committed to prison, with permission of the jailer, I visited NAT on Tuesday the 1st November, when, without being questioned at all, he commenced his narrative in the following words:—Sir,—You have asked me to give a history of the motives which induced me to undertake the late insurrection, as you call it—To do so I must go back to the days of my infancy, and even before I was born. I was thirty-one years of age the 2d of October last, and born the property of Benj. Turner, of this county. In my childhood a circumstance occurred which made an indelible impression on my mind, and laid the ground work of that enthusiasm, which has terminated so fatally to many, both white and black, and for which I am about to atone at the gallows. It is here necessary to relate this circumstance—trifling as it may seem, it was the commencement of that belief which has grown with time, and even now, sir, in this dungeon, helpless and forsaken as I am, I cannot divest myself of. Being at play with other children, when three or four years old, I was telling them something, which my mother overhearing, said it had happened before I was born—I stuck to my story, however, and related somethings which went, in her opinion, to confirm it—others being called on were greatly astonished, knowing that these things had happened, and caused them to say in my hearing, I surely would be a prophet, as the Lord had shewn me things that had happened before my birth. And my father and mother strengthened me in this my first impression, saying in my presence, I was intended for some great purpose, which they had always thought from certain marks on my head and breast—[a parcel of excrescences which I believe are not at all uncommon, particularly among negroes, as I have seen several with the same. In this case he has either cut them off or they have nearly disappeared]—My grandmother, who was very religious, and to whom I was much attached—my master, who belonged to the church, and other religious persons who visited the house, and whom I often saw at prayers, noticing the singularity of my manners, I suppose, and my uncommon intelligence for a child, remarked I had too much sense to be raised, and if I was, I would never be of any service to any one as a slave—To a mind like mine, restless, inquisitive and observant of everything that was passing, it is easy to suppose that religion was the subject to which it would be directed, and although this subject principally occupied my thoughts—there was nothing that I saw or heard of to which my attention was not directed—The manner in which I learned to read and write, not only had great influence on my own mind, as I acquired it with the most perfect ease, so much so, that I have no recollection whatever of learning the alphabet—but to the astonishment of the family, one day, when a book was shewn me to keep me from crying, I began spelling the names of different objects—this was a source of wonder to all in the neighborhood, particularly the blacks—and this learning was constantly improved at all opportunities—when I got large enough to go to work, while employed, I was reflecting on many things that would present themselves to my imagination, and whenever an opportunity occurred of looking at a book, when the school children were getting their lessons, I would find many things that the fertility of my own imagination had depicted to me before; all my time, not devoted to my master's service, was spent either in prayer, or in making experiments in casting different things in moulds made of earth, in attempting to make paper, gunpowder, and many other experiments, that although I could not perfect, yet convinced me of its practicability if I had the means.[Footnote: When questioned as to the manner of manufacturing those different articles, he was found well informed on the subject.] I was not addicted to stealing in my youth, nor have ever been—Yet such was the confidence of the negroes in the neighborhood, even at this early period of my life, in my superior judgment, that they would often carry me with them when they were going on any roguery, to plan for them. Growing up among them, with this confidence in my superior judgment, and when this, in their opinions, was perfected by Divine inspiration, from the circumstances already alluded to in my infancy, and which belief was ever afterwards zealously inculcated by the austerity of my life and manners, which became the subject of remark by white and black.—Having soon discovered to be great, I must appear so, and therefore studiously avoided mixing in society, and wrapped myself in mystery, devoting my time to fasting and prayer—By this time, having arrived to man's estate, and hearing the scriptures commented on at meetings, I was struck with that particular passage which says: "Seek ye the kingdom of Heaven and all things shall be added unto you."[1] I reflected much on this passage, and prayed daily for light on this subject—As I was praying one day at my plough, the spirit spoke to me, saying, "Seek ye the kingdom of Heaven and all things shall be added unto you." Question—what do you mean by the Spirit. Ans. The Spirit

[1] Slightly imperfect memory of either Matt. 6:33 or Luke 12:31.

that spoke to the prophets in former days—and I was greatly astonished, and for two years prayed continually, whenever my duty would permit—and then again I had the same revelation, which fully confirmed me in the impression that I was ordained for some great purpose in the hands of the Almighty. Several years rolled round, in which many events occurred to strengthen me in this my belief. At this time I reverted in my mind to the remarks made of me in my childhood, and the things that had been shewn me—and as it had been said of me in my childhood by those by whom I had been taught to pray, both white and black, and in whom I had the greatest confidence, that I had too much sense to be raised, and if I was, I would never be of any use to any one as a slave. Now finding I had arrived to man's estate, and was a slave, and these revelations being made known to me, I began to direct my attention to this great object, to fulfil the purpose for which, by this time, I felt assured I was intended. Knowing the influence I had obtained over the minds of my fellow servants, (not by the means of conjuring and such like tricks—for to them I always spoke of such things with contempt) but by the communion of the Spirit whose revelations I often communicated to them, and they believed and said my wisdom came from God. I now began to prepare them for my purpose, by telling them something was about to happen that would terminate in fulfilling the great promise that had been made to me—About this time I was placed under an overseer, from whom I ran away—and after remaining in the woods thirty days, I returned, to the astonishment of the negroes on the plantation, who thought I had made my escape to some other part of the country, as my father had done before. But the reason of my return was, that the Spirit appeared to me and said I had my wishes directed to the things of this world, and not to the kingdom of Heaven, and that I should return to the service of my earthly master—"For he who knoweth his Master's will, and doeth it not, shall be beaten with many stripes, and thus have I chastened you."[2] And the negroes found fault, and murmured against me, saying that if they had my sense they would not serve any master in the world. And about this time I had a vision—and I saw white spirits and black spirits engaged in battle, and the sun was darkened—the thunder rolled in the Heavens, and blood flowed in streams—and I heard a voice saying, "Such is your luck, such you are called to see, and let it come rough or smooth, you must surely bear it." I now withdrew myself as much as my situation would permit, from the intercourse of my fellow servants, for the avowed purpose of serving the Spirit more fully—and it appeared to me, and reminded me of the things it had already shown me, and that it would then reveal to me the knowledge of the elements, the revolution of the planets, the operation of tides, and changes of the seasons. After this revelation in the year 1825, and the knowledge of the elements being made known to me, I sought more than ever to obtain true holiness before the great day of judgment should appear, and then I began to receive the true knowledge of faith. And from the first steps of righteousness until the last, was I made perfect; and the Holy Ghost was with me, and said, "Behold me as I stand in the Heavens"—and I looked and saw the forms of men in different attitudes—and there were lights in the sky to which the children of darkness gave other names than what they

[2] See Luke 12:47.

really were—for they were the lights of the Saviour's hands, stretched forth from east to west, even as they were extended on the cross on Calvary for the redemption of sinners. And I wondered greatly at these miracles, and prayed to be informed of a certainty of the meaning thereof—and shortly afterwards, while laboring in the field, I discovered drops of blood on the corn as though it were dew from heaven—and I communicated it to many, both white and black, in the neighborhood—and I then found on the leaves in the woods hieroglyphic characters, and numbers, with the forms of men in different attitudes, portrayed in blood, and representing the figures I had seen before in the heavens. And now the Holy Ghost had revealed itself to me, and made plain the miracles it had shown me—For as the blood of Christ had been shed on this earth, and had ascended to heaven for the salvation of sinners, and was now returning to earth again in the form of dew—and as the leaves on the trees bore the impression of the figures I had seen in the heavens, it was plain to me that the Saviour was about to lay down the yoke he had borne for the sins of men, and the great day of judgment was at hand. About this time I told these things to a white man, (Etheldred T. Brantley) on whom it had a wonderful effect—and he ceased from his wickedness, and was attacked immediately with a cutaneous eruption, and blood ozed from the pores of his skin, and after praying and fasting nine days, he was healed, and the Spirit appeared to me again, and said, as the Saviour had been baptised so should we be also—and when the white people would not let us be baptised by the church, we went down into the water together, in the sight of many who reviled us, and were baptised by the Spirit—After this I rejoiced greatly, and gave thanks to God. And on the 12th of May, 1828, I heard a loud noise in the heavens, and the Spirit instantly appeared to me and said the Serpent was loosened, and Christ had laid down the yoke he had borne for the sins of men, and that I should take it on and fight against the Serpent, for the time was fast approaching when the first should be last and the last should be first. Ques. Do you not find yourself mistaken now? Ans. Was not Christ crucified. And by signs in the heavens that it would make known to me when I should commence the great work—and until the first sign appeared, I should conceal it from the knowledge of men—And on the appearance of the sign, (the eclipse of the sun last February) I should arise and prepare myself, and slay my enemies with their own weapons. And immediately on the sign appearing in the heavens, the seal was removed from my lips, and I communicated the great work laid out for me to do, to four in whom I had the greatest confidence, (Henry, Hark, Nelson, and Sam)—It was intended by us to have begun the work of death on the 4th July last—Many were the plans formed and rejected by us, and it affected my mind to such a degree, that I fell sick, and the time passed without our coming to any determination how to commence—Still forming new schemes and rejecting them, when the sign appeared again, which determined me not to wait longer. Since the commencement of 1830, I had been living with Mr. Joseph Travis, who was to me a kind master, and placed the greatest confidence in me; in fact, I had no cause to complain of his treatment to me. On Saturday evening, the 20th of August, it was agreed between Henry, Hark and myself, to prepare a dinner the next day for the men we expected, and then to concert a plan, as we had not yet determined on any. Hark, on the following morning, brought a pig, and Henry brandy, and being joined by Sam, Nelson, Will and Jack, they prepared in the woods a dinner, where, about three o'clock,

I joined them. Q. Why were you so backward in joining them. A. The same reason that had caused me not to mix with them for years before. I saluted them on coming up, and asked Will how came he there, he answered, his life was worth no more than others, and his liberty as dear to him. I asked him if he thought to obtain it? He said he would, or lose his life. This was enough to put him in full confidence. Jack, I knew, was only a tool in the hands of Hark, it was quickly agreed we should commence at home (Mr. J. Travis') on that night, and until we had armed and equipped ourselves, and gathered sufficient force, neither age nor sex was to be spared, (which was invariably adhered to.) We remained at the feast, until about two hours in the night, when we went to the house and found Austin; they all went to the cider press and drank, except myself. On returning to the house, Hark went to the door with an axe, for the purpose of breaking it open, as we knew we were strong enough to murder the family, if they were awaked by the noise; but reflecting that it might create an alarm in the neighborhood, we determined to enter the house secretly, and murder them whilst sleeping. Hark got a ladder and set it against the chimney, on which I ascended, and hoisting a window, entered and came down stairs, unbarred the door, and removed the guns from their places. It was then observed that I must spill the first blood. On which, armed with a hatchet, and accompanied by Will, I entered my master's chamber, it being dark, I could not give a death blow, the hatchet glanced from his head, he sprang from the bed and called his wife, it was his last word, Will laid him dead, with a blow of his axe, and Mrs. Travis shared the same fate, as she lay in bed. The murder of this family, five in number, was the work of a moment, not one of them awoke; there was a little infant sleeping in a cradle, that was forgotten, until we had left the house and gone some distance, when Henry and Will returned and killed it; we got here, four guns that would shoot, and several old muskets, with a pound or two of powder. We remained some time at the barn, where we paraded; I formed them in a line as soldiers, and after carrying them through all the manoeuvres I was master of, marched them off to Mr. Salathul Francis', about six hundred yards distant. Sam and Will went to the door and knocked. Mr. Francis asked who was there, Sam replied it was him, and he had a letter for him, on which he got up and came to the door; they immediately seized him, and dragging him out a little from the door, he was dispatched by repeated blows on the head; there was no other white person in the family. We started from there for Mrs. Reese's, maintaining the most perfect silence on our march, where finding the door unlocked, we entered, and murdered Mrs. Reese in her bed, while sleeping; her son awoke, but it was only to sleep the sleep of death, he had only time to say who is that, and he was no more. From Mrs. Reese's we went to Mrs. Turner's, a mile distant, which we reached about sunrise, on Monday morning. Henry, Austin, and Sam, went to the still, where, finding Mr. Peebles, Austin shot him, and the rest of us went to the house; as we approached, the family discovered us, and shut the door. Vain hope! Will, with one stroke of his axe, opened it, and we entered and found Mrs. Turner and Mrs. Newsome in the middle of a room, almost frightened to death. Will immediately killed Mrs. Turner, with one blow of his axe. I took Mrs. Newsome by the hand, and with the sword I had when I was apprehended, I struck her several blows over the head, but not being able to kill her, as the sword was dull. Will turning around and discovering it, despatched her also. A general destruction of property and search for money and ammunition, always succeeded the murders. By this time my company amounted to fifteen, and nine men mounted, who started for Mrs. Whitehead's, (the other six were to go through a byway to Mr. Bryant's, and rejoin us at Mrs. Whitehead's,) as we approached the house we discovered Mr. Richard Whitehead standing in the cotton patch, near the lane fence; we called him over into the lane, and Will, the executioner, was near at hand, with his fatal axe, to send him to an untimely grave. As we pushed on to the house, I discovered someone run round the garden, and thinking it was some of the white family, I pursued them, but finding it was a servant girl belonging to the house, I returned to commence the work of death, but they whom I left, had not been idle; all the family were already murdered, but Mrs. Whitehead and her daughter Margaret. As I came round to the door I saw Will pulling Mrs. Whitehead out of the house, and at the step he nearly severed her head from her body, with his broad axe. Miss Margaret, when I discovered her, had concealed herself in the corner, formed by the projection of the cellar cap from the house; on my approach she fled, but was soon overtaken, and after repeated blows with a sword, I killed her by a blow on the head, with a fence rail. By this time, the six who had gone by Mr. Bryant's, rejoined us, and informed me they had done the work of death assigned them. We again divided, part going to Mr. Richard Porter's, and from thence to Nathaniel Francis', the others to Mr. Howell Harris', and Mr. T. Doyle's. On my reaching Mr. Porter's, he had escaped with his family. I understood there, that the alarm had already spread, and I immediately returned to bring up those sent to Mr. Doyle's, and Mr. Howell Harris'; the party I left going on to Mr. Francis', having told them I would join them in that neighborhood. I met these sent to Mr. Doyle's and Mr. Harris' returning, having met Mr. Doyle on the road and killed him; and learning from some who joined them, that Mr. Harris was from home, I immediately pursued the course taken by the party gone on before; but knowing they would complete the work of death and pillage, at Mr. Francis' before I could get there, I went to Mr. Peter Edwards', expecting to find them there, but they had been here also. I then went to Mr. John T. Barrow's, they had been here and murdered him. I pursued on their track to Capt. Newt Harris', where I found the greater part mounted, and ready to start; the men now amounting to about forty, shouted and hurrahed as I rode up, some were in the yard, loading their guns, others drinking. They said Captain Harris and his family had escaped, the property in the house they destroyed, robbing him of money and other valuables. I ordered them to mount and march instantly, this was about nine or ten o'clock, Monday morning. I proceeded to Mr. Levi Waller's, two or three miles distant. I took my station in the rear, and as it 'twas my object to carry terror and devastation wherever we went, I placed fifteen or twenty of the best armed and most to be relied on, in front, who generally approached the houses as fast as their horses could run; this was for two purposes, to prevent their escape and strike terror to the inhabitants—on this account I never got to the houses, after leaving Mrs. Whitehead's, until the murders were committed, except in one case. I sometimes got in sight in time to see the work of death completed, viewed the mangled bodies as they lay, in silent satisfaction, and immediately started in quest of other victims—Having murdered Mrs. Waller and ten children, we started for Mr. William Williams'—having killed him and two little boys that were there; while engaged in this, Mrs. Williams fled and got some distance from the house, but she was pursued, overtaken, and compelled to get up behind one of the company, who brought her back, and after showing her the mangled body of her lifeless husband, she was told to get down and lay by his side, where she was shot dead. I then started for Mr. Jacob Williams, where the family were murdered—Here we found a young man named Drury, who had come on business with Mr. Williams—he was pursued, overtaken and shot. Mrs. Vaughan was the next place we visited—and after murdering the family here, I determined on starting for Jerusalem—Our number amounted now to fifty or sixty, all mounted and armed with guns, axes, swords and clubs—On reaching Mr. James W. Parker's gate, immediately on the road leading to Jerusalem, and about three miles distant, it was proposed to me to call there, but I objected, as I knew he was gone to Jerusalem, and my object was to reach there as soon as possible; but some of the men having relations at Mr. Parker's it was agreed that they might call and get his people. I remained at the gate on the road, with seven or eight; the others going across the field to the house, about half a mile off. After waiting some time for them, I became impatient, and started to the house for them, and on our return we were met by a party of white men, who had pursued our bloodstained track, and who had fired on those at the gate, and dispersed them, which I knew nothing of, not having been at that time rejoined by any of them—Immediately on discovering the whites, I ordered my men to halt and form, as they appeared to be alarmed—The white men, eighteen in number, approached us in about one hundred yards, when one of them fired, (this was against the positive orders of Captain Alexander P. Peete, who commanded, and who had directed the men to reserve their fire until within thirty paces) And I discovered about half of them retreating, I then ordered my men to fire and rush on them; the few remaining stood their ground until we approached within fifty yards, when they fired and retreated. We pursued and overtook some of them who we thought we left dead; (they were not killed) after pursuing them about two hundred yards, and rising a little hill, I discovered they were met by another party, and had halted, and were re-loading their guns, (this was a small party from Jerusalem who knew the negroes were in the field, and had just tied their horses to await their return to the road, knowing that Mr. Parker and family were in Jerusalem, but knew nothing of the party that had gone in with Captain Peete; on hearing the firing they immediately rushed to the spot and arrived just in time to arrest the progress of these barbarous villains, and save the lives of their friends and fellow citizens.) Thinking that those who retreated first, and the party who fired on us at fifty or sixty yards distant, had all only fallen back to meet others with ammunition. As I saw them re-loading their guns, and more coming up than I saw at first, and several of my bravest men being wounded, the others became panick struck and squandered over the field; the white men pursued and fired on us several times. Hark had his horse shot under him, and I caught another for him as it was running by me; five or six of my men were wounded, but none left on the field; finding myself defeated here I instantly determined to go through a private way, and cross the Nottoway river at the Cypress Bridge, three miles below Jerusalem, and attack that place in the rear, as I expected they would look for me on the other road, and I had a great desire to get there to procure arms and ammunition. After going a short distance in this private way, accompanied by about twenty men, I overtook two or three who told me the others were dispersed in every direction. After trying in vain to collect a sufficient force to proceed to

Jerusalem, I determined to return, as I was sure they would make back to their old neighborhood, where they would rejoin me, make new recruits, and come down again. On my way back, I called at Mrs. Thomas's, Mrs. Spencer's, and several other places, the white families having fled, we found no more victims to gratify our thirst for blood, we stopped at Majr. Ridley's quarter for the night, and being joined by four of his men, with the recruits made since my defeat, we mustered now about forty strong. After placing out sentinels, I laid down to sleep, but was quickly roused by a great racket; starting up, I found some mounted, and others in great confusion; one of the sentinels having given the alarm that we were about to be attacked, I ordered some to ride round and reconnoitre, and on their return the others being more alarmed, not knowing who they were, fled in different ways, so that I was reduced to about twenty again; with this I determined to attempt to recruit, and proceed on to rally in the neighborhood, I had left. Dr. Blunt's was the nearest house, which we reached just before day; on riding up the yard, Hark fired a gun. We expected Dr. Blunt and his family were at Maj. Ridley's, as I knew there was a company of men there; the gun was fired to ascertain if any of the family were at home; we were immediately fired upon and retreated, leaving several of my men. I do not know what became of them, as I never saw them afterwards. Pursuing our course back and coming in sight of Captain Harris', where we had been the day before, we discovered a party of white men at the house, on which all deserted me but two, (Jacob and Nat,) we concealed ourselves in the woods until near night, when I sent them in search of Henry, Sam, Nelson, and Hark, and directed them to rally all they could, at the place we had had our dinner the Sunday before, where they would find me, and I accordingly returned there as soon as it was dark and remained until Wednesday evening, when discovering white men riding around the place as though they were looking for someone, and none of my men joining me, I concluded Jacob and Nat had been taken, and compelled to betray me. On this I gave up all hope for the present; and on Thursday night after having supplied myself with provisions from Mr. Travis's, I scratched a hole under a pile of fence rails in a field, where I concealed myself for six weeks, never leaving my hiding place but for a few minutes in the dead of night to get water which was very near; thinking by this time I could venture out, I began to go about in the night and eaves drop the houses in the neighborhood; pursuing this course for about a fortnight and gathering little or no intelligence, afraid of speaking to any human being, and returning every morning to my cave before the dawn of day. I know not how long I might have led this life, if accident had not betrayed me, a dog in the neighborhood passing by my hiding place one night while I was out, was attracted by some meat I had in my cave, and crawled in and stole it, and was coming out just as I returned. A few nights after, two negroes having started to go hunting with the same dog, and passed that way, the dog came again to the place, and having just gone out to walk about, discovered me and barked, on which thinking myself discovered, I spoke to them to beg concealment. On making myself known they fled from me. Knowing then they would betray me, I immediately left my hiding place, and was pursued almost incessantly until I was taken a fortnight afterwards by Mr. Benjamin Phipps, in a little hole I had dug out with my sword, for the purpose of concealment, under the top of a fallen tree. On Mr. Phipps'

discovering the place of my concealment, he cocked his gun and aimed at me. I requested him not to shoot and I would give up, upon which he demanded my sword. I delivered it to him, and he brought me to prison. During the time I was pursued, I had many hair breadth escapes, which your time will not permit you to relate. I am here loaded with chains, and willing to suffer the fate that awaits me.

Chapter Nineteen

LAFCADIO HEARN (1850–1904)

In Lafcadio Hearn's account of a voudou ceremony, we encounter a vivid first-person depiction of African rituals, music and belief systems in nineteenth-century Louisiana from the perspective of a white European observer. His evocation of the Gothicized landscapes surrounding Lake Ponchartrain, with flickering campfires casting grotesque shadows, and his description of the voudou "queen" convey the simultaneous fear and fascination with which these rites were regarded.

Text: W. H. Coleman (Compiler), *Historical Sketch Book and Guide to New Orleans and Environs* (New York: Will H. Coleman), 229–31.

ST. JOHN'S EVE—VOUDOUISM (1875)

St. John's eve[1] is specially devoted to the worship of the Voudous. It is on that night that they congregate at some secret meeting-place on Lake Pontchartrain—changed from time to time—and hold their religious dances and impious ceremonies of worshipping the prince of evil, for, in their theology, the devil is God, and it is to him they pray. Voudouism is rapidly dying out, even among the negroes of Louisiana, but, for all that, a negro is frightened to death if he is "hoodooed," and with reason. The secret magic of the Voudous was nothing more than an acquaintance with a number of subtle vegetable poisons, which they brought with them from Africa, and which caused their victims to fade gradually away, and die of exhaustion.

Every St. John's eve thousands of persons visit the lake ends in the hope of coming upon the Voudous, but few succeed in finding them.

On St. John's eve, last year, the night was dark, and on the eastern sky hung a black cloud, from which now and then burst flashes of lightning, which lit up the road, the bayou and the surrounding swamp with a lurid glow, in fit introduction to what was to follow. The scene on the lake coast from Spanish Fort to Milneburg,[2] was one which cannot easily be forgotten. All along the shore, at intervals scarcely more than 300 yards, groups of men and women could be seen standing around blazing pine-knot fires, their dark copper-colored faces weirdly gilded by the red flames and their black forms thus illuminated appearing gigantic and supernatural against the opaque background of the lake and sky on one side and the mystical darkness just tinged with starlight of the seemingly limitless swamps on the other. Some of the men were stripped to the waist, and

[1] June 23. The feast celebrates the birth of John the Baptist, assumed to be June 24.

[2] New Orleans neighborhoods on Lake Pontchartrain.

all were gesticulating with animation, or seemed to be in waiting for something. Along the road at various intervals were negresses standing by small tables where gombo[3] and coffee were dispensed.

Between Spanish Fort and Milneburg, the shore was crowded with negroes, who seemed to be enjoying themselves laughing, talking and romping like children, but the music which came from the shanty where a dance had evidently been started, sounded like that of an ordinary negro ball.

As soon as the purlieus of Milneburg were left, the way down the Lake shore toward the now brilliant bonfires was difficult, for in the darkness one had to pick his steps. Between the Lake on the one side and the swamp on the other there was a belt of land not more than fifty feet across, and in some places this was diminished by more than half, by the encroachment of Pontchartrain's waves. There was no roadway, but simply a devious by-path which wended around stumps and mud holes in a most irregular manner.

After some ten minutes' walk there came to the ear the faintest sound as of a drum beaten rhythmically, and on listening a chorus of voices could be heard.

Behind, the hundreds of small watchfires along the shore twinkled like stars in the distance, and where they were built upon little points of land they were reflected in the water so brightly the duplication added a peculiar weirdness to the scene.

Pursuing the same path was a party of Creole negroes,[4] the men carrying musical instruments and the women laden with coffeepots and tin buckets of gombo. They were not inclined to talk and, when asked where the Voudou dance was to take place, answered that they knew nothing about it.

Passing around a little willow copse that grew almost in the lake there opened to the view a scene Doré[5] would have delighted to paint. The belt of land here was about 100 feet in width, and in the middle of this little plot was burning a large fire. Grouped around it were some thirty or forty negroes, the rising and falling of the flames giving a grotesqueness to their figures that was as curious as it was entertaining. There shadows stretched out over the rushes and reeds of the swamp, and their faces brought out in effect looked wild enough to satisfy any lover of the wild and mysterious.

Built half over the swamps and half on the land stood a small hut or, to give it all its pretensions, a house of two rooms. It was like most of the fishermen's cabins seen along the Lake, but rather more roomy.

Through the open window there came quite a flood of light, and a song was heard chanted, it seemed by some eight or ten voices.

It was about three-quarters of a mile below Milneburg, and the place was appropriately selected, for certainly no more dismal and dreary spot could have been found. Citywards the swamp, with its funereal cypress, stretched in gloomy perspective, while in front,

---

3 Gombo, i.e., gumbo, a famous Louisiana stew of African origin, consisting of seafood or meat and vegetables.

4 Creole is a term with shifting meanings in Louisiana, but here means speakers of French or French-Caribbean dialect.

5 Gustave Doré (1832–1887), a French artist known especially for his moody, atmospheric illustrations for literary texts, including the Bible, and works by Milton, Dante and Poe.

lapping the rushes and stumps, the ripples in the Lake came in, the water appearing almost black from the vegetable matter held in suspension.

Near the fire were two or three tables laden with gombo and dishes of rice, while on the embers hissed pots of coffee.

When the group near them was approached they gave evidence of uneasiness at the appearance of the party, there being no white persons present.

A few words in Creole patois made the negroes feel more at ease, and when a cup of coffee was purchased they ceased to look suspiciously on the new arrivals.

The music in the house began with renewed vigor at this time, and there was by general consent a movement thither. It was nearly midnight.

The wide gallery on the front was soon thronged, and it was noticed but few were allowed to enter the large room which formed the eastern side of the building. The door was closed, and a stout young negress guarded it on the inside.

A few words from Chief Bachemin in creole proved an *open sesame*, and the door was opened just wide enough to permit the party to enter one at a time. With their entrance the music ceased and all eyes were turned upon the new comers.

A bright mulatto man came forward and, in good English, said that if the gentlemen desired to remain they would have to obey the orders that had been given. It would spoil the charm if they did not take off their coats.

Accordingly the coats were removed.

Seated on the floor with their legs crossed beneath them were about twenty-five negro men and women, the men in their shirt sleeves, and the women with their heads adorned with the traditional head handkerchief or *tignon*.[6]

In the centre of the floor there was spread a small tablecloth, at the corners of which two tallow candles were placed, being held in position by a bed of their own grease.

As a centre-piece, on the cloth, there was a shallow Indian basket filled with weeds, or, as they call them, herbs. Around the basket were diminutive piles of white beans and corn, and just outside of these a number of small bones, whether human or not could not be told. Some curiously wrought bunches of feathers were the next ornamentations near the edge of the cloth, and outside of all several saucers with small cakes in them.

The only person enjoying the aristocratic privilege of a chair was a bright *cafe au lait* woman of about forty-eight, who sat in one corner of the room looking on the scene before her with an air of dignity. She said but little, but beside her two old and wrinkled negresses whispered to her continually. She was of extremely handsome figure, and her features showed that she was not of the class known in old times as field hands. She was evidently raised about the plantation house. She was neatly attired tired in a blue calico dotted with white, and on her head a brilliant tignon was gracefully tied.

On inquiry it was learned that her name was Malvina Latour,[7] and that she was the queen.

---

6 A piece of cloth worn as a kind of turban headdress.

7 Voudou Queen after the death of Marie Laveau, also subject of an essay by Hearn.

As soon as the visitors had squatted down in their places against the wall an old negro man, whose wool was white with years, began scraping on a two-stringed sort of a fiddle. The instrument had a long neck, and its body was not more than three inches in diameter, being covered with brightly mottled snake skin. This was the signal to two young mulattoes beside him, who commenced to beat with their thumbs on little drums made of gourds and covered with sheepskin.

These tam-tams gave forth a short, hollow note of peculiar sound, and were fit accompaniments of the primitive fiddle. As if to inspire those present with the earnestness of the occasion, the old darkey rolled his eyes around the room and then, stamping his foot three times, exclaimed: "*A present commencez!*"[8]

Rising and stepping out toward the middle of the floor a tall and sinewy negro called the attention of all to him. He looked a Hercules, and his face was anything but attractive.

Nervous with restrained emotion, he commenced at first in a low voice, which gradually became louder and louder, a song, one stanza of which ran as follows:

Mallé couri dan déser,
Mallé marché dan savane,
Mallé marché su piquan d'oré—
Mallé oir ça ya di moin!

Sangé moin dan l'abitation ci la la?
Mo gagnain soutchien la Louisiane,
Mallé oir ça ya di moin!

Which can be translated as follows:

I will wander into the desert
I will march through the prairie
I will walk upon the golden thorn—[9]
Who is there who can stop me?

To change me from this plantation?
I have the support of Louisiana—
Who is there who can say no to me?

As he sang he seemed to grow in stature and his eyes began to roll in a sort of wild frenzy. There was ferocity in every word, boldness and defiance in every gesture.

Keeping time to his song the tam-tams and fiddle gave a weird and savagely monotonous accompaniment that it was easy to believe was not unlike like the savage music of Africa.

---

[8] French: Now begin!

[9] Compare the 1969 song "I Walk on Gilded Splinters" by the late Dr. John (Malcolm John Rebennack Jr., 1941–2019). Thanks to Thomas A. Klinger of Tulane University for noting this connection.

When it became time for all to join in the refrain he waved his arms, and then from every throat went up:

"Mallé oir ça ya *di moin!*"

He had hardly ended the fourth stanza before two women, uttering a loud cry, joined their leader on the floor, and these three began a march around the room. As the song progressed, an emaciated young negro stepped out, and amid the shouts of all, fell in behind the others.

The last addition to the wild dancers was most affected of all, and in a sort of delirium he picked up two of the candles and marched on with them in his hand. When he arrived opposite the queen she gave him something to drink out of a bottle. After swallowing some he retained a mouthful which, with a peculiar blowing sound, he spurted in a mist from his lips, holding the candle so as to catch the vapor. As it was alcohol it blazed up, and this attempt at necromancy was hailed with a shout.

Then commenced the regular Voudou dance with all its twistings and contortions. Two of the women fell exhausted to the floor in a frenzy and frothing at the mouth, and the emaciated young man was carried out of the room unconscious.

Chapter Twenty

GEORGE WASHINGTON CABLE (1844–1925)

Many of Cable's *Strange True Stories of Louisiana* (1890) are as truly Gothic as any fiction he wrote, and perhaps as anything in this volume.

Salomé Müller was a German immigrant child who was separated from her family, sold into slavery and grew up *believing that she was black*. She was freed after a lengthy court battle, and her saga was widely reported.

Slavery in the Americas depended on the legal fiction that a person was either black or white. Yet after generations of racial mixing, the reality, observable by anyone, was that there were people of every shade in between. There are many stories of people of color passing as white, and other stories of people, like Grace King's "Little Convent Girl," involuntarily crossing the color line from white to black. Salomé Müller's sad story is a *reductio ad absurdum* of Southern racial dogma, and exposes the artificial construction upon which slavery was based.

Text: George Washington Cable, *Strange True Stories of Louisiana* (New York: Charles Scribner's Sons, 1889), 145–91.

SALOME MÜLLER, THE WHITE SLAVE (1818–45)

I. Salome and Her Kindred

She may be living yet, in 1889. For when she came to Louisiana, in 1818, she was too young for the voyage to fix itself in her memory. She could not, to-day, be more than seventy-five.

In Alsace, France, on the frontier of the Department of Lower Rhine, about twenty English miles from Strasburg,[1] there was in those days, as I suppose there still is, a village called Langensoultz.[2] The region was one of hills and valleys and of broad, flat meadows yearly overflowed by the Rhine. It was noted for its fertility; a land of wheat and wine, hop-fields, flax-fields, hay-stacks, and orchards.

It had been three hundred and seventy years under French rule,[3] yet the people were still, in speech and traditions, German. Those were not the times to make them French. The land swept by Napoleon's wars, their firesides robbed of fathers and sons by the

1 Strasbourg.

2 Presumably in Langensoultzbach, in the northeast Rhine region of France.

3 In the early seventeenth century, the French consolidated their military and political control of Alsace, though German was still widely spoken and German cultural norms still prevailed.

conscription, the awful mortality of the Russian campaign,[4] the emperor's waning star, Waterloo[5]—these were not the things or conditions to give them comfort in French domination. There was a widespread longing among them to seek another land where men and women and children were not doomed to feed the ambition of European princes.

In the summer of 1817 there lay at the Dutch port of Helder[6]—for the great ship-canal that now lets the largest vessels out from Amsterdam was not yet constructed—a big, foul, old Russian ship which a certain man had bought purposing to crowd it full of emigrants to America.

These he had expected to find up the Rhine, and he was not disappointed. Hundreds responded from Alsace; some in Strasburg itself, and many from the surrounding villages, grain-fields, and vineyards. They presently numbered nine hundred, husbands, wives, and children. There was one family named Thomas, with a survivor of which I conversed in 1884. And there was Eva Kropp, née Hillsler, and her husband, with their daughter of fifteen, named for her mother. Also Eva Kropp's sister Margaret and her husband, whose name does not appear. And there were Koelhoffer and his wife, and Frau Schultzheimer. There is no need to remember exact relationships. All these except the Thomases were of Langensoultz.

As they passed through another village some three miles away they were joined by a family of name not given, but the mother of which we shall know by and by, under a second husband's name, as Madame Fleikener. And there too was one Wagner, two generations of whose descendants were to furnish each a noted journalist to New Orleans. I knew the younger of these in my boyhood as a man of, say, fifty. And there was young Frank Schuber, a good, strong-hearted, merry fellow who two years after became the husband of the younger Eva Kropp; he hailed from Strasburg; I have talked with his grandson. And lastly there were among the Langensoultz group two families named Müller.

The young brothers Henry and Daniel Müller were by birth Bavarians. They had married, in the Hillsler family, two sisters of Eva and Margaret. They had been known in the village as lockmaker[7] Müller and shoemaker Müller. The wife of Daniel, the shoemaker, was Dorothea. Henry, the locksmith, and his wife had two sons, the elder ten years of age and named for his uncle Daniel, the shoemaker. Daniel and Dorothea had four children. The eldest was a little boy of eight years, the youngest was an infant, and between these were two little daughters, Dorothea and Salome.

And so the villagers were all bound closely together, as villagers are apt to be. Eva Kropp's young daughter Eva was godmother to Salome. Frau Koelhoffer had lived on a farm about an hour's walk from the Müllers and had not known them; but Frau Schultzheimer was a close friend, and had been a schoolmate and neighbor of Salome's

---

[4] Napoleon's Russian campaign resulted in heavy losses (estimated at 500,000 French and 400,000 Russian casualties).

[5] The 1815 battle marking Napoleon's final defeat.

[6] A city in the northern Netherlands, now known as Den Helder.

[7] Locksmith.

mother. The husband of her who was afterward Madame Fleikener was a nephew of the Müller brothers, Frank Schuber was her cousin, and so on.

[In sections II and III Cable tells of the terrible sufferings of the immigrant families. The broker who took their money absconded, leaving them destitute in Amsterdam. Eventually they sail on three ships, their fare paid by the Dutch government. But food and fresh water run out, there is sickness aboard and many die in the passage.—Eds.]

IV. Sold into Bondage

They were fever-struck and famine-wasted. But February was near its end, and they were in the Gulf of Mexico. At that time of year its storms have lulled and its airs are the perfection of spring; March is a kind of May. And March came.

They saw other ships now every day; many of them going their way. The sight cheered them; the passage had been lonely as well as stormy. Their own vessels, of course,—the other two,—they had not expected to see, and had not seen. They did not know whether they were on the sea or under it.

At length pilot-boats began to appear. One came to them and put a pilot on board. Then the blue water turned green, and by and by yellow. A fringe of low land was almost right ahead. Other vessels were making for the same lighthouse towards which they were headed, and so drew constantly nearer to one another. The emigrants line the bulwarks, watching the nearest sails. One ship is so close that some can see the play of waters about her bows. And now it is plain that her bulwarks, too, are lined with emigrants who gaze across at them. She glides nearer, and just as the cry of recognition bursts from this whole company the other one yonder suddenly waves caps and kerchiefs and sends up a cheer. Their ship is the *Johanna.*

Do we dare draw upon fancy? We must not. The companies did meet on the water, near the Mississippi's mouth, though whether first inside or outside the stream I do not certainly gather. But they met; not the two vessels only, but the three. They were towed up the river side by side, the *Johanna* here, the *Captain Grone* there, and the other ship between them. Wagner, who had sailed on the galiot, was still alive. Many years afterwards he testified:

"We all arrived at the Balize [the river's mouth] the same day. The ships were so close we could speak to each other from on board our respective ships. We inquired of one another of those who had died and of those who still remained."

Madame Fleikener said the same:

"We hailed each other from the ships and asked who lived and who had died. The father and mother of Madame Schuber [Kropp and his wife] told me Daniel Müller and family were on board."

But they had suffered loss. Of the Johanna's 700 souls only 430 were left alive. Henry Müller's wife was dead. Daniel Müller's wife, Dorothea, had been sick almost from the start; she was gone, with the babe at her bosom. Henry was left with his two boys, and Daniel with his one and his little Dorothea and Salome. Grandsteiner, the supercargo,[8] had lived; but of 1800 homeless poor whom the Dutch king's gilders had

[8] Captain or foreman.

paid him to bring to America, foul ships and lack of food and water had buried 1200 in the sea.

The vessels reached port and the passengers prepared to step ashore, when to their amazement and dismay Grandsteiner laid the hand of the law upon them and told them they were "redemptioners." A redemptioner was an emigrant whose services for a certain period were liable to be sold to the highest bidder for the payment of his passage to America. It seems that in fact a large number of those on board the Johanna had in some way really become so liable; but it is equally certain that of others, the Kropps, the Schultzheimers, the Koelhoffers, the Müllers, and so on, the transportation had been paid for in advance, once by themselves and again by the Government of Holland. Yet Daniel Müller and his children were among those held for their passage money.

Some influential German residents heard of these troubles and came to the rescue. Suits were brought against Grandsteiner, the emigrants remaining meanwhile on the ships. Mr. Grymes was secured as counsel in their cause; but on some account not now remembered by survivors scarce a week had passed before they were being sold as redemptioners.[9] At least many were, including Daniel Müller and his children.

Then the dispersion began. The people were bound out before notaries and justices of the peace, singly and in groups, some to one, some to two years' service, according to age. "They were scattered,"—so testified Frank Schuber twenty-five years afterwards,—"scattered about like young birds leaving a nest, without knowing anything of each other." They were "taken from the ships," says, the jungfrau Hemin, "and went here and there so that one scarcely knew where the other went."

Many went no farther than New Orleans or its suburbs, but settled, some in and about the old rue Chartres—the Thomas family, for example; others in the then new faubourg Marigny, where Eva Kropp's daughter, Salome's young cousin Eva, for one, seems to have gone into domestic service. Others, again, were taken out to plantations near the city; Madame Fleikener to the well-known estate of Maunsell White, Madame Schultzheimer to the locally famous Hopkins plantation, and so on.

But others were carried far away; some, it is said, even to Alabama. Madame Hemin was taken a hundred miles up the river, to Baton Rouge, and Henry Müller and his two little boys went on to Bayou Sara, and so up beyond the State's border and a short way into Mississippi.

When all his relatives were gone Daniel Müller was still in the ship with his little son and daughters. Certainly he was not a very salable redemptioner with his three little motherless children about his knees. But at length, some fifteen days after the arrival of the ships, Frank Schuber met him on the old customhouse wharf with his little ones and was told by him that he, Müller, was going to Attakapas.[10] About the same time, or a little later, Müller came to the house where young Eva Kropp, afterwards Schuber's wife, dwelt, to tell her good-bye. She begged to be allowed to keep Salome. During the

[9] Bondservants.

[10] A trading post in South Louisiana, now St. Martinville. It was part of Orleans Parish (County), defined by the US government after the Louisiana Purchase.

sickness of the little one's mother and after the mother's death she had taken constant maternal care of the pretty, black-eyed, olive-skinned godchild. But Müller would not leave her behind.

V. The Lost Orphans

The prospective journey was the same that we saw Suzanne and Françoise, Joseph and Alix, take with toil and danger, yet with so much pleasure, in 1795. The early company went in a flatboat; these went in a round-bottom boat. The journey of the latter was probably the shorter. Its adventures have never been told, save one line. When several weeks afterwards the boat returned, it brought word that Daniel Müller had one day dropped dead on the deck and that his little son had fallen overboard and was drowned. The little girls had presumably been taken on to their destination by whoever had been showing the way; but that person's name and residence, if any of those left in New Orleans had known them, were forgotten. Only the wide and almost trackless region of Attakapas was remembered, and by people to whom every day brought a struggle for their own existence. Besides, the children's kindred were bound as redemptioners.

Those were days of rapid change in New Orleans. The redemptioners worked their way out of bondage into liberty. At the end of a year or two those who had been taken to plantations near by returned to the city. The town was growing, but the upper part of the river front in faubourg Ste. Marie, now in the heart of the city, was still lined with brick-yards, and thitherward cheap houses and opportunities for market gardening drew the emigrants. They did not colonize, however, but merged into the community about them, and only now and then, casually, met one another. Young Schuber was an exception; he throve as a butcher in the old French market, and courted and married the young Eva Kropp. When the fellow-emigrants occasionally met, their talk was often of poor shoemaker Müller and his lost children.

No clear tidings of them came. Once the children of some Germans who had driven cattle from Attakapas to sell them in the shambles at New Orleans corroborated to Frank Schuber the death of the father; but where Salome and Dorothea were they could not say, except that they were in Attakapas.

Frank and Eva were specially diligent inquirers after Eva's lost godchild; as also was Henry Müller up in or near Woodville, Mississippi. He and his boys were, in their small German way, prospering. He made such effort as he could to find the lost children. One day in the winter of 1820–21 he somehow heard that there were two orphan children named Miller—the Müllers were commonly called Miller—in the town of Natchez, some thirty-five miles away on the Mississippi. He bought a horse and wagon, and, leaving his own children, set out to rescue those of his dead brother. About midway on the road from Woodville to Natchez the Homochitto Creek runs through a swamp which in winter overflows. In here Müller lost his horse. But, nothing daunted, he pressed on, only to find in Natchez the trail totally disappear.

Again, in the early spring of 1824, a man driving cattle from Attakapas to Bayou Sara told him of two little girls named Müller living in Attakapas. He was planning another and bolder journey in search of them, when he fell ill; and at length, without telling his sons, if he knew, where to find their lost cousins, he too died.

Years passed away. Once at least in nearly every year young Daniel Miller—the "u" was dropped—of Woodville came down to New Orleans. At such times he would seek out his relatives and his father's and uncle's old friends and inquire for tidings of the lost children. But all in vain. Frank and Eva Schuber too kept up the inquiry in his absence, but no breath of tidings came. On the city's south side sprung up the new city of Lafayette, now the Fourth District of New Orleans, and many of the aforetime redemptioners moved thither. Its streets near the river became almost a German quarter. Other German immigrants, hundreds and hundreds, landed among them and in the earlier years many of these were redemptioners. Among them one whose name will always be inseparable from the history of New Orleans has a permanent place in this story.

VI. Christian Roselius

One morning many years ago, when some business had brought me into a corridor of one of the old court buildings facing the Place d'Armes,[11] a loud voice from within one of the court-rooms arrested my own and the general ear. At once from all directions men came with decorous haste towards the spot whence it proceeded. I pushed in through a green door into a closely crowded room and found the Supreme Court of the State in session. A short, broad, big-browed man of an iron sort, with silver hair close shorn from a Roman head, had just begun his argument in the final trial of a great case that had been before the court for many years, and the privileged seats were filled with the highest legal talent, sitting to hear him. It was a famous will case [26], and I remember that he was quoting from "King Lear" as I entered.

"Who is that?" I asked of a man packed against me in the press.

"Roselius," he whispered; and the name confirmed my conjecture: the speaker looked like all I had once heard about him. Christian Roselius[12] came from Brunswick, Germany, a youth of seventeen, something more than two years later than Salome Müller and her friends. Like them he came an emigrant under the Dutch flag, and like them his passage was paid in New Orleans by his sale as a redemptioner. A printer bought his services for two years and a half. His story is the good old one of courage, self-imposed privations, and rapid development of talents. From printing he rose to journalism, and from journalism passed to the bar. By 1836, at thirty-three years of age, he stood in the front rank of that brilliant group where Grymes[13] was still at his best. Before he was forty he had been made attorney-general of the State. Punctuality, application, energy, temperance, probity, bounty, were the strong features of his character. It was a common thing for him to give his best services free in the cause of the weak against the strong.

---

[11] The original French name of Jackson Square.

[12] Christian Roselius (1803–1873) was a Louisiana lawyer, attorney general of Louisiana from 1841 to 1843.

[13] John Randolph Grymes (1786–1854), New Orleans attorney.

As an adversary he was decorous and amiable, but thunderous, heavy-handed, derisive if need be, and inexorable. A time came for these weapons to be drawn in defense of Salome Müller.

FOOTNOTES: [26] The will of R.D. Shepherd.

VII. Miller *versus* Belmonte

In 1843 Frank and Eva Schuber had moved to a house on the corner of Jackson and Annunciation streets. [27] They had brought up sons, two at least, who were now old enough to be their father's mainstay in his enlarged business of "farming" (leasing and subletting) the Poydras market. The father and mother and their kindred and companions in long past misfortunes and sorrows had grown to wealth and standing among the German-Americans of New Orleans and Lafayette. The little girl cousin of Salome Müller, who as a child of the same age had been her playmate on shipboard at the Helder and in crossing the Atlantic, and who looked so much like Salome, was a woman of thirty, the wife of Karl Rouff.

One summer day she was on some account down near the lower limits of New Orleans on or near the river front, where the population was almost wholly a lower class of Spanish people. Passing an open door her eye was suddenly arrested by a woman of about her own age engaged in some humble service within with her face towards the door.

Madame Karl paused in astonishment. The place was a small drinking-house, a mere *cabaret*; but the woman! It was as if her aunt Dorothea, who had died on the ship twenty-five years before, stood face to face with her alive and well. There were her black hair and eyes, her olive skin, and the old, familiar expression of countenance that belonged so distinctly to all the Hillsler family. Madame Karl went in.

"My name," the woman replied to her question, "is Mary." And to another question, "No; I am a yellow girl.[14] I belong to Mr. Louis Belmonti, who keeps this 'coffee-house.' He has owned me for four or five years. Before that? Before that, I belonged to Mr. John Fitz Müller, who has the saw-mill down here by the convent. I always belonged to him." Her accent was the one common to English-speaking slaves.

But Madame Karl was not satisfied. "You are not rightly a slave. Your name is Müller. You are of pure German blood. I knew your mother. I know you. We came to this country together on the same ship, twenty-five years ago."

"No," said the other; "you must be mistaking me for some one else that I look like." But Madame Karl: "Come with me. Come up into Lafayette and see if I do not show you to others who will know you the moment they look at you."

The woman enjoyed much liberty in her place and was able to accept this invitation. Madame Karl took her to the home of Frank and Eva Schuber.

Their front door steps were on the street. As Madame Karl came up to them Eva stood in the open door much occupied with her approach, for she had not seen her for

[14] A woman of mixed race.

two years. Another woman, a stranger, was with Madame Karl. As they reached the threshold and the two old-time friends exchanged greetings, Eva said:

"Why, it is two years since last I saw you. Is that a German woman?—I know her!"

"Well," said Madame Karl, "if you know her, who is she?"

"My God!" cried Eva,—"the long-lost Salome Müller!"

"I needed nothing more to convince me," she afterwards testified in court. "I could recognize her among a hundred thousand persons."

Frank Schuber came in, having heard nothing. He glanced at the stranger, and turning to his wife asked:

"Is not that one of the girls who was lost?"

"It is," replied Eva; "it is. It is Salome Müller!"

On that same day, as it seems, for the news had not reached them, Madame Fleikener and her daughter—they had all become madams in Creole America—had occasion to go to see her kinswoman, Eva Schuber. She saw the stranger and instantly recognized her, "because of her resemblance to her mother."

They were all overjoyed. For twenty-five years dragged in the mire of African slavery, the mother of quadroon children and ignorant of her own identity, they nevertheless welcomed her back to their embrace, not fearing, but hoping, she was their long-lost Salome.

But another confirmation was possible, far more conclusive than mere recognition of the countenance. Eva knew this. For weeks together she had bathed and dressed the little Salome every day. She and her mother and all Henry Müller's family had known, and had made it their common saying, that it might be difficult to identify the lost Dorothea were she found; but if ever Salome were found they could prove she was Salome beyond the shadow of a doubt. It was the remembrance of this that moved Eva Schuber to say to the woman:

"Come with me into this other room." They went, leaving Madame Karl, Madame Fleikener, her daughter, and Frank Schuber behind. And when they returned the slave was convinced, with them all, that she was the younger daughter of Daniel and Dorothea Müller. We shall presently see what fixed this conviction.

The next step was to claim her freedom. She appears to have gone back to Belmonti, but within a very few days, if not immediately, Madame Schuber and a certain Mrs. White—who does not become prominent—followed down to the cabaret. Mrs. White went out somewhere on the premises, found Salome at work, and remained with her, while Madame Schuber confronted Belmonti, and, revealing Salome's identity and its proofs, demanded her instant release.

Belmonti refused to let her go. But while doing so he admitted his belief that she might be of pure white blood and of right entitled to freedom. He confessed having gone back to John F. Müller [28] soon after buying her and proposing to set her free; but Müller, he said, had replied that in such a case the law required her to leave the country. Thereupon Belmonti had demanded that the sale be rescinded, saying: "I have paid you my money for her."

"But," said Müller, "I did not sell her to you as a slave. She is as white as you or I, and neither of us can hold her if she chooses to go away."

Such at least was Belmonti's confession, yet he was as far from consenting to let his captive go after this confession was made as he had been before. He seems actually to have kept her for a while; but at length she went boldly to Schuber's house, became one of his household, and with his advice and aid asserted her intention to establish her freedom by an appeal to law. Belmonti replied with threats of public imprisonment, the chain-gang, and the auctioneer's block.

Salome, or Sally, for that seems to be the nickname by which her kindred remembered her, was never to be sold again; but not many months were to pass before she was to find herself, on her own petition and bond of $500, a prisoner, by the only choice the laws allowed her, in the famous calaboose, not as a criminal, but as sequestered goods in a sort of sheriff's warehouse. Says her petition: "Your petitioner has good reason to believe that the said Belmonti intends to remove her out of the jurisdiction of the court during the pendency of the suit"; wherefore not he but she went to jail. Here she remained for six days and was then allowed to go at large, but only upon giving still another bond and security, and in a much larger sum than she had ever been sold for.

The original writ of sequestration[15] lies before me as I write, indorsed as follows:

		No. 23,041.
Sally Miller	}	Sequestrian
vs.		Sigur, Caperton
Louis Belmonti.		Bonford.

Received 24th January, 1844, and on the 26th of the same month sequestered the body of the plaintiff and committed her to prison for safe keeping; but on the 1st February, 1844, she was released from custody, having entered bond in the sum of one thousand dollars with Francis Schuber as the security conditioned according to law, and which bond is herewith returned this 3d February, 1844.

B.F. LEWIS, d'y sh'ff.

Inside is the bond with the signatures, Frantz Schuber in German script, and above in English,

THE COURT PAPERS.

handwritten text

Also the writ, ending in words of strange and solemn irony: "In the year of our Lord one thousand eight hundred and forty-four and in the sixty-eighth year of the Independence of the United States."

We need not follow the history at the slow gait of court proceedings. At Belmonti's petition John F. Miller was called in warranty; that is, made the responsible party in Belmonti's stead. There were "prayers" and rules, writs and answers, as the cause slowly gathered shape for final contest. Here are papers of date February 24 and 29—it was leap year—and April 1, 2, 8, and 27. On the 7th of May Frank Schuber asked leave, and on the 14th was allowed, to substitute another bondsman in his place in order that he himself might qualify as a witness; and on the 23d of May the case came to trial.

[15] A document remanding her in custody.

VIII. The Trial

It had already become famous. Early in April the press of the city, though in those days unused to giving local affairs more than the feeblest attention, had spoken of this suit as destined, if well founded, to develop a case of "unparalleled hardship, cruelty, and oppression." The German people especially were aroused and incensed. A certain newspaper spoke of the matter as the case "that had for several days created so much excitement throughout the city." The public sympathy was with Salome.

But by how slender a tenure was it held! It rested not on the "hardship, cruelty, and oppression" she had suffered for twenty years, but only on the fact, which she might yet fail to prove, that she had suffered these things without having that tincture of African race which, be it ever so faint, would entirely justify, alike in the law and in the popular mind, treatment otherwise counted hard, cruel, oppressive, and worthy of the public indignation.

And now to prove the fact. In a newspaper of that date appears the following: Hon. A.M. Buchanan, Judge.

> Sally Miller
> *vs.* } No. 23,041.
> Belmonti.
> This cause came on to-day for trial before the court,
> Roselius and Upton for plaintiff, Canon for defendant, Grymes and
> Micou for warrantor; when after hearing evidence the same is
> continued until to-morrow morning at 11 o'clock.

Salome's battle had begun. Besides the counsel already named, there were on the slave's side a second Upton and a Bonford, and on the master's side a Sigur, a Caperton, and a Lockett. The redemptioners[16] had made the cause their own and prepared to sustain it with a common purse.

Neither party had asked for a trial by jury; the decision was to come from the bench.

The soldier, in the tableaux of Judge Buchanan's life, had not dissolved perfectly into the justice, and old lawyers of New Orleans remember him rather for unimpeachable integrity than for fine discrimination, a man of almost austere dignity, somewhat quick in temper.

Before him now gathered the numerous counsel, most of whose portraits have long since been veiled and need not now be uncovered. At the head of one group stood Roselius, at the head of the other, Grymes. And for this there were good reasons. Roselius, who had just ceased to be the State's attorney-general, was already looked upon as one of the readiest of all champions of the unfortunate. He was in his early prime, the first full spread of his powers, but he had not forgotten the little Dutch brig Jupiter, or the days when he was himself a redemptioner. Grymes, on the other side, had had to do—as we have seen—with these same redemptioners before. The uncle and the father of this same Sally Miller, so called, had been chief witnesses in the suit for their liberty and

[16] Bound servants, or those who had worked as such.

hers, which he had—blamelessly, we need not doubt—lost some twenty-five years before. Directly in consequence of that loss Salome had gone into slavery and disappeared. And now the loser of that suit was here to maintain that slavery over a woman who, even if she should turn out not to be the lost child, was enough like to be mistaken for her. True, causes must have attorneys, and such things may happen to any lawyer; but here was a cause which in our lights to-day, at least, had on the defendant's side no moral right to come into court.

One other person, and only one, need we mention. Many a New York City lawyer will recall in his reminiscences of thirty years ago a small, handsome, gold-spectacled man with brown hair and eyes, noted for scholarship and literary culture; a brilliant pleader at the bar, and author of two books that became authorities, one on trade-marks, the other on prize law. Even some who do not recollect him by this description may recall how the gifted Frank Upton—for it is of him I write—was one day in 1863 or 1864 struck down by apoplexy while pleading in the well-known Peterhoff case. Or they may remember subsequently his constant, pathetic effort to maintain his old courtly mien against his resultant paralysis. This was the young man of about thirty, of uncommon masculine beauty and refinement, who sat beside Christian Roselius as an associate in the cause of Sally Miller versus Louis Belmonti.

FOOTNOTES:

[27] Long since burned down.

[28] The similarity in the surnames of Salome and her master is odd, but is accidental and without significance.

IX. The Evidence

We need not linger over the details of the trial. The witnesses for the prosecution were called. First came a Creole woman, so old that she did not know her own age, but was a grown-up girl in the days of the Spanish governor-general Galvez, sixty-five years before. She recognized in the plaintiff the same person whom she had known as a child in John F. Miller's domestic service with the mien, eyes, and color of a white person and with a German accent. Next came Madame Hemin, who had not known the Müllers till she met them on the Russian ship and had not seen Salome since parting from them at Amsterdam, yet who instantly identified her "when she herself came into the court-room just now." "Witness says," continues the record, "she perceived the family likeness in plaintiff's face when she came in the door."

The next day came Eva and told her story; and others followed, whose testimony, like hers, we have anticipated. Again and again was the plaintiff recognized, both as Salome and as the girl Mary, or Mary Bridget, who for twenty years and upward had been owned in slavery, first by John F. Miller, then by his mother, Mrs. Canby, and at length by the cabaret keeper Louis Belmonti. If the two persons were but one, then for twenty years at least she had lived a slave within five miles, and part of the time within two, of her kindred and of freedom.

That the two persons were one it seemed scarcely possible to doubt. Not only did every one who remembered Salome on shipboard recognize the plaintiff as she, but others, who had quite forgotten her appearance then, recognized in her the strong family likeness of the Müllers. This likeness even witnesses for the defense had to admit. So, on Salome's side, testified Madame Koelhoffer, Madame Schultzheimer, and young Daniel Miller (Müller) from Mississippi. She was easily pointed out in the throng of the crowded court-room.

And then, as we have already said, there was another means of identification which it seemed ought alone to have carried with it overwhelming conviction. But this we still hold in reserve until we have heard the explanation offered by John F. Miller both in court and at the same time in the daily press in reply to its utterances which were giving voice to the public sympathy for Salome.

It seems that John Fitz Miller was a citizen of New Orleans in high standing, a man of property, money, enterprises, and slaves. John Lawson Lewis, commanding-general of the State militia, testified in the case to Mr. Miller's generous and social disposition, his easy circumstances, his kindness to his eighty slaves, his habit of entertaining, and the exceptional fineness of his equipage. Another witness testified that complaints were sometimes made by Miller's neighbors of his too great indulgence of his slaves. Others, ladies as well as gentlemen, corroborated these good reports, and had even kinder and higher praises for his mother, Mrs. Canby. They stated with alacrity, not intending the slightest imputation against the gentleman's character, that he had other slaves even fairer of skin than this Mary Bridget, who nevertheless, "when she was young," they said, "looked like a white girl." One thing they certainly made plain—that Mr. Miller had never taken the Müller family or any part of them to Attakapas or knowingly bought a redemptioner.

He accounted for his possession of the plaintiff thus: In August, 1822, one Anthony Williams, being or pretending to be a negro-trader and from Mobile, somehow came into contact with Mr. John Fitz Miller in New Orleans. He represented that he had sold all his stock of slaves except one girl, Mary Bridget, ostensibly twelve years old, and must return at once to Mobile. He left this girl with Mr. Miller to be sold for him for his (Williams's) account under a formal power of attorney so to do, Mr. Miller handing him one hundred dollars as an advance on her prospective sale. In January, 1823, Williams had not yet been heard from, nor had the girl been sold; and on the 1st of February Mr. Miller sold her to his own mother, with whom he lived—in other words, to himself, as we shall see. In this sale her price was three hundred and fifty dollars and her age was still represented as about twelve. "From that time she remained in the house of my mother," wrote Miller to the newspapers, "as a domestic servant" until 1838, when "she was sold to Belmonti."

Mr. Miller's public statement was not as full and candid as it looked. How, if the girl was sold to Mrs. Canby, his mother—how is it that Belmonti bought her of Miller himself? The answer is that while Williams never re-appeared, the girl, in February, 1835, "the girl Bridget," now the mother of three children, was with these children bought back again by that same Mr. Miller from the entirely passive Mrs. Canby, for the same three hundred and fifty dollars; the same price for the four which he had got, or had seemed to get, for the mother alone when she was but a child of twelve years. Thus had Mr. Miller become the owner of the woman, her two sons, and her daughter, had had her service for the keeping, and had never paid but one hundred dollars. This point he prudently overlooked in his public statement. Nor did he count it necessary to emphasize the further fact that when this slave-mother was about twenty-eight years old and her little daughter had died, he sold her alone, away from her two half-grown sons, for ten times what he had paid for her, to be the bond-woman of the wifeless keeper of a dram-shop.

But these were not the only omissions. Why had Williams never come back either for the slave or for the proceeds of her sale? Mr. Miller omitted to state, what he knew well enough, that the girl was so evidently white that Williams could not get rid of her, even to him, by an open sale. When months and years passed without a word from Williams, the presumption was strong that Williams knew the girl was not of African tincture, at least within the definition of the law, and was content to count the provisional transfer to Miller equivalent to a sale.

Miller, then, was—heedless enough, let us call it—to hold in African bondage for twenty years a woman who, his own witnesses testified, had every appearance of being a white person, without ever having seen the shadow of a title for any one to own her, and with everything to indicate that there was none. Whether he had any better right to own the several other slaves whiter than this one whom those same witnesses of his were forward to state he owned and had owned, no one seems to have inquired. Such were the times; and it really was not then remarkable that this particular case should involve a lady noted for her good works and a gentleman who drove "the finest equipage in New Orleans."

One point, in view of current beliefs of to-day, compels attention. One of Miller's witnesses was being cross-examined. Being asked if, should he see the slave woman among white ladies, he would not think her white, he replied:

"I cannot say. There are in New Orleans many white persons of dark complexion and many colored persons of light complexion." The question followed:

"What is there in the features of a colored person that designates them to be such?"

"I cannot say. Persons who live in countries where there are many colored persons acquire an instinctive means of judging that cannot be well explained."

And yet neither this man's "instinct" nor that of any one else, either during the whole trial or during twenty years' previous knowledge of the plaintiff, was of the least value to determine whether this poor slave was entirely white or of mixed blood. It was more utterly worthless than her memory. For as to that she had, according to one of Miller's own witnesses, in her childhood confessed a remembrance of having been brought "across the lake"; but whether that had been from Germany, or only from Mobile, must be shown in another way. That way was very simple, and we hold it no longer in suspense.

X. The Crowning Proof

"If ever our little Salome is found," Eva Kropp had been accustomed to say, "we shall know her by two hair moles about the size of a coffee-bean, one on the inside of each thigh, about midway up from the knee. Nobody can make those, or take them away without leaving the tell-tale scars." And lo! when Madame Karl brought Mary Bridget to Frank Schuber's house, and Eva Schuber, who every day for weeks had bathed and dressed her godchild on the ship, took this stranger into another room apart and alone, there were the birth-marks of the lost Salome.

This incontestable evidence the friends of Salome were able to furnish, but the defense called in question the genuineness of the marks.

The verdict of science was demanded, and an order of the court issued to two noted physicians, one chosen by each side, to examine these marks and report "the nature, appearance, and cause of the same." The kindred of Salome chose Warren Stone, probably the greatest physician and surgeon in one that New Orleans has ever known.[17] Mr. Grymes's client chose a Creole gentleman almost equally famed, Dr. Armand Mercier.[18]

Dr. Stone died many years ago; Dr. Mercier, if I remember aright, in 1885. When I called upon Dr. Mercier in his office in Girod street in the summer of 1883, to appeal to his remembrance of this long-forgotten matter, I found a very noble-looking, fair old gentleman whose abundant waving hair had gone all to a white silken floss with age. He sat at his desk in persistent silence with his strong blue eyes fixed steadfastly upon me while I slowly and carefully recounted the story. Two or three times I paused inquiringly; but he faintly shook his head in the negative, a slight frown of mental effort gathering for a moment between the eyes that never left mine. But suddenly he leaned forward and drew his breath as if to speak. I ceased, and he said:

"My sister, the wife of Pierre Soulé, refused to become the owner of that woman and her three children because they were so white!" He pressed me eagerly with an enlargement of his statement, and when he paused I said nothing or very little; for, sad to say, he had only made it perfectly plain that it was not the girl Mary Bridget whom he was recollecting, but *another case.*

He did finally, though dimly, call to mind having served with Dr. Stone in such a matter as I had described. But later I was made independent of his powers of recollection, when the original documents of the court were laid before me. There was the certificate of the two physicians. And there, over their signatures, "Mercier d.m.p." standing first, in a bold heavy hand underscored by a single broad quill-stroke, was this "Conclusion":

"1. These marks ought to be considered as noevi materni.

"2. They are congenital; or, in other words, the person was born with them.

"3. There is no process by means of which artificial spots bearing all the character of the marks can be produced."

Handwritten conclusion number 3 and signatures of Mercier dmp and Dr. Stone.

---

[17] Warren Stone (1808–1872), founder of the Medical College of Louisiana, now Tulane University.

[18] Armand Mercier (1813–1885), a prominent New Orleans physician trained in Paris.

XI. Judgment

[The judge rules that the evidence is insufficient to free Salome. However, the case is appealed to the Louisiana Supreme Court.—Eds.]

XII. Before the Supreme Court

[The Louisiana Supreme Court rules, in 1845, that the defense had failed to prove that Salome was of African descent, and thus should be set free.—Eds.]

... Salome being free, her sons were, by law, free also. But they could only be free mulattoes, went to Tennessee and Kentucky, were heard of once or twice as stable-boys to famous horses, and disappeared. A Mississippi River pilot, John Given by name, met Salome among her relatives, and courted and married her. As might readily be supposed, this alliance was only another misfortune to Salome, and the pair separated. Salome went to California. Her cousin, Henry Schuber, tells me he saw her in 1855 in Sacramento City, living at last a respected and comfortable life.

Chapter Twenty-One

GEORGE WASHINGTON CABLE (1844–1925)

In "The Haunted House in Royal Street," Cable describes the various incarnations of a mansion in New Orleans, which was even, for a time, a school. In the section below, Cable tells of the time when the house was presided over by the notorious Madame Lalurie, a woman of uncertain background who gained admission to New Orleans society through her great beauty, wealth and charm.

She also was a secret sadist, who committed acts of brutality on her slaves. When the secrets of the house were at last revealed, the slave-owning citizens of New Orleans rioted and drove her from the city.

This story, like that of Salome Müller, was known throughout the South.

Text: George Washington Cable, Strange True Stories of Louisiana (New York: Charles Scribner's Sons, 1889), 200–219.

THE "HAUNTED HOUSE" IN ROYAL STREET

1831–82

II. Madame Lalaurie

On the 30th of August, 1831, before Octave de Armas, notary, one E. Soniat Dufossat sold this property to a Madame Lalaurie. She may have dwelt in the house earlier than this, but here is where its tragic history begins. Madame Lalaurie was still a beautiful and most attractive lady, though bearing the name of a third husband. Her surname had been first McCarty,—a genuine Spanish-Creole name, although of Irish origin, of course,—then Lopez, or maybe first Lopez and then McCarty, and then Blanque. She had two daughters, the elder, at least, the issue of her first marriage.

The house is known to this day as Madame Blanque's house,—which, you notice, it never was,—so distinctly was she the notable figure in the household. Her husband was younger than she. There is strong sign of his lesser importance in the fact that he was sometimes, and only sometimes, called doctor—Dr. Louis Lalaurie. The graces and graciousness of their accomplished and entertaining mother quite outshone his step-daughters as well as him. To the frequent and numerous guests at her sumptuous board these young girls seemed comparatively unanimated, if not actually unhappy. Not so with their mother. To do her full share in the upper circles of good society, to dispense the pleasures of drawing-room and dining-room with generous frequency and captivating amiability, was the eager pursuit of a lady who nevertheless kept the management of her money affairs, real estate, and slaves mainly in her own hands. Of slaves she had ten, and housed most of them in the tall narrow wing that we have already noticed.

We need not recount again the state of society about her at that time. The description of it given by the young German duke whom we quoted without date in the story of "Salome Muller" belongs exactly to this period. Grymes stood at the top and front of things. John Slidell was already shining beside him. They were co-members of the Elkin Club, then in its glory. It was trying energetically to see what incredible quantities of Madeira it could drink. Judge Mazereau was "avocat-général" and was being lampooned by the imbecile wit of the singers and dancers of the calinda in Congo Square. The tree-planted levee was still populous on summer evenings with promenaders and loungers. The quadroon caste was in its dying splendor, still threatening the moral destruction of private society, and hated—as only woman can hate enemies of the hearthstone—by the proud, fair ladies of the Creole pure-blood, among whom Madame Lalaurie shone brilliantly. Her elegant house, filled with "furniture of the most costly description,"—says the "New Orleans Bee" of a date which we shall come to,—stood central in the swirl of "downtown" gayety, public and private. From Royal into Hospital street, across Circus street—rue de la Cirque—that was a good way to get into Bayou Road, white, almost as snow, with its smooth, silent pavement of powdered shells. This road followed the slow, clear meanderings of Bayou St. Jean, from red-roofed and embowered suburb St. Jean to the lake, the swamp of giant, grizzly bearded cypresses hugging it all the way, and the whole five miles teeming with gay, swift carriages, some filled with smokers, others with ladies and children, the finest equipage of all being, as you may recollect, that of John Fitz Miller. He was at that very time master of Salome Muller, and of "several others fairer than Salome." He belongs in the present story only here in this landscape, and here not as a typical, but only as an easily possible, slaveholder. For that matter, Madame Lalaurie, let it be plainly understood, was only another possibility, not a type. The two stories teach the same truth: that a public practice is answerable for whatever can happen easier with it than without it, no matter whether it must, or only may, happen. However, let the moral wait or skip it entirely if you choose: a regular feature of that bright afternoon throng was Madame Lalaurie's coach with the ever-so-pleasant Madame Lalaurie inside and her sleek black coachman on the box.

"Think," some friend would say, as he returned her courteous bow—"think of casting upon that woman the suspicion of starving and maltreating her own house-servants! Look at that driver; his skin shines with good keeping. The truth is those jealous Americans"—

There was intense jealousy between the Americans and the Creoles. The Americans were just beginning in public matters to hold the odds. In private society the Creoles still held power, but it was slipping from them even there. Madame Lalaurie was a Creole. Whether Louisiana or St. Domingo born was no matter; she should not be criticised by American envy! Nor would the Creoles themselves go nosing into the secretest privacy of her house.

"Why, look you, it is her common practice, even before her guests, to leave a little wine in her glass and hand it, with some word of kindness, to the slave waiting at her back. Thin and hollow-chested—the slaves? Yes, to be sure: but how about your rich uncle, or my dear old mother: are they not hollow-chested? Well!"

But this kind of logic did not satisfy everybody, not even every Creole; and particularly not all her neighbors. The common populace too had unflattering beliefs.

"Do you see this splendid house? Do you see those attic windows? There are slaves up there confined in chains and darkness and kept at the point of starvation."

A Creole gentleman, M. Montreuil, who seems to have been a neighbor, made several attempts to bring the matter to light, but in vain. Yet rumors and suspicious indications grew so rank that at length another prominent citizen, an "American" lawyer, who had a young Creole studying law in his office, ventured to send him to the house to point out to Madame Lalaurie certain laws of the State. For instance there was Article XX. of the old Black Code: "Slaves who shall not be properly fed, clad, and provided for by their masters, may give information thereof to the attorney-general or the Superior Council, or to all the other officers of justice of an inferior jurisdiction, and may put the written exposition of their wrongs into their hands; upon which information, and even ex officio, should the information come from another quarter, the attorney-general shall prosecute said masters," etc. But the young law student on making his visit was captivated by the sweetness of the lady whom he had been sent to warn against committing unlawful misdemeanors, and withdrew filled with indignation against any one who could suspect her of the slightest unkindness to the humblest living thing.

III. A Terrible Revelation

The house that joined Madame Lalaurie's premises on the eastern side had a staircase window that looked down into her little courtyard. One day all by chance the lady of that adjoining house was going up those stairs just when the keen scream of a terrified child resounded from the next yard. She sprung to the window, and, looking down, saw a little negro girl about eight years old run wildly across the yard and into the house, with Madame Lalaurie, a cow-hide whip in her hand, following swiftly and close upon her.

They disappeared; but by glimpses through the dark lattices and by the sound of the tumult, the lady knew that the child was flying up stairway after stairway, from gallery to gallery, hard pressed by her furious mistress. Soon she heard them rise into the belvedere and the next instant they darted out upon the roof. Down into its valleys and up over its ridges the little fugitive slid and scrambled. She reached the sheer edge, the lady at the window hid her face in her hands, there came a dull, jarring thud in the paved court beneath, and the lady, looking down, saw the child lifted from the ground and borne out of sight, limp, silent, dead.

She kept her place at the window. Hours passed, the day waned, darkness settled down. Then she saw a torch brought, a shallow hole was dug,—as it seemed to her; but in fact a condemned well of slight depth, a mere pit, was uncovered,—and the little broken form was buried. She informed the officers of justice. From what came to light at a later season, it is hard to think that in this earlier case the investigation was more than superficial. Yet an investigation was made, and some legal action was taken against Madame Lalaurie for cruelty to her slaves. They were taken from her and—liberated? Ah! no. They were sold by the sheriff, bid in by her relatives, and by them sold back to her. Let us believe that this is what occurred, or at least was shammed; for unless we do we must accept the implication of a newspaper statement of two or three years afterwards, and the confident impression of an aged Creole gentleman and notary still living who was an eye-witness to much of this story, that all Madame Lalaurie ever suffered for this part of her hideous misdeeds was a fine. Lawyers will doubtless remind us that Madame Lalaurie was not legally chargeable with the child's death. The lady at the window was not the only witness who might have been brought. A woman still living, who after the civil war was for years a domestic in this "haunted house," says her husband, now long dead, then a lad, was passing the place when the child ran out on the roof, and he saw her scrambling about on it seeking to escape. But he did not see the catastrophe that followed. No one saw more than what the law knows as assault; and the child was a slave.

Miss Martineau, in her short account of the matter,[1] which she heard in New Orleans and from eye-witnesses only a few years after it had occurred, conjectures that Madame Lalaurie's object in buying back these slaves was simply to renew her cruelties upon them. But a much easier, and even kinder, guess would be that they knew things about her that had not been and must not be told, if she could possibly prevent it. A high temper, let us say, had led her into a slough of misdoing to a depth beyond all her expectation, and the only way out was on the farther side.

Yet bring to bear all the generous conjecture one can, and still the fact stands that she did starve, whip, and otherwise torture these poor victims. She even mistreated her daughters for conveying to them food which she had withheld. Was she not insane? One would hope so; but we cannot hurry to believe just what is most comfortable or kindest. That would be itself a kind of "emotional insanity." If she was insane, how about her husband? For Miss Martineau, who was told that he was no party to her crimes, was misinformed; he was as deep in the same mire as passive complicity could carry him. If she was insane her insanity stopped abruptly at her plump, well-fed coachman. He was her spy against all others. And if she was insane, then why did not her frequent guests at table suspect it?

All that society knew was that she had carried her domestic discipline to excess, had paid dearly for it, and no doubt was desisting and would henceforth desist from that kind of thing. Enough allowance can hardly be made in our day for the delicacy society felt about prying into one of its own gentleman or lady member's treatment of his or her own servants. Who was going to begin such an inquiry—John Fitz Miller?

And so time passed, and the beautiful and ever sweet and charming Madame Lalaurie—whether sane or insane we leave to the doctors, except Dr. Lalaurie—continued to drive daily, yearly, on the gay Bayou Road, to manage her business affairs, and to gather bright groups around her tempting board, without their suspicion that she kept her cook in the kitchen by means of a twenty-four-foot chain fastened to her person and to the wall or floor.

---

[1] Harriet Martineau (1802–1876) was a prolific English writer of novels, travel books and studies in philosophy, sociology and economics. The account of Madame Lalaurie is in *Retrospect of Western Travel* (1838).

And yet let this be said to the people's credit, that public suspicion and indignation steadily grew. But they were still only growing when one day, the both of April, 1834, the aged cook,—she was seventy,—chained as she was, purposely set the house on fire. It is only tradition that, having in a dream the night before seen the drawing-room window curtains on fire, she seized the happy thought and made the dream a reality. But it is in the printed record of the day that she confessed the deed to the mayor of the city.

The desperate stratagem succeeds. The alarm of fire spreads to the street and a hundred men rush, in, while a crowd throngs the streets. Some are neighbors, some friends, some strangers. One is M. Montreuil, the gentleman who has so long been watching his chance to bring the law upon the house and its mistress. Young D——, a notary's clerk, is another. And another is Judge Canonge—Aha! And there are others of good and well-known name!

The fire has got a good start; the kitchen is in flames; the upper stories are filling with smoke. Strangers run to the place whence it all comes and fall to fighting the fire. Friends rally to the aid of Monsieur and Madame Lalaurie. The pretty lady has not lost one wit—is at her very best. Her husband is as passive as ever.

"This way," she cries; "this way! Take this—go, now, and hurry back, if you please. This way!" And in a moment they are busy carrying out, and to places of safety, plate, jewels, robes, and the lighter and costlier pieces of furniture. "This way, please, gentlemen; that is only the servants' quarters."

The servants' quarters—but where are the servants?

Madame's answers are witty but evasive. "Never mind them now—save the valuables!"

Somebody touches Judge Canonge—"Those servants are chained and locked up and liable to perish."

"Where?"

"In the garret rooms."

He hurries towards them, but fails to reach them, and returns, driven back and nearly suffocated by the smoke. He looks around him—this is no sketch of the fancy; we have his deposition sworn before a magistrate next day—and sees some friends of the family. He speaks to them:

"I am told"—so and so—"can it be? Will you speak to Monsieur or to Madame?" But the friends repulse him coldly.

He turns and makes fresh inquiries of others. He notices two gentlemen near him whom he knows. One is Montreuil. "Here, Montreuil, and you, Fernandez, will you go to the garret and search? I am blind and half smothered." Another—he thinks it was Felix Lefebre—goes in another direction, most likely towards the double door between the attics of the house and wing. Montreuil and Fernandez come back saying they have searched thoroughly and found nothing. Madame Lalaurie begs them, with all her sweetness, to come other ways and consider other things. But here is Lefebre. He cries, "I have found some of them! I have broken some bars, but the doors are locked!"

Judge Canonge hastens through the smoke. They reach the spot.

"Break the doors down!" Down come the doors. The room they push into is a "den." They bring out two negresses. One has a large heavy iron collar at the neck and heavy irons on her feet. The fire is subdued now, they say, but the search goes on. Here is

M. Guillotte; he has found another victim in another room. They push aside a mosquito-net and see a negro woman, aged, helpless, and with a deep wound in the head.

Some of the young men lift her and carry her out.

Judge Canonge confronts Doctor Lalaurie again:

"Are there slaves still in your garret, Monsieur?" And the doctor "replies with insulting tone that 'There are persons who would do much better by remaining at home than visiting others to dictate to them laws in the quality of officious friends.'"

The search went on. The victims were led or carried out. The sight that met the public eye made the crowd literally groan with horror and shout with indignation. "We saw," wrote the editor of the "Advertiser" next day, "one of these miserable beings. The sight was so horrible that we could scarce look upon it. The most savage heart could not have witnessed the spectacle unmoved. He had a large hole in his head; his body from head to foot was covered with scars and filled with worms! The sight inspired us with so much horror that even at the moment of writing this article we shudder from its effects. Those who have seen the others represent them to be in a similar condition." One after another, seven dark human forms were brought forth, gaunt and wild-eyed with famine and loaded with irons, having been found chained and tied in attitudes in which they had been kept so long that they were crippled for life.

It must have been in the first rush of the inside throng to follow these sufferers into the open air and sunlight that the quick-witted Madame Lalaurie clapped to the doors of her house with only herself and her daughters—possibly the coachman also—inside, and nothing but locks and bars to defend her from the rage of the populace. The streets under her windows—Royal street here, Hospital yonder—and the yard were thronged. Something by and by put some one in mind to look for buried bodies. There had been nine slaves besides the coachman; where were the other two? A little digging brought their skeletons to light—an adult's out of the soil, and the little child's out of the "condemned well"; there they lay. But the living seven—the indiscreet crowd brought them food and drink in fatal abundance, and before the day was done two more were dead. The others were tenderly carried—shall we say it?—to prison;—to the calaboose. Thither "at least two thousand people" flocked that day to see, if they might, these wretched sufferers.

A quiet fell upon the scene of the morning's fire. The household and its near friends busied themselves in getting back the jewelry, plate, furniture, and the like, the idle crowd looking on in apathy and trusting, it may be, to see arrests made. But the restoration was finished and the house remained close barred; no arrest was made. As for Dr. Lalaurie, he does not appear in this scene. Then the crowd, along in the afternoon, began to grow again; then to show anger and by and by to hoot and groan, and cry for satisfaction.

IV. The Lady's Flight

The old Bayou Road saw a strange sight that afternoon. Down at its farther end lay a little settlement of fishermen and Spanish moss gatherers, pot-hunters, and shrimpers, around a custom-house station, a lighthouse, and a little fort. There the people who drove out in carriages were in the habit of alighting and taking the cool air of the lake, and sipping lemonades, wines, and ices before they turned homeward again along the crowded way that they had come. In after years the place fell into utter neglect. The customs station was removed, the fort was dismantled, the gay carriage people drove on the "New Shell Road" and its tributaries, Bienville and Canal streets, Washington and Carrollton avenues, and sipped and smoked in the twilights and starlights of Carrollton Gardens and the "New Lake End." The older haunt, once so bright with fashionable pleasure-making, was left to the sole illumination of "St. John Light" and the mongrel life of a bunch of cabins branded Crabtown, and became, in popular superstition at least, the yearly rendezvous of the voodoos. Then all at once in latter days it bloomed out in electrical, horticultural, festal, pyrotechnical splendor as "Spanish Fort," and the carriages all came rolling back.

So, whenever you and——visit Spanish Fort and stroll along the bayou's edge on the fort side, and watch the broad schooners glide out through the bayou's mouth and into the open water, you may say: "Somewhere just along this bank, within the few paces between here and yonder, must be where that schooner lay, moored and ready to sail for Mandeville the afternoon that Madame Lalaurie, fleeing from the mob," etc.

For on that afternoon, when the people surrounded the house, crying for vengeance, she never lost, it seems, her cunning. She and her sleek black coachman took counsel together, and his plan of escape was adopted. The early afternoon dinner-hour of those times came and passed and the crowd still filled the street, but as yet had done nothing. Presently, right in the midst of the throng, her carriage came to the door according to its well-known daily habit at that hour, and at the same moment the charming Madame Lalaurie, in all her pretty manners and sweetness of mien, stepped quickly across the sidewalk and entered the vehicle.

The crowd was taken all aback. When it gathered its wits the coach-door had shut and the horses were starting. Then her audacity was understood.

"She is getting away!" was the cry, and the multitude rushed upon her. "Seize the horses!" they shouted, and dashed at the bits and reins. The black driver gave the word to his beasts, and with his coach whip lashed the faces of those who sprung forward. The horses reared and plunged, the harness held, and the equipage was off. The crowd went with it.

"Turn the coach over!" they cry, and attempt it, but fail. "Drag her out!"

They try to do it, again and again, but in vain; away it rattles! Away it flashes! down Hospital street, past Bourbon, Dauphine, Burgundy, and the Rampart, with the crowd following, yelling, but fast growing thin and thinner.

"Stop her! Stop her! Stop that carriage! Stop that *carriage*!"

In vain! On it spins! Out upon the Bayou Road come the pattering hoofs and humming wheels—not wildly driven, but just at their most telling speed—into the whole whirling retinue of fashionable New Orleans out for its afternoon airing. Past this equipage; past that one; past half a dozen; a dozen; a score! Their inmates sit chatting in every sort of mood over the day's sensation, when—what is this? A rush from behind, a whirl of white dust, and—"As I live, there she goes now, on her regular drive! What scandalous speed! and—see here! they are after her!" Past fifty gigs and coaches; past a hundred; around this long bend in the road; around that one. Good-bye, pursuers! Never a chance to cut her off, the swamp forever on the right, the bayou on the left; she is getting away, getting away! the crowd is miles behind! The lake is reached. The road ends. What next? The coach dashes up to the bayou's edge and stops. Why just here? Ah! because just here so near the bayou's mouth a schooner lies against the bank. Is Dr. Lalaurie's hand in this? The coachman parleys a moment with the schooner-master and hands him down a purse of gold. The coach-door is opened, the lady alights, and is presently on the vessel's deck. The lines are cast off, the great sails go up, the few lookers-on are there without reference to her and offer no interruption; a little pushing with poles lets the wind fill the canvas, and first slowly and silently, and then swiftly and with a grateful creaking of cordage and spars, the vessel glides out past the lighthouse, through the narrow opening, and stands away towards the northern horizon, below which, some thirty miles away, lies the little watering-place of Mandeville with roads leading as far away northward as one may choose to fly. Madame Lalaurie is gone!

The brave coachman—one cannot help admiring the villain's intrepidity—turned and drove back towards the city. What his plan was is not further known. No wonder if he thought he could lash and dash through the same mob again. But he mistook. He had not reached town again when the crowd met him. This time they were more successful. They stopped the horses—killed them. What they did with the driver is not told; but one can guess. They broke the carriage into bits. Then they returned to the house.

They reached it about 8 o'clock in the evening. The two daughters had just escaped by a window. The whole house was locked and barred; "hermetically sealed," says "L'Abeille" of the next morning. The human tempest fell upon it, and "in a few minutes," says "The Courier," "the doors and windows were broken open, the crowd rushed in, and the work of destruction began." "Those who rush in are of all classes and colors" continues "The Courier" of next day; but "No, no!" says a survivor of to-day who was there and took part; "we wouldn't have allowed that!" In a single hour everything movable disappeared or perished. The place was rifled of jewelry and plate; china was smashed; the very stair-balusters were pulled piece from piece; hangings, bedding and table linen were tossed into the streets; and the elegant furniture, bedsteads, wardrobes, buffets, tables, chairs, pictures, "pianos," says the newspaper, were taken with pains to the third-story windows, hurled out and broken—"smashed into a thousand pieces"—upon the ground below. The very basements were emptied, and the floors, wainscots, and iron balconies damaged as far as at the moment they could be. The sudden southern nightfall descended, and torches danced in the streets and through the ruined house. The débris was gathered into hot bonfires, feather-beds were cut open, and the pavements covered with a thick snow of feathers. The night wore on, but the mob persisted. They mounted and battered the roof; they defaced the inner walls. Morning found them still at their senseless mischief, and they were "in the act of pulling down the walls when the sheriff and several citizens interfered and put an end to their work."

It was proposed to go at once to the houses of others long suspected of like cruelties to their slaves. But against this the highest gentility of the city alertly and diligently opposed themselves. Not at all because of sympathy with such cruelties. The single reason has its parallel in our own day. It was the fear that the negroes would be thereby encouraged to seek by violence those rights which their masters thought it not expedient to give them.

The movement was suppressed, and the odious parties were merely warned that they were watched.

Madame Lalaurie, we know by notarial records, was in Mandeville ten days after, when she executed a power of attorney in favor of her New Orleans business agent, in which act she was "authorized and assisted by her husband, Louis Lalaurie." So he disappears.

His wife made her way to Mobile—some say to the North—and thence to Paris. Being recognized and confronted there, she again fled. The rest of her story is tradition, but comes very directly. A domestic in a Creole family that knew Madame Lalaurie—and slave women used to enjoy great confidence and familiarity in the Creole households at times—tells that one day a letter from France to one of the family informed them that Madame Lalaurie, while spending a season at Pau, had engaged with a party of fashionable people in a boar-hunt, and somehow meeting the boar while apart from her companions had been set upon by the infuriated beast, and too quickly for any one to come to her rescue had been torn and killed. If this occurred after 1836 or 1837 it has no disagreement with Harriet Martineau's account, that at the latter date Madame Lalaurie was supposed to be still "skulking about some French province under a false name."

The house remained untouched for at least three years, "ornamented with various writings expressive of indignation and just punishment." The volume of "L'Abeille"[2] containing this account seems to have been abstracted from the city archives. It was in the last week of April or the first week of May, 1836, that Miss Martineau saw the house. It "stands," she wrote about a year later, "and is meant to stand, in its ruined state. It was the strange sight of its gaping windows and empty walls, in the midst of a busy street, which excited my wonder, and was the cause of my being told the story the first time. I gathered other particulars afterwards from eye-witnesses."

So the place came to be looked upon as haunted. In March, 1837, Madame Lalaurie's agent sold the house to a man who held it but a little over three months and then sold it at the same price that he had paid—only fourteen thousand dollars. The notary who made the earlier act of sale must have found it interesting. He was one of those who had helped find and carry out Madame Lalaurie's victims. It did not change hands again for twenty-five years. And then—in what state of repair I know not—it was sold at an advance equal to a yearly increase of but six-sevenths of one per cent, on the purchase price of the gaping ruin sold in 1837. There is a certain poetry in notarial records. But we will not delve for it now. Idle talk of strange sights and sounds crowded out of notice any true history the house may have had in those twenty-five years, or until war had destroyed that slavery to whose horridest possibilities the gloomy pile, even when restored and renovated, stood a ghost-ridden monument. Yet its days of dark romance were by no means ended.

2 French: Bee. A New Orleans newspaper.

Chapter Twenty-Two

CHARLES W. CHESNUTT (1858–1932)

In the African diaspora, enslaved peoples brought elements of their religion, which over time blended with Christianity. The resulting beliefs and practices differed according to African origins and the version of Christianity that was assimilated. In the Spanish Caribbean, the result was called *santería*, which has evolved into a recognized religion. In French islands and Louisiana, *voudou* (or *voudoun*) was the result; in the English-speaking South, *conjure*.

In this essay, Charles Chesnutt discusses his knowledge of conjure, which he both absorbed uncritically as a child in North Carolina and studied as an adult. The practices of conjure shown here are helpful in understanding not only Chesnutt's conjure tales but also E. Levi Brown's "At the Hermitage."

Text: Charles W. Chesnutt, *Stories, Novels, & Essays* (New York: Library of America, 2002), 864–71.

SUPERSTITIONS AND FOLK-LORE OF THE SOUTH

During a recent visit to North Carolina, after a long absence, I took occasion to inquire into the latter-day prevalence of the old-time belief in what was known as "conjuration" or "goopher," my childish recollection of which I have elsewhere embodied into a number of stories. The derivation of the word "goopher" I do not know, nor whether any other writer than myself has recognized its existence, though it is in frequent use in certain parts of the South. The origin of this curious superstition itself is perhaps more easily traceable. It probably grew, in the first place, out of African fetichism, which was brought over from the dark continent along with the dark people. Certain features, too, suggest a distant affinity with Voodooism, or snake worship, a cult which seems to have been indigenous to tropical America. These beliefs, which in the place of their origin had all the sanctions of religion and social custom, became, in the shadow of the white man's civilization, a pale reflection of their former selves. In time, too, they were mingled and confused with the witchcraft and ghost lore of the white man, and the tricks and delusions of the Indian conjurer. In the old plantation days they flourished vigorously, though discouraged by the "great house," and their potency was well established among the blacks and the poorer whites. Education, however, has thrown the ban of disrepute upon witchcraft and conjuration. The stern frown of the preacher, who looks upon superstition as the ally of the Evil One; the scornful sneer of the teacher, who sees in it a part of the livery of bondage, have driven this quaint combination of ancestral traditions to the remote chimney corners of old black aunties, from which it is difficult for the stranger to unearth them. Mr. Harris, in his Uncle Remus stories, has, with fine literary discrimination, collected and put into pleasing and enduring form, the plantation stories which dealt with animal lore, but so little attention has been paid to those dealing with so-called conjuration, that they seem in a fair way to disappear, without leaving a trace behind. The loss may not be very great, but these vanishing traditions might furnish valuable data for the sociologist, in the future study of racial development. In writing, a few years ago, the volume entitled *The Conjure Woman*, I suspect that I was more influenced by the literary value of the material than by its sociological bearing, and therefore took, or thought I did, considerable liberty with my subject. Imagination, however, can only act upon data—one must have somewhere in his consciousness the ideas which he puts together to form a connected whole. Creative talent, of whatever grade, is, in the last analysis, only the power of rearrangement—there is nothing new under the sun. I was the more firmly impressed with this thought after I had interviewed half a dozen old women, and a genuine "conjure doctor;" for I discovered that the brilliant touches, due, I had thought, to my own imagination, were after all but dormant ideas, lodged in my childish mind by old Aunt This and old Uncle That, and awaiting only the spur of imagination to bring them again to the surface. For instance, in the story, "Hot-foot Hannibal," there figures a conjure doll with pepper feet. Those pepper feet I regarded as peculiarly my own, a purely original creation. I heard, only the other day, in North Carolina, of the consternation struck to the heart of a certain dark individual upon finding upon his door-step a rabbit's foot—a good omen in itself perhaps—to which a malign influence had been imparted by tying to one end of it, in the form of a cross, two small pods of red pepper!

Most of the delusions connected with this belief in conjuration grow out of mere lack of enlightenment. As primeval men saw a personality behind every natural phenomenon, and found a god or a devil in wind, rain, and hail, in lightning, and in storm, so the untaught man or woman who is assailed by an unusual ache or pain, some strenuous symptom of serious physical disorder, is prompt to accept the suggestion, which tradition approves, that some evil influence is behind his discomfort; and what more natural than to conclude that some rival in business or in love has set this force in motion?

Relics of ancestral barbarism are found among all peoples, but advanced civilization has at least shaken off the more obvious absurdities of superstition. We no longer attribute insanity to demoniac possession, nor suppose that a king's touch can cure scrofula. To many old people in the South, however, any unusual ache or pain is quite as likely to have been caused by some external evil influence as by natural causes. Tumors, sudden swellings due to inflammatory rheumatism or the bites of insects, are especially open to suspicion. Paralysis is proof positive of conjuration. If there is any doubt, the "conjure doctor" invariably removes it. The credulity of ignorance is his chief stock in trade—there is no question, when he is summoned, but that the patient has been tricked.[1]

The means of conjuration are as simple as the indications. It is a condition of all witch stories that there must in some way be contact, either with the person, or with

[1] Cursed.

some object or image intended to represent the person to be affected; or, if not actual contact, at least close proximity. The charm is placed under the door-sill, or buried under the hearth, or hidden in the mattress of the person to be conjured. It may be a crude attempt to imitate the body of the victim, or it may consist merely of a bottle, or a gourd, or a little bag, containing a few rusty nails, crooked pins, or horsehairs. It may be a mysterious mixture thrown surreptitiously upon the person to be injured, or merely a line drawn across a road or path, which line it is fatal for a certain man or woman to cross. I heard of a case of a laboring man who went two miles out of his way, every morning and evening, while going to and from his work, to avoid such a line drawn for him by a certain powerful enemy.

Some of the more gruesome phases of the belief in conjuration suggest possible poisoning, a knowledge of which baleful art was once supposed to be widespread among the imported Negroes of the olden time. The blood or venom of snakes, spiders, and lizards is supposed to be employed for this purpose. The results of its administration are so peculiar, however, and so entirely improbable, that one is supposed to doubt even the initial use of poison, and figure it in as part of the same general delusion. For instance, a certain man "swelled up all over" and became "pieded," that is, pied or spotted. A white physician who was summoned thought that the man thus singularly afflicted was poisoned, but did not recognize the poison nor know the antidote. A conjure doctor, subsequently called in, was more prompt in his diagnosis. The man, he said, was poisoned with a lizard, which at that very moment was lodged somewhere in the patient's anatomy.[2] The lizards and snakes in these stories, by the way, are not confined to the usual ducts and cavities of the human body, but seem to have freedom of movement throughout the whole structure. This lizard, according to the "doctor," would start from the man's shoulder, descend to his hand, return to the shoulder, and pass down the side of the body to the leg. When it reached the calf of the leg the lizard's head would appear right under the skin. After it had been perceptible for three days the lizard was to be cut out with a razor, or the man would die. Sure enough, the lizard manifested its presence in the appointed place at the appointed time; but the patient would not permit the surgery, and at the end of three days paid with death the penalty of his obstinacy. Old Aunt Harriet told me, with solemn earnestness, that she herself had taken a snake from her own arm, in sections, after a similar experience. Old Harriet may have been lying, but was, I imagine, merely self-deluded. Witches, prior to being burned, have often confessed their commerce with the Evil One. Why should Harriet hesitate to relate a simple personal experience which involved her in no blame whatever?

Old Uncle Jim, a shrewd, hard old sinner, and a palpable fraud, who did not, I imagine, believe in himself to any great extent, gave me some private points as to the manner in which these reptiles were thus transferred to the human system. If a snake or a lizard be killed, and a few drops of its blood be dried upon a plate or in a gourd, the person next eating or drinking from the contaminated vessel will soon become the unwilling landlord of a reptilian tenant. There are other avenues, too, by which the

[2] See E. Levi Brown's "At the Hermitage" in this collection.

reptile may gain admittance; but when expelled by the conjure doctor's arts or medicines, it always leaves at the point where it entered. This belief may have originally derived its existence from the fact that certain tropical insects sometimes lay their eggs beneath the skins of animals, or even of men, from which it is difficult to expel them until the larvae are hatched. The chico or "jigger" of the West Indies and the Spanish Main is the most obvious example.

Old Aunt Harriet—last name uncertain, since she had borne those of her master, her mother, her putative father, and half a dozen husbands in succession, no one of which seemed to take undisputed precedence—related some very remarkable experiences. She at first manifested some reluctance to speak of conjuration, in the lore of which she was said to be well versed; but by listening patiently to her religious experiences—she was a dreamer of dreams and a seer of visions—I was able now and then to draw a little upon her reserves of superstition, if indeed her religion itself was much more than superstition.

"W'en I wuz a gal 'bout eighteen er nineteen," she confided, "de w'ite folks use' ter sen' me ter town ter fetch vegetables. One day I met a' ole conjuh man name' Jerry Macdonal', an' he said some rough, ugly things ter me. I says, says I, 'You mus' be a fool.' He did n' say nothin', but jes' looked at me wid 'is evil eye. Wen I come 'long back, dat ole man wuz stan'in' in de road in front er his house, an' w'en he seed me he stoop' down an' tech' de groun', jes' lack he wuz pickin' up somethin', an' den went 'long back in 'is ya'd. De ve'y minute I step' on de spot he tech', I felt a sha'p pain shoot thoo my right foot, it tu'n't under me, an' I fell down in de road. I pick' myself up' an' by de time I got home, my foot wuz swoll' up twice its nachul size. I cried an' cried an' went on, fer I knowed I'd be'n trick' bv dat ole man. Dat night in my sleep a voice spoke ter me an' says: 'Go an' git a plug er terbacker. Steep it in a skillet er wa'm water. Strip it lengthways, an' bin' it ter de bottom er yo' foot'. I never didn' use terbacker, an' I laid dere, an' says I ter myse'f, 'My Lawd, w'at is dat, Wat is dat!' Soon ez my foot got kind er easv, dat voice up an' speaks ag'in: 'Go an' git a plug er terbacker. Steep it in a skillet er wa'm water, an' bin' it ter de bottom er yo' foot'.' I scramble' ter my feet, got de money out er my pocket, woke up de two little boys sleepin' on de flo', an' tol' 'em ter go ter de sto' an' git me a plug er terbacker. Dey didn' want ter go, said de sto' wuz shet, an' de sto' keeper gone ter bed. But I chased 'em fo'th, an' dey found' de sto' keeper an' fetch' de terbacker—dey sho' did. I soaked it in de skillet, an' stripped it 'long by degrees, till I got ter de en', w'en I boun' it under my foot an' roun' mv ankle. Den I kneel' down an' prayed, an' next mawnin' de swelin' wuz all gone! Dat voice wus de Spirit er de Lawd talkin' ter me, it sho' wuz! De Lawd have mussy upon us, praise his Holy Name!"

Very obviously Harriet had sprained her ankle while looking at the old man instead of watching the path, and the hot fomentation had reduced the swelling. She is not the first person to hear spirit voices in his or her own vagrant imaginings.

On another occasion, Aunt Harriet's finger swelled up "as big as a corn-cob." She at first supposed the swelling to be due to a felon. She went to old Uncle Julius Lutterloh, who told her that some one had tricked her. "My Lawd!" she exclaimed, "how did they fix my finger?" He explained that it was done while in the act of shaking hands. "Doctor" Julius opened the finger with a sharp knife and showed Harriet two seeds at the bottom of the incision. He instructed her to put a poultice of red onions on the wound over night, and in the morning the seeds would come out. She was then to put the two seeds in a skillet, on the right hand side of the fire-place, in a pint of water, and let them simmer nine mornings, and on the ninth morning she was to let all the water simmer out, and when the last drop should have gone, the one that put the seeds in her hand was to go out of this world! Harriet, however, did not pursue the treatment to the bitter end. The seeds, once extracted, she put into a small phial which she corked up tightly and put carefully away in her bureau drawer. One morning she went to look at them, and one of them was gone. Shortly afterwards the other disappeared. Aunt Harriet has a theory that she had been tricked by a woman of whom her husband of that time was unduly fond, and that the faithless husband had returned the seeds to their original owner. A part of the scheme of conjuration is that the conjure doctor can remove the spell and put it back upon the one who laid it. I was unable to learn, however, of any instance where this extreme penalty had been insisted upon.

It is seldom that any of these old Negroes will admit that he or she possesses the power to conjure, though those who can remove spells are very willing to make their accomplishment known, and to exercise it for a consideration. The only professional conjure doctor whom I met was old Uncle Jim Davis, with whom I arranged a personal interview. He came to see me one evening, but almost immediately upon his arrival a minister called. The powers of light prevailed over those of darkness, and Jim was dismissed until a later time, with a commission to prepare for me a conjure "hand" or good luck charm, of which, he informed some of the children about the house, who were much interested in the proceedings, I was very much in need. I subsequently secured the charm, for which, considering its potency, the small sum of silver it cost me was no extravagant outlay. It is a very small bag of roots and herbs, and, if used according to directions, is guaranteed to insure me good luck and "keep me from losing my job." The directions require it to be wet with spirits nine mornings in succession, to be carried on the person, in a pocket on the right hand side, care being taken that it does not come in contact with any tobacco. When I add that I procured, from an equally trustworthy source, a genuine graveyard rabbit's foot, I would seem to be reasonably well protected against casual misfortune. I shall not, however, presume upon this immunity, and shall omit no reasonable precaution which the condition of my health or my affairs may render prudent.

An interesting conjure story which I heard, involves the fate of a lost voice. A certain woman's lover was enticed away by another woman, who sang very sweetly, and who, the jilted one suspected, had told lies about her. Having decided upon the method of punishment for this wickedness, the injured woman watched the other closely, in order to find a suitable opportunity for carrying out her purpose, but in vain, for the fortunate one, knowing of her enmity, would never speak to her or remain near her. One day the jilted woman plucked a red rose from her garden, and hid herself in the bushes near her rival's cabin. Very soon an old woman came by, who was accosted by the woman in hiding, and requested to hand the red rose to the woman of the house. The old woman, suspecting no evil, took the rose and approached the house, the other woman following her closely, but keeping herself always out of sight. When the old woman, having reached the door and called out the mistress of the house, delivered the rose as requested, the recipient thanked the giver in a loud voice, knowing the old woman to be somewhat deaf. At the moment she spoke, the woman in hiding reached up and caught her rival's voice, and clasping it tightly in her right hand, escaped, unseen, to her own cabin. At the same same instant the afflicted woman missed her voice, and felt a sharp pain shoot through her left arm, just below the elbow. She at first suspected the old woman of having tricked her through the medium of the red rose, but was subsequently informed by a conjure doctor that her voice had been stolen, and that the old woman was innocent. For the pain he gave her a bottle of medicine, of which nine drops were to be applied three times a day, and rubbed in with the first two fingers of the right hand, care being taken not to let any other part of the hand touch the arm, as this would render the medicine useless. By the aid of a mirror, in which he called up her image, the conjure doctor ascertained who was the guilty person. He sought her out and charged her with the crime which she promptly denied. Being pressed, however, she admitted her guilt. The doctor insisted upon immediate restitution. She expressed her willingness, and at the same time her inability to comply—she had taken the voice, but did not possess the power to restore it. The conjure doctor was obdurate and at once placed a spell upon her which is to remain until the lost voice is restored. The case is still pending, I understand; I shall sometime take steps to find out how it terminates.

How far a story like this is original, and how far a mere reflection of familiar wonder stories, is purely a matter of speculation. When the old mammies would tell the tales of Br'er Rabbit and Br'er Fox to the master's children, these in turn would no doubt repeat the fairy tales which they had read in books or heard from their parents' lips. The magic mirror is as old as literature. The inability to restore the stolen voice is foreshadowed in the *Arabian Nights*, when the "Open Sesame" is forgotten. The act of catching the voice has a simplicity which stamps it as original, the only analogy of which I can at present think being the story of later date, of the words which were frozen silent during the extreme cold of an Arctic winter, and became audible again the following summer when they had thawed out.

Chapter Twenty-Three

W. E. B. DU BOIS (1868–1963)

W. E. B. Du Bois, the first African American to earn a PhD at Harvard, was a leading historian, sociologist and controversial public intellectual for many decades.

"Of the Black Belt" is a chapter from *The Souls of Black Folk*, a foundational text of African American intellectual history. It was written during the nadir of postbellum life for black Southerners, when the brief gains of Reconstruction had been suppressed by Jim Crow segregation laws and lynching. *The Souls of Black Folk* was published in 1903, the year after Thomas Dixon's *The Leopard's Spots*, the first novel in Dixon's popular Ku Klux Klan trilogy.

Apologists for slavery had rewritten Southern history and erased much of African American experience. Du Bois takes us on a tour of a Georgia county that is, at every point, steeped in the history of the three races that inhabited this land. He shows a countryside that had once enriched slave-owning cotton growers but is now impoverished by poor soil management, a depressed cotton market, absentee ownership and the lingering consequences of the war. We see ruined plantations, fallen great houses and the survivors—black and white—of the old era. Such stories have nourished generations of Southern writers.

Text: *The Souls of Black Folk* (Chicago, IL: A. C. McClurg, 1903).

OF THE BLACK BELT

> I am black but comely, O ye daughters of
> Jerusalem,
> As the tents of Kedar, as the curtains of
> Solomon.
> Look not upon me, because I am black,
> Because the sun hath looked upon me:
> My mother's children were angry with me;
> They made me the keeper of the vineyards;
> But mine own vineyard have I not kept.

THE SONG OF SOLOMON[1]

Out of the North the train thundered, and we woke to see the crimson soil of Georgia stretching away bare and monotonous right and left. Here and there lay straggling,

1 Song of Sol. 1:5–6.

unlovely villages, and lean men loafed leisurely at the depots; then again came the stretch of pines and clay. Yet we did not nod, nor weary of the scene; for this is historic ground. Right across our track, three hundred and sixty years ago, wandered the cavalcade of Hernando de Soto, looking for gold and the Great Sea; and he and his foot-sore captives disappeared yonder in the grim forests to the west.[2] Here sits Atlanta, the city of a hundred hills, with something Western, something Southern, and something quite its own, in its busy life. Just this side Atlanta is the land of the Cherokees and to the southwest, not far from where Sam Hose[3] was crucified, you may stand on a spot which is to-day the centre of the Negro problem,—the centre of those nine million men who are America's dark heritage from slavery and the slave-trade.

Not only is Georgia thus the geographical focus of our Negro population, but in many other respects, both now and yesterday, the Negro problems have seemed to be centered in this State. No other State in the Union can count a million Negroes among its citizens,—a population as large as the slave population of the whole Union in 1800; no other State fought so long and strenuously to gather this host of Africans. Oglethorpe[4] thought slavery against law and gospel; but the circumstances which gave Georgia its first inhabitants were not calculated to furnish citizens over-nice in their ideas about rum and slaves. Despite the prohibitions of the trustees, these Georgians, like some of their descendants, proceeded to take the law into their own hands; and so pliant were the judges, and so flagrant the smuggling, and so earnest were the prayers of Whitefield, that by the middle of the eighteenth century all restrictions were swept away,[5] and the slave-trade went merrily on for fifty years and more.

Down in Darien, where the Delegal riots took place some summers ago,[6] there used to come a strong protest against slavery from the Scotch Highlanders; and the Moravians of Ebenezer did not like the system. But not till the Haytian Terror of Toussaint was the trade in men even checked; while the national statute of 1808 did not suffice to stop it. How the Africans poured in!—fifty thousand between 1790 and 1810, and then, from Virginia and from smugglers, two thousand a year for many years more. So the thirty thousand Negroes of Georgia in 1790 doubled in a decade,—were over a hundred thousand in 1810, had reached two hundred thousand in 1820, and half a million at the time of the war. Thus like a snake the black population writhed upward.

---

2 Hernando De Soto (1500–1542) mounted an expedition to North America (1539–42) that passed through Georgia in 1540. De Soto died somewhere on the western bank of the Mississippi River.

3 Sam Hose (ca. 1875–1899) killed his employer, apparently in self-defense. He was taken from custody by a mob, mutilated and burned alive.

4 James Edward Oglethorpe (1696–1765), founder of the colony of Georgia.

5 George Whitefield (or Whitfield, 1714–1770) was an English clergyman and one of the founders of Methodism. He was immensely popular in the English colonies, where he traveled widely and preached before large audiences. Whitefield advocated that slavery be legalized in Georgia, where he had founded an orphanage, and the legalization occurred in 1751.

6 Riots in August 1899, following the arrest of Henry Delegal, a black man, for allegedly raping a white woman.

But we must hasten on our journey. This that we pass as we near Atlanta is the ancient land of the Cherokees,—that brave Indian nation which strove so long for its fatherland, until Fate and the United States Government drove them beyond the Mississippi.[7] If you wish to ride with me you must come into the "Jim Crow Car." There will be no objection,—already four other white men, and a little white girl with her nurse, are in there. Usually the races are mixed in there; but the white coach is all white. Of course this car is not so good as the other, but it is fairly clean and comfortable. The discomfort lies chiefly in the hearts of those four black men yonder—and in mine.

We rumble south in quite a business-like way. The bare red clay and pines of Northern Georgia begin to disappear, and in their place appears a rich rolling land, luxuriant, and here and there well tilled. This is the land of the Creek Indians; and a hard time the Georgians had to seize it. The towns grow more frequent and more interesting, and brand-new cotton mills rise on every side. Below Macon the world grows darker; for now we approach the Black Belt,—that strange land of shadows, at which even slaves paled in the past, and whence come now only faint and half-intelligible murmurs to the world beyond. The "Jim Crow Car" grows larger and a shade better; three rough field-hands and two or three white loafers accompany us, and the newsboy still spreads his wares at one end. The sun is setting, but we can see the great cotton country as we enter it,—the soil now dark and fertile, now thin and gray, with fruit-trees and dilapidated buildings,—all the way to Albany.

At Albany, in the heart of the Black Belt, we stop. Two hundred miles south of Atlanta, two hundred miles west of the Atlantic, and one hundred miles north of the Great Gulf lies Dougherty County, with ten thousand Negroes and two thousand whites. The Flint River winds down from Andersonville, and, turning suddenly at Albany, the county-seat, hurries on to join the Chattahoochee and the sea. Andrew Jackson knew the Flint well, and marched across it once to avenge the Indian Massacre at Fort Mims.[8] That was in 1814, not long before the battle of New Orleans; and by the Creek treaty that followed this campaign, all Dougherty County, and much other rich land, was ceded to Georgia. Still, settlers fought shy of this land, for the Indians were all about, and they were unpleasant neighbors in those days. The panic of 1837,[9] which Jackson bequeathed to Van Buren, turned the planters from the impoverished lands of Virginia, the Carolinas, and east Georgia, toward the West. The Indians were removed to Indian Territory, and settlers poured into these coveted lands to retrieve their broken fortunes. For a radius of a hundred miles about Albany, stretched a great fertile land, luxuriant with forests of pine, oak, ash, hickory, and poplar; hot with the sun and damp with the rich black swamp-land; and here the corner-stone of the Cotton Kingdom was laid.

Albany is to-day a wide-streeted, placid, Southern town, with a broad sweep of stores and saloons, and flanking rows of homes,—whites usually to the north, and blacks to

---

7 The Indian Removal Act was passed by Congress on May 28, 1830.

8 On August 29, 1813, the "red stick" faction of the Creeks overwhelmed Ft. Mims and killed most of its defenders.

9 A financial crisis, followed by a major recession that lasted until the mid-1840s.

the south. Six days in the week the town looks decidedly too small for itself, and takes frequent and prolonged naps. But on Saturday suddenly the whole county disgorges itself upon the place, and a perfect flood of black peasantry pours through the streets, fills the stores, blocks the sidewalks, chokes the thoroughfares, and takes full possession of the town. They are black, sturdy, uncouth country folk, good-natured and simple, talkative to a degree, and yet far more silent and brooding than the crowds of the Rhine-pfalz, or Naples, or Cracow. They drink considerable quantities of whiskey, but do not get very drunk; they talk and laugh loudly at times, but seldom quarrel or fight. They walk up and down the streets, meet and gossip with friends, stare at the shop windows, buy coffee, cheap candy, and clothes, and at dusk drive home—happy? well no, not exactly happy, but much happier than as though they had not come.

Thus Albany is a real capital,—a typical Southern county town, the centre of the life of ten thousand souls; their point of contact with the outer world, their centre of news and gossip, their market for buying and selling, borrowing and lending, their fountain of justice and law. Once upon a time we knew country life so well and city life so little, that we illustrated city life as that of a closely crowded country district. Now the world has well-nigh forgotten what the country is, and we must imagine a little city of black people scattered far and wide over three hundred lonesome square miles of land, without train or trolley, in the midst of cotton and corn, and wide patches of sand and gloomy soil.

It gets pretty hot in Southern Georgia in July,—a sort of dull, determined heat that seems quite independent of the sun; so it took us some days to muster courage enough to leave the porch and venture out on the long country roads, that we might see this unknown world. Finally we started. It was about ten in the morning, bright with a faint breeze, and we jogged leisurely southward in the valley of the Flint. We passed the scattered box-like cabins of the brickyard hands, and the long tenement-row facetiously called "The Ark," and were soon in the open country, and on the confines of the great plantations of other days. There is the "Joe Fields place"; a rough old fellow was he, and had killed many a "nigger" in his day. Twelve miles his plantation used to run,—a regular barony. It is nearly all gone now; only straggling bits belong to the family, and the rest has passed to Jews and Negroes. Even the bits which are left are heavily mortgaged, and, like the rest of the land, tilled by tenants. Here is one of them now,—a tall brown man, a hard worker and a hard drinker, illiterate, but versed in farmlore, as his nodding crops declare. This distressingly new board house is his, and he has just moved out of yonder moss-grown cabin with its one square room.

From the curtains in Benton's house, down the road, a dark comely face is staring at the strangers; for passing carriages are not every-day occurrences here. Benton is an intelligent yellow man with a good-sized family, and manages a plantation blasted by the war and now the broken staff of the widow. He might be well-to-do, they say; but he carouses too much in Albany. And the half-desolate spirit of neglect born of the very soil seems to have settled on these acres. In times past there were cotton-gins and machinery here; but they have rotted away.

The whole land seems forlorn and forsaken. Here are the remnants of the vast plantations of the Sheldons, the Pellots, and the Rensons; but the souls of them are passed. The houses lie in half ruin, or have wholly disappeared; the fences have flown, and the families are wandering in the world. Strange vicissitudes have met these whilom masters. Yonder stretch the wide acres of Bildad Reasor; he died in war-time, but the upstart overseer hastened to wed the widow. Then he went, and his neighbors too, and now only the black tenant remains; but the shadow-hand of the master's grand-nephew or cousin or creditor stretches out of the gray distance to collect the rack-rent remorselessly, and so the land is uncared-for and poor. Only black tenants can stand such a system, and they only because they must. Ten miles we have ridden to-day and have seen no white face.

A resistless feeling of depression falls slowly upon us, despite the gaudy sunshine and the green cottonfields. This, then, is the Cotton Kingdom,—the shadow of a marvellous dream. And where is the King? Perhaps this is he,—the sweating ploughman, tilling his eighty acres with two lean mules, and fighting a hard battle with debt. So we sit musing, until, as we turn a corner on the sandy road, there comes a fairer scene suddenly in view,—a neat cottage snugly ensconced by the road, and near it a little store. A tall bronzed man rises from the porch as we hail him, and comes out to our carriage. He is six feet in height, with a sober face that smiles gravely. He walks too straight to be a tenant,—yes, he owns two hundred and forty acres. "The land is run down since the boom-days of eighteen hundred and fifty," he explains, and cotton is low. Three black tenants live on his place, and in his little store he keeps a small stock of tobacco, snuff, soap, and soda, for the neighborhood. Here is his gin-house with new machinery just installed. Three hundred bales of cotton went through it last year. Two children he has sent away to school. Yes, he says sadly, he is getting on, but cotton is down to four cents; I know how Debt sits staring at him.

Wherever the King may be, the parks and palaces of the Cotton Kingdom have not wholly disappeared. We plunge even now into great groves of oak and towering pine, with an undergrowth of myrtle and shrubbery. This was the "home-house" of the Thompsons,—slave-barons who drove their coach and four in the merry past. All is silence now, and ashes, and tangled weeds. The owner put his whole fortune into the rising cotton industry of the fifties, and with the falling prices of the eighties he packed up and stole away. Yonder is another grove, with unkempt lawn, great magnolias, and grass-grown paths. The Big House stands in half-ruin, its great front door staring blankly at the street, and the back part grotesquely restored for its black tenant. A shabby, well-built Negro he is, unlucky and irresolute. He digs hard to pay rent to the white girl who owns the remnant of the place. She married a policeman, and lives in Savannah.

Now and again we come to churches. Here is one now,—Shepherd's, they call it,—a great whitewashed barn of a thing, perched on stilts of stone, and looking for all the world as though it were just resting here a moment and might be expected to waddle off down the road at almost any time. And yet it is the centre of a hundred cabin homes; and sometimes, of a Sunday, five hundred persons from far and near gather here and talk and eat and sing. There is a schoolhouse near,—a very airy, empty shed; but even this is an improvement, for usually the school is held in the church. The churches vary from log-huts to those like Shepherd's, and the schools from nothing to this little house that sits demurely on the county line. It is a tiny plank-house, perhaps ten by twenty, and has within a double row of rough unplaned benches, resting mostly on legs, sometimes on boxes. Opposite the door is a square home-made desk. In one corner are the ruins of a stove, and in the other a dim blackboard. It is the cheerfulest schoolhouse I have seen in Dougherty, save in town. Back of the schoolhouse is a lodgehouse two stories high and not quite finished. Societies meet there,—societies "to care for the sick and bury the dead"; and these societies grow and flourish.

We had come to the boundaries of Dougherty, and were about to turn west along the county-line, when all these sights were pointed out to us by a kindly old man, black, white-haired, and seventy. Forty-five years he had lived here, and now supports himself and his old wife by the help of the steer tethered yonder and the charity of his black neighbors. He shows us the farm of the Hills just across the county line in Baker,—a widow and two strapping sons, who raised ten bales (one need not add "cotton" down here) last year. There are fences and pigs and cows, and the soft-voiced, velvet-skinned young Memnon, who sauntered half-bashfully over to greet the strangers, is proud of his home. We turn now to the west along the county line. Great dismantled trunks of pines tower above the green cottonfields, cracking their naked gnarled fingers toward the border of living forest beyond. There is little beauty in this region, only a sort of crude abandon that suggests power,—a naked grandeur, as it were. The houses are bare and straight; there are no hammocks or easy-chairs, and few flowers. So when, as here at Rawdon's, one sees a vine clinging to a little porch, and home-like windows peeping over the fences, one takes a long breath. I think I never before quite realized the place of the Fence in civilization. This is the Land of the Unfenced, where crouch on either hand scores of ugly one-room cabins, cheerless and dirty. Here lies the Negro problem in its naked dirt and penury. And here are no fences. But now and then the crisscross rails or straight palings break into view, and then we know a touch of culture is near. Of course Harrison Gohagen,—a quiet yellow man, young, smooth-faced, and diligent,—of course he is lord of some hundred acres, and we expect to see a vision of well-kept rooms and fat beds and laughing children. For has he not fine fences? And those over yonder, why should they build fences on the rack-rented land? It will only increase their rent.

On we wind, through sand and pines and glimpses of old plantations, till there creeps into sight a cluster of buildings,—wood and brick, mills and houses, and scattered cabins. It seemed quite a village. As it came nearer and nearer, however, the aspect changed: the buildings were rotten, the bricks were falling out, the mills were silent, and the store was closed. Only in the cabins appeared now and then a bit of lazy life. I could imagine the place under some weird spell, and was half-minded to search out the princess. An old ragged black man, honest, simple, and improvident, told us the tale. The Wizard of the North—the Capitalist—had rushed down in the seventies to woo this coy dark soil. He bought a square mile or more, and for a time the field-hands sang, the gins groaned, and the mills buzzed. Then came a change. The agent's son embezzled the funds and ran off with them. Then the agent himself disappeared. Finally the new agent stole even the books, and the company in wrath closed its business and its houses, refused to sell, and let houses and furniture and machinery rust and rot. So the Waters-Loring plantation was stilled by the spell of dishonesty, and stands like some gaunt rebuke to a scarred land.

Somehow that plantation ended our day's journey; for I could not shake off the influence of that silent scene. Back toward town we glided, past the straight and thread-like pines, past a dark tree-dotted pond where the air was heavy with a dead sweet perfume. White slender-legged curlews flitted by us, and the garnet blooms of the cotton looked gay against the green and purple stalks. A peasant girl was hoeing in the field, white-turbaned and black-limbed. All this we saw, but the spell still lay upon us.

How curious a land is this,—how full of untold story, of tragedy and laughter, and the rich legacy of human life; shadowed with a tragic past, and big with future promise! This is the Black Belt of Georgia. Dougherty County is the west end of the Black Belt, and men once called it the Egypt of the Confederacy. It is full of historic interest. First there is the Swamp, to the west, where the Chickasawhatchee flows sullenly southward. The shadow of an old plantation lies at its edge, forlorn and dark. Then comes the pool; pendent gray moss and brackish waters appear, and forests filled with wildfowl. In one place the wood is on fire, smouldering in dull red anger; but nobody minds. Then the swamp grows beautiful; a raised road, built by chained Negro convicts, dips down into it, and forms a way walled and almost covered in living green. Spreading trees spring from a prodigal luxuriance of undergrowth; great dark green shadows fade into the black background, until all is one mass of tangled semi-tropical foliage, marvellous in its weird savage splendor. Once we crossed a black silent stream, where the sad trees and writhing creepers, all glinting fiery yellow and green, seemed like some vast cathedral,—some green Milan builded of wildwood. And as I crossed, I seemed to see again that fierce tragedy of seventy years ago. Osceola,[10] the Indian-Negro chieftain, had risen in the swamps of Florida, vowing vengeance. His war-cry reached the red Creeks of Dougherty, and their war-cry rang from the Chattahoochee to the sea. Men and women and children fled and fell before them as they swept into Dougherty. In yonder shadows a dark and hideously painted warrior glided stealthily on,—another and another, until three hundred had crept into the treacherous swamp. Then the false slime closing about them called the white men from the east. Waist-deep, they fought beneath the tall trees, until the war-cry was hushed and the Indians glided back into the west. Small wonder the wood is red.

Then came the black slaves. Day after day the clank of chained feet marching from Virginia and Carolina to Georgia was heard in these rich swamp lands. Day after day the songs of the callous, the wail of the motherless, and the muttered curses of the wretched echoed from the Flint to the Chickasawhatchee, until by 1860 there had risen in West Dougherty perhaps the richest slave kingdom the modern world ever knew. A hundred and fifty barons commanded the labor of nearly six thousand Negroes, held sway over farms with ninety thousand acres tilled land, valued even in times of cheap soil at three millions of dollars. Twenty thousand bales of ginned cotton went yearly to England, New and Old; and men that came there bankrupt made money and grew rich. In a single decade the cotton output increased four-fold and the value of lands was tripled. It was the heyday of the nouveau riche, and a life of careless extravagance among the masters.

[10] Osceola, aka Billy Powell (1804–1838), was a racially mixed Creek who moved as a child to Florida after the defeat of the Creeks in 1814. He joined the Seminoles and was a leader of that tribe's resistance to the US army. He was captured and died in military custody in Charleston.

Four and six bobtailed thoroughbreds rolled their coaches to town; open hospitality and gay entertainment were the rule. Parks and groves were laid out, rich with flower and vine, and in the midst stood the low wide-halled "big house," with its porch and columns and great fireplaces.

And yet with all this there was something sordid, something forced,—a certain feverish unrest and recklessness; for was not all this show and tinsel built upon a groan? "This land was a little Hell," said a ragged, brown, and grave-faced man to me. We were seated near a roadside blacksmith shop, and behind was the bare ruin of some master's home. "I've seen niggers drop dead in the furrow, but they were kicked aside, and the plough never stopped. Down in the guard-house, there's where the blood ran."

With such foundations a kingdom must in time sway and fall. The masters moved to Macon and Augusta, and left only the irresponsible overseers on the land. And the result is such ruin as this, the Lloyd "home-place":—great waving oaks, a spread of lawn, myrtles and chestnuts, all ragged and wild; a solitary gate-post standing where once was a castle entrance; an old rusty anvil lying amid rotting bellows and wood in the ruins of a blacksmith shop; a wide rambling old mansion, brown and dingy, filled now with the grandchildren of the slaves who once waited on its tables; while the family of the master has dwindled to two lone women, who live in Macon and feed hungrily off the remnants of an earldom. So we ride on, past phantom gates and falling homes,—past the once flourishing farms of the Smiths, the Gandys, and the Lagores,—and find all dilapidated and half ruined, even there where a solitary white woman, a relic of other days, sits alone in state among miles of Negroes and rides to town in her ancient coach each day.

This was indeed the Egypt of the Confederacy,—the rich granary whence potatoes and corn and cotton poured out to the famished and ragged Confederate troops as they battled for a cause lost long before 1861. Sheltered and secure, it became the place of refuge for families, wealth, and slaves. Yet even then the hard ruthless rape of the land began to tell. The red-clay sub-soil already had begun to peer above the loam. The harder the slaves were driven the more careless and fatal was their farming. Then came the revolution of war and Emancipation, the bewilderment of Reconstruction,—and now, what is the Egypt of the Confederacy, and what meaning has it for the nation's weal or woe?

It is a land of rapid contrasts and of curiously mingled hope and pain. Here sits a pretty blue-eyed quadroon hiding her bare feet; she was married only last week, and yonder in the field is her dark young husband, hoeing to support her, at thirty cents a day without board. Across the way is Gatesby, brown and tall, lord of two thousand acres shrewdly won and held. There is a store conducted by his black son, a blacksmith shop, and a ginnery. Five miles below here is a town owned and controlled by one white New Englander. He owns almost a Rhode Island county, with thousands of acres and hundreds of black laborers. Their cabins look better than most, and the farm, with machinery and fertilizers, is much more business-like than any in the county, although the manager drives hard bargains in wages. When now we turn and look five miles above, there on the edge of town are five houses of prostitutes,—two of blacks and three of whites; and in one of the houses of the whites a worthless black boy was harbored too openly two years ago; so he was hanged for rape. And here, too, is the high whitewashed fence of the "stockade," as the county prison is called; the white folks say it is ever full of black criminals,—the black folks say that only colored boys are sent to jail, and they not because they are guilty, but because the State needs criminals to eke out its income by their forced labor.

Immigrants are heirs of the slave baron in Dougherty; and as we ride westward, by wide stretching cornfields and stubby orchards of peach and pear, we see on all sides within the circle of dark forest a Land of Canaan. Here and there are tales of projects for money-getting, born in the swift days of Reconstruction,—"improvement" companies, wine companies, mills and factories; most failed, and foreigners fell heir. It is a beautiful land, this Dougherty, west of the Flint. The forests are wonderful, the solemn pines have disappeared, and this is the "Oakey Woods," with its wealth of hickories, beeches, oaks and palmettos. But a pall of debt hangs over the beautiful land; the merchants are in debt to the wholesalers, the planters are in debt to the merchants, the tenants owe the planters, and laborers bow and bend beneath the burden of it all. Here and there a man has raised his head above these murky waters. We passed one fenced stock-farm with grass and grazing cattle, that looked very home-like after endless corn and cotton. Here and there are black free-holders: there is the gaunt dull-black Jackson, with his hundred acres. "I says, 'Look up! If you don't look up you can't get up,'" remarks Jackson, philosophically. And he's gotten up. Dark Carter's neat barns would do credit to New England. His master helped him to get a start, but when the black man died last fall the master's sons immediately laid claim to the estate. "And them white folks will get it, too," said my yellow gossip.

I turn from these well-tended acres with a comfortable feeling that the Negro is rising. Even then, however, the fields, as we proceed, begin to redden and the trees disappear. Rows of old cabins appear filled with renters and laborers,—cheerless, bare, and dirty, for the most part, although here and there the very age and decay makes the scene picturesque. A young black fellow greets us. He is twenty-two, and just married. Until last year he had good luck renting; then cotton fell, and the sheriff seized and sold all he had. So he moved here, where the rent is higher, the land poorer, and the owner inflexible; he rents a forty-dollar mule for twenty dollars a year. Poor lad!—a slave at twenty-two. This plantation, owned now by a foreigner, was a part of the famous Bolton estate. After the war it was for many years worked by gangs of Negro convicts,—and black convicts then were even more plentiful than now; it was a way of making Negroes work, and the question of guilt was a minor one. Hard tales of cruelty and mistreatment of the chained freemen are told, but the county authorities were deaf until the free-labor market was nearly ruined by wholesale migration. Then they took the convicts from the plantations, but not until one of the fairest regions of the "Oakey Woods" had been ruined and ravished into a red waste, out of which only a Yankee or an immigrant could squeeze more blood from debt-cursed tenants.

No wonder that Luke Black, slow, dull, and discouraged, shuffles to our carriage and talks hopelessly. Why should he strive? Every year finds him deeper in debt. How strange that Georgia, the world-heralded refuge of poor debtors, should bind her own to sloth and misfortune as ruthlessly as ever England did! The poor land groans with its birth-pains, and brings forth scarcely a hundred pounds of cotton to the acre, where fifty years ago it yielded eight times as much. Of his meagre yield the tenant pays from a quarter to a third in rent, and most of the rest in interest on food and supplies bought on credit. Twenty years yonder sunken-cheeked, old black man has labored under that system, and now, turned day-laborer, is supporting his wife and boarding himself on his wages of a dollar and a half a week, received only part of the year.

The Bolton convict farm formerly included the neighboring plantation. Here it was that the convicts were lodged in the great log prison still standing. A dismal place it still remains, with rows of ugly huts filled with surly ignorant tenants. "What rent do you pay here?" I inquired. "I don't know,—what is it, Sam?" "All we make," answered Sam. It is a depressing place,—bare, unshaded, with no charm of past association, only a memory of forced human toil,—now, then, and before the war. They are not happy, these black men whom we meet throughout this region. There is little of the joyous abandon and playfulness which we are wont to associate with the plantation Negro. At best, the natural good-nature is edged with complaint or has changed into sullenness and gloom. And now and then it blazes forth in veiled but hot anger. I remember one big red-eyed black whom we met by the roadside. Forty-five years he had labored on this farm, beginning with nothing, and still having nothing. To be sure, he had given four children a common-school training, and perhaps if the new fence-law had not allowed unfenced crops in West Dougherty he might have raised a little stock and kept ahead. As it is, he is hopelessly in debt, disappointed, and embittered. He stopped us to inquire after the black boy in Albany, whom it was said a policeman had shot and killed for loud talking on the sidewalk. And then he said slowly: "Let a white man touch me, and he dies; I don't boast this,—I don't say it around loud, or before the children,—but I mean it. I've seen them whip my father and my old mother in them cotton-rows till the blood ran; by—" and we passed on.

Now Sears, whom we met next lolling under the chubby oak-trees, was of quite different fibre. Happy?—Well, yes; he laughed and flipped pebbles, and thought the world was as it was. He had worked here twelve years and has nothing but a mortgaged mule. Children? Yes, seven; but they hadn't been to school this year,—couldn't afford books and clothes, and couldn't spare their work. There go part of them to the fields now,—three big boys astride mules, and a strapping girl with bare brown legs. Careless ignorance and laziness here, fierce hate and vindictiveness there;—these are the extremes of the Negro problem which we met that day, and we scarce knew which we preferred.

Here and there we meet distinct characters quite out of the ordinary. One came out of a piece of newly cleared ground, making a wide detour to avoid the snakes. He was an old, hollow-cheeked man, with a drawn and characterful brown face. He had a sort of self-contained quaintness and rough humor impossible to describe; a certain cynical earnestness that puzzled one. "The niggers were jealous of me over on the other place," he said, "and so me and the old woman begged this piece of woods, and I cleared it up myself. Made nothing for two years, but I reckon I've got a crop now." The cotton looked tall and rich, and we praised it. He curtsied low, and then bowed almost to the ground, with an imperturbable gravity that seemed almost suspicious. Then he continued, "My mule died last week,"—a calamity in this land equal to a devastating fire in town,—"but a white man loaned me another." Then he added, eyeing us, "Oh, I gets along with white folks." We turned the conversation. "Bears? deer?" he answered, "well, I should say there were," and he let fly a string of brave oaths, as he told hunting-tales of the swamp. We left him standing still in the middle of the road looking after us, and yet apparently not noticing us.

The Whistle place, which includes his bit of land, was bought soon after the war by an English syndicate, the "Dixie Cotton and Corn Company." A marvellous deal of style their factor put on, with his servants and coach-and-six; so much so that the concern soon landed in inextricable bankruptcy. Nobody lives in the old house now, but a man comes each winter out of the North and collects his high rents. I know not which are the more touching,—such old empty houses, or the homes of the masters' sons. Sad and bitter tales lie hidden back of those white doors,—tales of poverty, of struggle, of disappointment. A revolution such as that of '63 is a terrible thing; they that rose rich in the morning often slept in paupers' beds. Beggars and vulgar speculators rose to rule over them, and their children went astray. See yonder sad-colored house, with its cabins and fences and glad crops! It is not glad within; last month the prodigal son of the struggling father wrote home from the city for money. Money! Where was it to come from? And so the son rose in the night and killed his baby, and killed his wife, and shot himself dead. And the world passed on.

I remember wheeling around a bend in the road beside a graceful bit of forest and a singing brook. A long low house faced us, with porch and flying pillars, great oaken door, and a broad lawn shining in the evening sun. But the window-panes were gone, the pillars were worm-eaten, and the moss-grown roof was falling in. Half curiously I peered through the unhinged door, and saw where, on the wall across the hall, was written in once gay letters a faded "Welcome."

Quite a contrast to the southwestern part of Dougherty County is the northwest. Soberly timbered in oak and pine, it has none of that half-tropical luxuriance of the southwest. Then, too, there are fewer signs of a romantic past, and more of systematic modern land-grabbing and money-getting. White people are more in evidence here, and farmer and hired labor replace to some extent the absentee landlord and rack-rented tenant. The crops have neither the luxuriance of the richer land nor the signs of neglect so often seen, and there were fences and meadows here and there. Most of this land was poor, and beneath the notice of the slave-baron, before the war. Since then his poor relations and foreign immigrants have seized it. The returns of the farmer are too small to allow much for wages, and yet he will not sell off small farms. There is the Negro Sanford; he has worked fourteen years as overseer on the Ladson place, and "paid out enough for fertilizers to have bought a farm," but the owner will not sell off a few acres.

Two children—a boy and a girl—are hoeing sturdily in the fields on the farm where Corliss works. He is smooth-faced and brown, and is fencing up his pigs. He used to run a successful cotton-gin, but the Cotton Seed Oil Trust has forced the price of ginning so low that he says it hardly pays him. He points out a stately old house over the way as the home of "Pa Willis." We eagerly ride over, for "Pa Willis" was the tall and powerful black Moses who led the Negroes for a generation, and led them well. He was a Baptist preacher, and when he died, two thousand black people followed him to the grave; and now they preach his funeral sermon each year His widow lives here,—a weazened, sharp-featured little woman, who curtsied quaintly as we greeted her. Further on lives Jack Delson, the most prosperous Negro farmer in the county. It is a joy to meet him,—a great broad-shouldered, handsome black man, intelligent and jovial. Six hundred and fifty acres he owns, and has eleven black tenants. A neat and tidy home nestled in a flower-garden, and a little store stands beside it.

We pass the Munson place, where a plucky white widow is renting and struggling; and the eleven hundred acres of the Sennet plantation, with its Negro overseer. Then the character of the farms begins to change. Nearly all the lands belong to Russian Jews; the overseers are white, and the cabins are bare board-houses scattered here and there. The rents are high, and day-laborers and "contract" hands abound. It is a keen, hard struggle for living here, and few have time to talk. Tired with the long ride, we gladly drive into Gillonsville. It is a silent cluster of farmhouses standing on the crossroads, with one of its stores closed and the other kept by a Negro preacher. They tell great tales of busy times at Gillonsville before all the railroads came to Albany; now it is chiefly a memory. Riding down the street, we stop at the preacher's and seat ourselves before the door. It was one of those scenes one cannot soon forget:—a wide, low, little house, whose motherly roof reached over and sheltered a snug little porch. There we sat, after the long hot drive, drinking cool water,—the talkative little storekeeper who is my daily companion; the silent old black woman patching pantaloons and saying never a word; the ragged picture of helpless misfortune who called in just to see the preacher; and finally the neat matronly preacher's wife, plump, yellow, and intelligent. "Own land?" said the wife; "well, only this house." Then she added quietly. "We did buy seven hundred acres across up yonder, and paid for it; but they cheated us out of it. Sells was the owner." "Sells!" echoed the ragged misfortune, who was leaning against the balustrade and listening, "he's a regular cheat. I worked for him thirty-seven days this spring, and he paid me in cardboard checks which were to be cashed at the end of the month. But he never cashed them,—kept putting me off. Then the sheriff came and took my mule and corn and furniture—" "Furniture? But furniture is exempt from seizure by law." "Well, he took it just the same," said the hard-faced man.

INDEX

Absalom, Absalom! (Faulkner) 19
Africanism 1
Alcuin (C. B. Brown) 151
Arthur Mervyn (C. B. Brown) 151
"At La Glorieuse" (Davis) 3, 115–31
"At the Hermitage" (E. L. Brown) 3, 97–107, 115, 207, 209n2, 215

Balcony Stories (King) 91
Bayou Folk (Chopin) 109
Bear, The (Faulkner) 47
"Belles Demoiselles Plantation" (Cable) 55–67
Beloved (Morrison) 3
"Big Bear of Arkansas, The" (Thorpe) 47
Bissette, Cyrille 7
"Black Belt, Of the" (DuBois) 4, 213–24
Brown, Charles Brockden 3, 151–57
  Alcuin 151
  Arthur Mervyn 151
  "On the Consequences of Abolishing the Slave Trade to the West Indian Colonies" 151–57
  Edgar Huntly 151
  Ormond 151
  Wieland 151
Brown, E. Levi, "At the Hermitage" 1, 3, 97–107, 115, 207, 209n2, 21
Burr, Aaron 159

Cable, George Washington 2, 3, 4, 55–67, 69, 91, 181–205
  "Belles Demoiselles Plantation" 55–67
  "The Haunted House on Royal Street" 197–205
  Old Creole Days 55–67
  "Salome Müller" 181–96
  Strange True Stories of Louisiana, 181–205
Chesnutt, Charles 3, 83–90, 97, 109, 207–12
  The Conjure Woman, 83–90, 208
  "The Dumb Witness" 83
  "The Marked Tree" 83
  "Po' Sandy" 3, 83–90
  "The Sheriff's Children" 83
  "Superstitions and Folk-Lore of the South" 207–12
Chopin, Kate 2, 3, 77, 109–13
  Bayou Folk 109–13
  "Désirée's Baby"' 109–13
  A Night in Arcady, 109
Clairveaux, Augustin 160n4
"Confessions of Nat Turner, The" (Gray) 3–4, 165–73
Confessions of Nat Turner, The (Styron) 165
conjure 83–90, 97, 103–7, 207–12. *See also* santería; voudoun (voudou)
Conjure Woman, The (Chesnutt) 83–90
Crevecoeur, J. Hector St. John de 3, 145–53
  Letters from an American Farmer 3, 145–53

Davis, M. E. M. 2–3, 115–31
  "At La Glorieuse" 2–3, 115–31
  Under Six Flags 115
Dessalines, Jean-Jacques 3, 147–49, 153, 160n2, 160n4, 162, 162n10
  "Proclamation, 28 April 1804" 147–49
"Désirée's Baby"' (Chopin) 109–13
De Soto, Hernando 214, 214n2
Dixon, Thomas 213
  The Leopard's Spots 213
Du Bois, W. E. B. 19, 213–24
  "Of the Black Belt" 213–24
  The Souls of Black Folk 213–24
"Dumb Witness, The" (Chesnutt) 83

Edgar Huntly (C. B. Brown) 151

"Fall of the House of Usher, The" (Poe) 2, 19–32, 71
Faulkner, William 19, 47
  Absalom, Absalom! 19
  The Bear 47

"Ghostly Kiss, The" (Hearn) 69–70
Godwin, William 151
Gray, Thomas Ruffin 3, 165–73
"The Confessions of Nat Turner" 3, 165–73

Haiti 2–3, 7–18, 147–49, 151–57, 159–63
"Haunted House on Royal Street, The" (Cable) 4, 197–205
Hearn, Lafcadio 3, 4, 175–79
"The Ghostly Kiss" 69–70
"St. Johns Eve—Voudouism" 175–79
Hemmings, Sally 145
Hose, Sam 214, 214n3
Howells, William D. and Alden, Henry Mills (eds) 97–107, 115–31
Shapes that Haunt the Dusk: Harper's Novelettes 97–107, 115–31

Indian Removal Act (1830) 215n7

Jefferson, Thomas 1, 145–46
Notes on the State of Virginia 145–46
Jim Crow laws (segregation) 2, 213, 215

King, Grace 3, 91–96
Balcony Stories 3, 91–96
"The Little Convent Girl" 3, 91–96

Le Clerc, General Charles 159, 159n2, 160, 160n7
Leopard's Spots, The (Dixon) 213
Letters from an American Farmer (Crèvecoeur) 135–43
Lewis, Henry Clay 3, 47–53
Odd Leaves from the Life of a Louisiana Swamp Doctor 3, 47–53
"A Struggle for Life" 3, 47–53
"Little Convent Girl, The" (King) 3, 91–96
L'Ouverture, Toussaint 147, 148, 148n3, 159n2, 162, 163, 163n11, 214

"Marked Tree, The" (Chesnutt) 83
Maroons 15, 15n9
Morrison, Toni 1, 1n1, 3
Beloved, 3
"Playing in the Dark" 1n1
"Mulatto, The" ("Le Mulâtre") (Séjour) 2, 7–18

New Orleans Picayune (newspaper) 55
Night in Arcady, A (Chopin) 109

"No Haid Pawn" (Page) 3, 71–81
Notes on the State of Virginia (Jefferson) 145–46

Odd Leaves from the Life of a Louisiana Swamp Doctor (Lewis) 47–53
Oglethorpe, James Edward 214, 214n4
Old Creole Days (Cable) 55–67
"On the Consequences of Abolishing the Slave Trade to the West Indian Colonies" (C. B. Brown) 151–57
Ormond (C. B. Brown) 151
Osceola (native American leader) 219, 219n10

Page, Thomas Nelson) 3, 71–81
"No Haid Pawn" 3, 71–81
Playing in the Dark (Morrison) 1n1
"Po' Sandy" (Chesnutt) 3, 83–90
Poe, Edgar Allan 2, 19–46, 71, 151, 176n3
"The Fall of the House of Usher" 2, 19–32, 71
"The System of Doctor Tarr and Professor Fether" 33–46
"Proclamation, 28 April 1804" (Dessalines) 3, 147–49, 162

Revue des Colonies (periodical) 7
Rochambeau, General Donatien-Marie-Joseph de Vimeur, vicomte de 159, 160, 160n7, 162

St. Domingue (St. Domingo). *See* Haiti
"St. Johns Eve—Voudouism" (Hearn) 175–79
"Salome Müller" (Cable) 181–96
Sansay, Leonora 1, 3, 159–63
Secret History; or, The Horrors of St. Domingo 159–63
santería 207. *See also* conjure, voudoun (voodoo)
Secret History; or, The Horrors of St. Domingo (Sansay) 159–63
Séjour, Victor 2, 7–18
"The Mulatto ("Le Mulâtre") 2, 7–18
Shapes that Haunt the Dusk: Harper's Novelettes (ed. Howells and Alden) 97–107, 115–31
"Sheriff's Children, The" (Chesnutt) 83
Sivils, Matthew vii, 105
Souls of Black Folk, The (DuBois) 213–24

Spirit of the Times, The (periodical) 47
Strange True Stories of Louisiana (Cable) 4, 181–205
"Struggle for Life, A" (Lewis) 3, 47–53
Styron, William 165
The Confessions of Nat Turner 165
"Superstitions and Folk-Lore of the South" (Chesnutt) 207–12
"System of Doctor Tarr and Professor Fether, The" (Poe) 1, 2, 33–46

Thorpe, T. B. 47
"The Big Bear of Arkansas" 47
Treville, Admiral Louis Rene Levassor de la Touche 160, 160n5
Turner, Nat 2, 3–4, 165–73. *See also* Gray, Thomas Ruffin
Twain, Mark (Samuel L. Clemens) 47

Under Six Flags (Davis) 115

Whitefield, George 214, 214n5
voudoun (voodoo) 4, 175–79. *See also* conjure, santería
Wieland (C. B. Brown) 151
Wollstonecraft, Mary 151

www.ingramcontent.com/pod-product-compliance
Lightning Source LLC
Chambersburg PA
CBHW051919110726
47902CB00002B/345